STEP BY STEP

STEP BY STEP

Focus on Stepfamilies

Margaret Robinson
and
Donna Smith

HARVESTER WHEATSHEAF

New York London Toronto Sydney Tokyo Singapore

in association with

STEPFAMILY

THE NATIONAL STEPFAMILY ASSOCIATION

Tel. 071–372 0844

First published 1993 by
Harvester Wheatsheaf
Campus 400, Maylands Avenue
Hemel Hempstead
Hertfordshire, HP2 7EZ
A division of
Simon & Schuster International Group

Typeset in 10½/12 pt Bembo by Photoprint

Printed and bound in Great Britain by Biddles

British Library Cataloguing in Publication Data

A catalogue record for this book is available from the British Library

ISBN 07450 1281 7 (hbk)
ISBN 07450 1282 5 (pbk)

1 2 3 4 5 97 96 95 94 93

For our grandchildren and stepgrandchildren, present and future:
Naima, Tyson, Chester and Polly

Contents

Foreword

Stepfamilies today could be seen as pioneers challenging cultural ideals about the family and promoting a new vision of family life and parenting as it is actually lived by so many behind the front door. Yet there have been stepfamilies for centuries. So what has changed? Changes in society have certainly been reflected in changes in daily living – smaller households, more mothers working outside the home, more couples separating and divorcing. There have also been changes in our understanding and perception of the notion of family duties and relationships, of marriage and divorce. There have been changes in the roles and responsibilities of men and women, of parents and grandparents and of the need and concerns of children through both their childhood and their young adulthood. In moments of optimism we can reflect on the known potential for love and harmony, peace and personal development that we know can be nurtured in families and stepfamilies. We can feel and value the care and support we receive and give not only to our immediate family and blood relatives but also to those with whom we have a relationship through community, extended kin or other relationships. In moments of pessimism we may feel isolated, alone and confused about what is expected of us – as men or women, as parents or partners.

The authors of this book have an abundance of expertise from their personal, professional and clinical experiences. They challenge us to consider what we understand by the concept of family and stepfamily. The historical overview reminds us that stepfamilies are not new but one of many family forms that have evolved over the centuries, adapting to society's needs as well as those of the children and adults within them. More important, it also highlights the fact that any individual stepfamily is perceived differently from the standpoint of each member of that stepfamily – whether adult or child – according to their gender and position in the family and where they are in their own life-cycle development and the stage of family or stepfamily life-cycle development. It is therefore particularly important for those trying to help stepfamilies to be aware of the particular stages that all members may be going through as so often a therapist will only be working with part of the whole stepfamily system. In addition, the perspective of the different stepfamily members may also be different from the beliefs and perceptions of the therapist. One of the most frequent complaints coming to the National Stepfamily Association is the assumption by many counsellors and therapists that a stepfamily is 'the same as' a family with two birth parents, or that a family where the parents are divorced is 'a broken family waiting to be fixed by remarriage'. Each stepfamily will have its own history and events that have shaped its beliefs, patterns of behaviour and emotional resilience and vulnerability. It is essential that anyone working with stepfamilies recognises the relevance of the different life-cycle stages and belief systems of all involved.

It is now over fifty years since the tentative introduction of family therapy, which treats members of a family as a unit with its own system. It is over ten years since the publication of a formative book on the changing family life cycle. I welcome the further evolution of this developmental and systemic approach of viewing the stepfamily in all its complexity and diversity – the coming together of different patterns of family behaviour and belief systems, with individuals at different stages of growth and maturity all nudging and jostling each other in an attempt to find some sort of equilibrium by which they can live in the same house and adjust to the starting and ending and the changing nature of relationships.

For many post-separation or post-divorce families sorting out the new routines and various roles and tasks of each member of the now two households is already difficult. To then combine either of those new households with another to create a stepfamily is indeed a challenge. Sharing parenting between parents no longer living together, or sharing the parenting between parent and step-parent where children are living full-time or regularly or occasionally visiting is only the beginning of many practical dilemmas that have to be addressed if all members are to survive with humour and sanity! Issues of death and loss cannot be ignored and can have their own potent impact on a stepfamily, sometimes the death of a parent coming before the creation of the stepfamily, and sometimes after its formation.

The public debate about the importance of the nuclear family and responsible parenting continues along with the moral panic over divorce and a rising incidence of cohabitation and of children born outside marriage. As our expectations of family and stepfamily are more openly discussed and challenged, it is becoming more acceptable to promote the idea of 'good enough' parenting as a more realistic goal for us all – whatever the shape or size or historical formation of the family household. This is particularly relevant for stepfamilies, where the diversity of demands and expectations of each individual are rarely likely to be met by the newly formed restructured household. Yet this diversity can also be a rich tapestry of new experiences and relationships that may enhance the emotional maturity of the adults and children within stepfamilies.

The Introduction opens with the statement that a stepfamily exists because another family ceases to exist. Families and stepfamilies are good enough if they meet the needs of those involved, for clearly if they do not, they remain vulnerable to future loss and disappointment. The range of losses that many families will have already experienced prior to becoming a stepfamily will probably come as a surprise to many readers. The hopes and expectations that adults, and sometimes the children, take into a stepfamily cannot be overestimated. Adults almost always have high ideals of a fresh start, of getting it right this time. At the same time, many children realise that their parent's new relationship and the acknowledgement of the stepfamily also mean the end of their fantasy – their parents will not now be re-united. The high hopes and celebrations of the adults and the mixed emotions and grieving of the children often symbolise the precariousness with which many stepfamilies embark on their journey into the future. Stepfamilies are not only about losses, however; they are also about gains. Children have an opportunity to have significant extra adults in their lives who care about them, who may offer opportunities and skills in addition to those provided by birth parents. Adults may experience a different form of relationship with children who are not theirs, much as when grandparents remark on the different relationship one has with a child and a grandchild – the possibility of enjoyment without all the responsibility!

Stepfamilies have always been a fact of life, but tended to be invisible, to disappear into the conventional family model. In the past they were usually formed because one of the parents had died. Nowadays stepfamily life is obviously complicated and diverse, with parents separating, divorcing and then forming one or more subsequent relationships bringing in their wake step-parents, stepchildren and additional extended family relationships. Some research studies suggest that children growing up in stepfamilies are at a disadvantage socially and emotionally. It is therefore critical that when the child or adult in a stepfamily turns for help whether from the educational, health, welfare or legal system, they receive sensitive, appropriate and informed help. What we need is research which also shows us some of the strengths and advantages that can come from growing up in a stepfamily. This book heralds a new vision towards understanding, promoting and supporting stepfamilies – one of the various forms of family structure and formations in which our children are now living. With an anticipated 2.5 million children in stepfamilies during this decade it is imperative that we start to move the vision forward into action. Being a step-parent, as you will learn from this book, can be hard work and needs all the support and understanding that can be mustered.

Erica De'Ath
Director, National Stepfamily Association

Acknowledgements

We wish to thank our families and friends for tolerating the obsession we sometimes burdened them with during the writing of this book. In preparing the references, we realised that there are many more we might have included, because our thinking and perceptions have been informed and influenced by many writers, therapists and teachers. We have, we are sure, unconsciously drawn upon many people whose names do not appear here. Others are absent because the knowledge they have contributed is indirectly significant to this work, but nevertheless important and helpful in thinking about the myriad issues relevant to stepfamilies. We are grateful to them and to the many people whose work in progress is contributing to the understanding of stepfamily life.

We want also to express our appreciation of the National Stepfamily Association and of its work in providing help and information directly to stepfamily members as well as to the general public. We especially wish to thank Erica De'Ath, Director of the Stepfamily Association, for encouraging us to carry this book through to completion; and to our editor, Clare Grist, for her very helpful support throughout, our grateful thanks. Special thanks are due also to Howard Stacey, solicitor, for his invaluable advice and guidance on legal issues in Chapter 5.

Case examples are drawn from our own experience or our own practices and are disguised to ensure anonymity. Permission to use examples from the telephone counselling service operated by the National Stepfamily Association has been granted by the Association.

Introduction and aims

A stepfamily exists because another family ceases to exist. Or to put it another way: stepfamilies are made up of parts of other families which have reformed because parents divorced or one parent died. A stepfamily begins with at least one of the adults being a stranger to the children. It is one of our aims here to describe in both theoretical and practical terms what stepfamilies are and how they live with dilemmas which appear to be beyond resolution. We do not suggest that answers can always be found – indeed many stepfamilies give up – but we attempt to understand and explain what makes the stepfamily experience an enormous challenge to both children and adults.

We hope this book will find readership with members of stepfamilies but also with people who work with and meet stepfamilies in their professional activities. Teachers who appreciate the fact that families have many different shapes and forms and that children are loyal to their families can be a positive force in a child's life. Health visitors, general practitioners, social workers, psychologists, occupational therapists, child-care workers in special schools and residential units or hospitals and many others may find indicators here for their encounters with stepfamilies which, we hope, will help to organise the welter of information and sheer complexity of stepfamilies into an understandable form.

Research into stepfamily life and books about the subject were both rather scarce until about the end of the 1970s. Ten to fifteen years of research and publication, increasing, to be sure, is not long. What we say here will be modified, elaborated and improved by others in time, especially with regard to law and social policy. We attempt in this book to provide an overview of both as they relate to the stepfamily in Britain in the 1990s. A social history of the stepfamily is needed, even overdue; but we are not social historians, although an historical perspective can be found here also. We wish to show how attitudes and expectations about marriage and remarriage have changed and that there is an interaction between socially acceptable behaviour in marriage and family practices and legislation. We aim to provide a perspective on the stepfamily which includes the development of legal and welfare matters in order to add some understanding to the question of 'how things got to be the way they are'.

The 'traditional' stepfamily is the family which is formed after a parent has died. The stepfamily which is prevalent in the 1990s follows parental separation and divorce; obviously, an historical and socio-legal perspective must include divorce law and practice. We ask whether social policy includes or ignores the existence of post-divorce stepfamilies. Income support and laws pertaining to maintenance of women and their dependent children imposes requirements which may cause hardship in stepfamilies. How far is this considered?

We are social workers and family therapists. We have experience of direct work with stepfamilies. Our principal aim is to widen the understanding of how stepfamilies survive or do not, and what the process of ending a family and forming a stepfamily involves in terms of emotional and psychological adjustments. The phases of development in stepfamilies will be described and examples from our own practices will be used as illustrations. We will strive to suggest ways an outside agent can help, but we will not shirk the mistakes we have made by providing only examples of success!

Finally, we hope to suggest to those who meet with stepfamilies and to stepfamilies themselves that there are positive things about this family form. There are good things about life in stepfamilies and it is our view that many people in the wider society expect only chaos and failure. Many research projects begin with a negative question, a proposal which assumes a deficit (Ganong and Coleman 1987), when approaching the stepfamily. The question 'What is difficult about the nuclear family?' is seldom posed, and while we are not posing it, we assume that many kinds of family forms are good places for both adults and children and that the nuclear family of two parents and their biological children is merely one of them.

There are many questions about divorce and its effects on children and adults and many about stepfamilies which perpetuate a negative cultural image and some damaging myths. We wish to provide greater awareness of the pressures on stepfamilies, but also greater awareness of satisfactions in stepfamily life. It is just possible that the stepfamily which survives the pressures of the early stages – the needs of children for continuity of contact with both their parents, sharing responsibilities and allowing previous connections to exist – provides a model for family life which is needed in a complex multicultural society, where differences are not only allowed but respected.

CHAPTER ONE

Stepfamilies – a new kind of family?

Past and present

The word family comes from the Latin *familia*; in Roman times this was a domestic rather than a kinship group. In the better-off households the male head of the household, the *paterfamilias* was regarded as the father of the family, although only a minority of its members were actually his kin. Until this century, many, if not most stepfamilies were created following the death and remarriage of one or both parents and were usually regarded as if they were nuclear families. Nowadays we use the word 'family' almost entirely in its most restrictive use, that is, 'the nuclear group of parents and children' rather than in its legal definition, although, increasingly, the stepfamily which is created following the divorce and remarriage of one or both parents is regarded as a variant form of family. This book attempts to consider the current family structures as well as some of the underlying beliefs and the emotional patterns of behaviour in a particular type of family, the stepfamily (Robinson 1980, 1991; Smith 1990).

Because most stepfamilies are created from a second relationship or remarriage, at least one partner, if not both, will have had experience of a first marital type of relationship from which children are born. The exception is the stepfamily which is created when a single mother who has not had what might be described as a living-in relationship marries or moves into a steady cohabitation, thus creating a stepfamily. As we indicated in the Introduction, the first marriage or partnership will have ended in loss either through death or divorce and the quality of that relationship and the manner of its ending will have relevance for the stepfamily which follows. It is therefore important to start this book, albeit briefly, with some account of the history of both marriage and divorce.

Marriage

Until the mid eighteenth century the population of England and Wales was predominantly rural, and mainly consisted of a patchwork of local face-to-face communities, each with their own traditions (Parker 1991). Many marriages, especially among the poor, were relatively informal and took a variety of forms, although recognised by the communities in which the couple lived. For the lower classes there were often trial marriages which usually ended in some kind of commitment when the woman became pregnant. These were distinguished from cohabitation, which was not regarded by either of the parties or by the community as a marital type relationship. There were also several ways of ending those which proved to be incompatible, such as jumping backwards over a broom, the main community concern being to ensure a male who provided for the women and children. Until that time, land was the predominant source of production of wealth, and therefore marriage for the landed gentry was important in that this safeguarded the transmission of their often rural estates so as to protect them for their descendants, usually through some form of patrimony. Parents, especially those of the lower landed gentry, effectively controlled the marriages of their children, particularly that of their eldest son, so as to protect their primogeniture. These marriages were usually more formal and recognised by Church and state as marriages carrying full religious and legal consequences, or informal in carrying only some religious and legal consequences (Parker 1991).

With the growth of merchant and industrial capital in the early eighteenth century, marriage became a critical alliance, that of different types of capital as distinct from that based on agriculture. Social historians differ as to the explanation of the origin of the affective marriage, based on romantic love and personal compatibility, the ideal of which began to arise among the moneyed classes during the early eighteenth century. These in turn led to the growth in clandestine marriages, which were soon regarded by the powerful patriarchal squirearchy with something of a moral panic, such as now accompanies the high divorce rate. Dissenters from the values of the Church and economic changes increased these concerns, and these led to the Marriage Act of 1753, which applied only to England and Wales, whereby the state attempted to prescribe that marriage in church was to be compulsory. This was not altogether successful and many evasive tactics were devised, perhaps the best known being the 'Gretna Green' marriage; although by 1836 the Scottish law required a three-week residence, which restricted such marriages to those elopers who were able to afford this.

The 1834 Poor Law Amendment Act introduced the poor-law regions as well as requiring the registration of births, marriages and deaths. This resulted in making a legal marriage necessary for many urban women, who therefore abandoned the plural marriages which had hitherto been the practice for many. The 1836 Civil Marriage Act which followed was intended both to engage the middle classes and to bring more bureaucratic control over the morals of the working class, particularly the women, largely so that they would not become dependent on the parish poor relief.

Remarriage

Until the late nineteenth and early twentieth century, the generally poor level of health resulted in a considerable number of deaths, leaving families either without a wage earner or without a mother to care for the children. Remarriage was therefore a common way of managing to preserve the family unit, and was often a matter of convenience rather than loving attachment. In most families the father's authority was not questioned, and this pattern continued in most stepfamilies, including the majority of families with a stepfather.

Except for the aristocracy, during the Middle Ages the attitude of the Catholic Church was generally disapproving towards remarriage following the death of one partner; and such a marriage was regarded as a private act which could not receive public sanction. The priest might give a blessing – though principally as a precaution – to the bride, bed and bechamber

(Ihinger Tallman and Pasley 1987). By the end of the Middle Ages the Church had changed its attitude, but, while approving of the remarriage of widowers, did not extend this approval to the remarriage of widows, which was accompanied by the use of pejorative terms for stepmothers. Even so, in spite of the partial change of Church attitude, such marriages were perceived with hostility by the community for a number of reasons:

- As first marriages symbolised the procreative career for the couple, many second marriages did not serve the function of reproduction.
- Such a remarriage meant that a young and as yet unmarried young woman (or man) was removed from eligibility, thus limiting the choice for other marrigeable young people.
- There was usually disapproval if such a remarriage was between partners who were unequal in age, status or wealth, as they often were.

There were a number of factors that affected the rate of remarriage, the most important of which were the sex and age of the surviving spouse and the number of dependent children. For those who did remarry there was generally a preference for a partner who had not previously been married rather than a widow or widower. Other indicators were social factors such as class, urban or rural domicile and the 'marriage market' (Ihinger Tallman and Pasley 1987). This was affected by availability of potential marriage partners from whom men or women and those in a particular age group are likely to choose. For example, potential brides generally chose to marry men who were slightly older than themselves; but if there were fewer eligible men for some reason (e.g. during and following a war) or a higher proportion of eligible women with whom they must compete, then the patterns of choice became limited and therefore changed.

By the late nineteenth and early twentieth centuries the success of British industry had resulted in improved wages and the availability of housing to rent, and therefore the standard of living was generally higher. Families were more stable and because of the relatively steady employment and working hours, many families had leisure hours to spend together.

Attitudes towards remarriage also changed: while, previously, hasty remarriages had been frowned upon by the local communities, more liberal views began to develop in both Church and state. Whatever social attitudes prevailed, remarriage and the experience of having a step-parent was a common one. Indeed, in pre-industrial England the average marriage lasted only about twenty years before either the husband or the wife died. It is therefore likely that as many as one-third of dependent children lost one or both parents in the high mortality rate of pre-industrial times, and probable that as many as one-quarter of all children had step-parents. Recent research shows that, in one family out of six, children were likely to have had a parent who died and that a third of these children later had a step-parent (Burchardt 1989).

The various terms for steprelationships originates from the Old English *steop* meaning 'bereaved', for instance stepchild, stepson, stepdaughter, stepfather or stepmother, and thus stepfamily which all emphasise the degree of affinity resulting from the remarriage of the parent.

Divorce

The teaching of the Roman Catholic doctrine has always been that a validly contracted marriage cannot be dissolved, and therefore divorce is prohibited. This doctrine underlay the ideology of the law of marriage in Europe for centuries until the Protestant Reformation and in some countries until recent times – indeed, the only European country which still has no divorce law is Ireland! However from the twelfth century canon law recognised that separations could be granted in circumstances which would not allow remarriage to take place.

The ecclesiastical courts could be sued for separation from bed and board – in effect, a judicial separation. Such suits were often brought by husbands in order to avoid paying alimony to an adulterous wife; and also by wives, often as a blackmail device in order to improve their financial position following a separation which had already occurred. Some were collusively brought by a husband, but agreed to by a wife in order to prepare for a parliamentary divorce.

Another way of ending a marriage, for those men who could afford it, was through a civil action by the injured for damages for Criminal Conversation, usually the adultery of his wife with a lover. These did not allow remarriage, but were often brought as a prelude to a parliamentary divorce. Sometimes they were the result of connivance between a husband and his wife, whose lover was of higher rank, the award of damages not being followed by a suit for divorce. Accounts of such 'Crim.Con.' cases, as they were known, made titillating reading in the equivalent of today's tabloid press!

An alternative way was an agreement to part by the two parties in a deed of separation which was drawn up by a conveyancer; but this judicial separation was also somewhat costly, nor did it allow remarriage.

For men who could not afford any of these remedies, yet had a home of their own and some income, a husband could eject his wife and lock her out of the household, setting up a new household elsewhere either with a mistress or through a bigamous clandestine or Church marriage, which were not easy to detect. For women and some of the poorer men there was little alternative but for one partner to leave home, and this was chosen by some battered, ill-treated or neglected wives, who sometimes eloped to start a new life with a lover.

There were also a number of wife sales, usually agreed between the parties, in which the husband publicly sold his wife (and sometimes also his children) to another man, who undertook legal responsibility for her upkeep.

The only way it was possible for a man to divorce his wife in order to remarry was a long and costly business. He first had to seek a separation through the ecclesiastical court and then by a private Act of Parliament had to seek a divorce which would allow him to remarry. Therefore it was only a few men, mostly wealthy aristocrats who were concerned about succession to their estates, who were able to divorce and remarry.

However, by the late eighteenth century there was increasing collusion and connivance in parliamentary divorces about which successive governments demonstrated mounting concern. This was reflected in various attempts to stem the rising tide of divorces, both by punishing female adultery and by the introduction of tighter procedures before divorce could be obtained.

The prevailing double sexual standards enabled men to seek to terminate their marriage by alleging misbehaviour on the part of their wives, who were not even allowed to give evidence to refute that called by their husbands. A case which aroused considerable public indignation was that of Caroline Norton, who lost the custody of her children and campaigned for the rights of women throughout much of the nineteenth century, winning the support of many influential parliamentarians, including Lord Melbourne (Stone 1990). It was largely as the result of her determination that the Infant Custody Act 1839 was passed, which removed the presumption of custody of children under the age of seven from father to mother.

There were other attempts at divorce reform which were only partially successful, although the Married Womens' Property Acts of 1870, 1874 and 1882 had the effect of giving women more control over their own property. A Royal Commission on Divorce in 1853 eventually led to the Divorce Reform Act 1857, though this was 'a botched and bungled job' (Stone 1990). It did, however, introduce the new Matrimonial Court, which had the power to award the custody of children to either parent. This was followed in 1873 by another Act, which allowed the Chancery Court to award custody as it saw fit. The 1857 Act also allowed the wife to be represented and appear in court and also to call witnesses in her own defence. It was much more difficult for wives to obtain a divorce, and even when they could do so they often lost the custody of their children because of the prevailing presumption that children were the possessions of their father.

During the early years of the twentieth century the opposition to the reform of the divorce law diminished. This was largely the result of the weakening of the power of the Church, the growing exasperation of the House of Lords with the collusions which were forced upon litigants and the growing movement for female enfranchisement, equal rights and opportunities. There was a Royal Commission in 1912 which resulted in a split; the majority report recommended three principles: equality of access for divorce for rich and poor and men and women; the idea that divorce should be a legal mopping-up process after the spiritual death of the marriage; and recognition that there is not necessarily any correlation between the level of sexual immorality and the number of divorces. However, the minority report opposed any proposals that would make divorce easier.

During 1913 and following the war there was a striking increase in divorce and there were various unsuccessful attempts to introduce reforms of the divorce law. This was eventually achieved in 1923 through a private bill which allowed wives to divorce their husbands on the grounds of adultery.

A further private member's bill, introduced in 1937, followed the recommendations of the 1912 Royal Commission and extended the grounds for which a divorce could be obtained by the addition of proof of desertion for three years, habitual drunkenness and incurable insanity. The Act also shifted the burden of proof of innocence to the petitioner, which diminished the collusion. A.P. Herbert, the playwright, in introducing the Act to Parliament, stated that its intention was to offer real support for marriage; to protect children; to remove hardship for the unhappily married; to reduce illicit unions; to eliminate unseemly litigation; to relieve the consciences of the clergy and to restore respect for the law. The grounds for divorce as introduced by the Herbert Act are still essentially the basis of the present divorce law, which will be considered below in the discussion on the legal framework for the dissolution of marriage.

Following the Second World War, there was a sharp rise in the rate of divorce, the trend rising from about 3 per 1,000 married couples in the mid 1960s to 12.8 in 1989 (*Social Trends* 1989; *Population Trends* 1990). The number of marriages involving at least one divorced partner has also increased from 34,000 to 151,000 (provisional figure) between 1961 and 1989, while the number involving a widow or widower has fallen from 29,000 to 18,000 over the same period (*Population Trends* 1990). There has also been a considerable increase in those couples who cohabit, especially among the younger age groups, and particularly among those of all ages following divorce, often resulting in the creation of (what are generally known as) *de facto* stepfamilies. Fewer stepfamilies are created following the death of a parent and remarriage of the surviving parent, and it seems very likely that there has been a rapid increase in those following parental divorce and remarriage of at least one parent. If current levels of divorce were to persist unchanged, then over one in three marriages which take place at the present time are likely to end in divorce. Although the remarriage rates have been dropping quite sharply over a relatively long period, most divorcees either remarry (particularly the older men) or (if younger) move into stable cohabitations after divorce. Despite the relentless increase in the proportions of couples who have divorced by each wedding anniversary for successive groups of couples, in the year 1989, of those who remarried, 96,000 men were either divorced or widowers and 93,700 of the women were widows or divorced women.

The modern family

In his elegant and witty historical account of divorce in England, Stone (1990) points out that 'there are four common words which have undergone considerable changes in meaning since the eighteenth century. . . . These are "family", 'friends", "marriage" and "divorce"' (p. 45). The modern family seems to be regarded with a kind of double vision: on the one hand, it is seen as the natural unit of parents and children, united in love, trust, mutual respect and fidelity (based originally on religious beliefs); and on the other, as a narrow cage, constrained by family members being considered merely as instruments of production, by the simultaneous destructive shaping of the identities of women and children and by a general cut-off from participation in the wider society. Other commentators have argued that we need to turn away from preoccupations with family size and structures towards a consideration of the emotional patterns within the family.

Modern marriage

Before considering the position of remarried couples, it is necessary to look at the changes in the patterns of first marriages. Marriage is a public declaration of a private agreement between two individuals. Most couples marrying for the first time still choose to be married in church, while others (particularly those who are remarrying) opt for a registry-office wedding. However, since the 1970s marriage rates have fallen and there are also increasing numbers of couples who move into steady cohabitation; indeed, this is virtually the norm between a first and second marriage. Until relatively recently, the conventions or rules regarding married life were generally understood and mostly accepted. Men and women became husband or wife, understood their roles and knew what was expected of them. During the immediate post-war period the ways in which husbands and wives organised their familial activities were often described as complementary (that is, separate but fitting together as a whole), independent (in which the activities were carried out as far as possible without reference to one another) or joint (in which either partner might at different times perform the same activity). These ways of organising their activities, whether within their home or outside it, were found to be linked with the couples' relationships within their kin networks (Bott 1968). In rural and long-established working-class areas, where there is a segregation of conjugal roles, there is a clear division between the tasks of males and females and these were often accompanied by close-knit kin networks. That is, they were closely connected in the sense that people known by a family also knew and met one another independently. The husbands in couples who had joint conjugal roles were more likely to be in professional, semi-professional or clerical occupations and the issue of whether or not the wife worked was a matter of negotiation between individual couples. (It is likely that it is these families who today would be among those where both husband and wife are in full-time employment.) Those families with joint conjugal roles were likely to share their domestic and child-care tasks, but had correspondingly more loose-knit connectedness (psychosocial links) with kin and other social networks. In between these two types of families were those described as intermediate, among which there was considerable variety in the occupations of the couples and their social connectedness. Their conjugal-role segregations also showed variety in that, though there was some defined division of labour, this was more flexible, and there was also involvement with extended family and community networks.

However, changes in society, perhaps most particularly the changing role of women, have led to corresponding changes in public and private expectations of marriage, although these may well be contradictory. In the public domain there are the role expectations which are often concealed in legislation such as fiscal legislation or that of social security, which tends to emphasise the traditional view of marriage. For instance, it is only since 1990 that husbands and wives have been taxed separately.

Until very recently the media have demonstrated an essentially idealised view of marriage, though this is now changing. In the private domain there is an increasing *expectation* of the companionate marriage or coupledom between good friends who in terms of power are relatively equal and who share an intimacy and care for one another as well as a sexual and procreative partnership, although it is evident that this is still far from the case for many. Indeed, perhaps the biggest task for individual adults nowadays is how to balance their own needs for personal development with those of their partnership as a couple, and also with being parents for their children as well as those as son or daughter in the extended families of an increasingly ageing population.

The substantial increase in the number of divorces has also resulted in the number of children experiencing the divorce of their parents (or step-parents) rising from just under 71,000 in 1971 through to a peak of 163,000 in 1980 to just under 148,000 in 1989. At the same time the number of divorces in families with young children has been increasing – the most common ages being three to eight. As marriage-registration records do not include details of children brought into marriage, by whatever means, it is difficult to know the numbers and ages of children of couples who remarry (Haskey, personal communication).

In modern times, therefore, some kind of family unit remains as popular as ever. However, an increasing proportion of family households seem to experience changes in members, usually connected with incoming step-parents, cohabitees, or stepchildren. Most of these are likely to be stepfamilies in ever-increasing numbers, whether the adults are married to each other or cohabiting. Assuming that current divorce rates were to persist unaltered, about one in four children would experience divorce at least once in their family, and perhaps more than once during their childhood years – up to the age of sixteen. Furthermore, most of these children might be expected to spend at least part of their childhood years in single-parent households, while many others will sooner or later join what might be described as full-time stepfamily households, usually with a stepfather. While the exact figures are not known, it seems likely that one in eight families with children is a stepfamily or a household in which the custodial parent is cohabiting within a committed relationship.

The legal framework – the dissolution of marriage

In view of such radical changes in the patterns of marriage and remarriage, it is important to consider how these have been reflected in family law relating to the dissolution of marriage which has also had to change in order to accommodate the social trends. Just as getting married is a public act, so getting divorced is too. Although it is not known how many married couples live separately without becoming divorced, most who decide to end their marriage do so as the result of engaging in a legal process which ultimately terminates their marriage.

During the nineteenth and the first half of the twentieth century it was generally considered that the state had a responsibility for buttressing the stability of marriage. However, the rising divorce rate since the Second World War has led to much criticism of the divorce laws of the time, and this resulted in various attempts at reform. Three private member's bills were introduced, each of which failed to reach the statute book. There was a Royal Commission (the Morton Commission (1956)) as well as the report of a group called together by the Archbishop of Canterbury (*Putting Asunder: A divorce law for contemporary society* (1966)) which paved the way for reform. Until the Divorce Reform Act of 1969 it was only possible to obtain a divorce by the petitioner proving that the respondent had committed one of several specified matrimonial offences, such as adultery, cruelty or desertion, for three years. The report of the Archbishop's group was referred to the Law Commission, who found that the doctrine of 'fault' not only caused considerable bitterness and distress to the divorcing parents and their children, but also led to spouses being unable to obtain a divorce and setting up illicit but stable unions with new partners. The Law Commission considered that the law should buttress rather than undermine the stability of marriage, but they were also of the view that a marriage which had become an empty legal shell should be destroyed with maximum fairness, minimum bitterness, distress and humiliation (*The Field of Choice* (1966)). The 1969 Divorce Reform Act was not implemented until 1971 and was consolidated within the Matrimonial Proceedings Act 1973. The present legal framework embodies both a doctrine of irretrievable breakdown of marriage and that of fault. The sole ground for obtaining a divorce is that of irretrievable breakdown of marriage, but this must be established by proving one or more of five 'facts', three of which are the old faults under a new guise – adultery, behaviour or desertion – plus two separation 'facts' (now amended). The petitioner for a divorce therefore alleges that the marriage has irretrievably broken down and seeks to prove that the behaviour of the respondent accords with one of the 'facts' (referred to in brackets) or that the parties have lived separately:

- The respondent has committed adultery and the petitioner therefore finds it intolerable to live with the respondent. (Adultery)
- The respondent has behaved in such a way that the petitioner cannot reasonably be expected to live with the respondent. (Behaviour)
- The respondent has deserted the petitioner for a continuous period of at least two years immediately preceding the presentation of the petition. (Desertion)
- The parties have lived separately and apart continuously for two years immediately preceding the petition and the respondent cannot agree to the granting of a decree. (Separation with agreement)
- The parties have lived separately and apart continuously for a period of five years immediately preceding the presentation of the petition. In order to petition under this 'fact' it is not necessary for the respondent to agree. (Separation without agreement)

In order to obtain a divorce quickly it is therefore necessary to resort to one of these fault-based 'facts' by alleging and proving that the respondent has either committed adultery or behaved unreasonably, and indeed that is what most petitioners do. By far the majority of petitioners for divorce are women (71 per cent of the 150,872 decrees absolute in 1989). Over half of those petitions which are granted solely to the wife are on the grounds of their husband's behaviour. When they do petition, men are more likely to do so on the grounds of their wife's adultery (45 per cent of the decrees granted solely to the husband). In order to obtain a decree the petitioner has to swear an affidavit, which is forwarded to the solicitors of the respondent for an answer. The respondent then may accept or refute the allegations by filing an answer or indeed may file his or her own petition alleging one of the facts. This is known as cross-petitioning. The petition (or petitions) are then presented to the court for the registrar to review.

Under the present divorce law, before a decree absolute can be given the judge is required to review the arrangements which divorcing parents propose as regards their children. While most parents are able to agree arrangements for custody and access, for some these become the battlefield on which the feelings of anger, bitterness and despair about the failure of their marriage erupt, sometimes with volcanic force. Many of these parents who become embroiled in bitter conflict are eventually able to come to an agreement, either with the help of their solicitors, and/or an out-of-court mediation service, or under the auspices of the civil-court units of the probation service. If this proves impossible, then eventually the courts, although generally reluctant to do so, will have to take over the decision making and 'award' the custody, care and control to one parent, while perhaps defining the periods of access for the other.

The present divorce law is generally considered to be unsatisfactory by both the legal profession and the general public and it does little to buttress the stability of marriage; indeed, it is doubtful whether the law can do so. As it stands, the law neither encourages reconciliation nor promotes negotiation between the couple as regards the future of the family. It does not deter hasty and acrimonious divorces nor does it allow marriages which have become an empty shell to be given a decent burial with the minimum of bitterness and maximum of fairness (Hoggett 1989). Following a White Paper 'Facing the future' (1988) the Law Commission has recently produced proposals – *Family Law: the Ground for Divorce* (1990) – and a draft bill for future legislation. They propose divorce as a process over time, known as process divorce, to be awarded by the courts, usually one year from the time of one or both parties making a statement to the court that their marriage has broken down. During the next eleven months the couple would be expected to consider and resolve all the practical and potential problems which result from the breakdown of the marriage, including the arrangements regarding the children, maintenance and the matrimonial home. At the end of this period, if one or both wanted a divorce, this would be granted, although exceptionally an extension might be made. The court would still scrutinise the arrangements and a hardship bar might be imposed, for instance for poorer women with children for whom no proper financial arrangements had been made by the husband. Usually a divorce decree would be made twelve months after the original statement had been filed with the court.

The Lord Chancellor has recently pointed out that while the law cannot save marriages which have decayed beyond repair, such a *process divorce* might give greater opportunity for reaching agreements which considered the needs of children. Such a change might also improve the chances of saving a marriage (Address to the National Family Conciliation Council 1990). Quoting the research relating to the results of divorce on children, he pointed out the additional effects on the children of being confronted with the result of the present fault-based law. This can mean that they must become aware of the reason for their parents' divorce being their unreasonable or adulterous behaviour.

The most important Act relating to children since 1933, the Children Act 1989, implemented in 1991, also changes the rights of children under private law. This introduces the concept of shared parental responsibility between married parents, which continues subsequent to a divorce. Unmarried fathers can acquire this either by agreement with the mother or through application to the court. It also introduces entirely new principles in decision making within the legal context with regard to children, which will be discussed more fully in a later chapter (Chapter 5).

During the late 1960s and early 1970s the remarriage figures for men reached a peak, while by 1987 the rate was comparable to that of the early 1960s. For women the remarriage rate has risen much more slowly. It is the younger women who are more likely to remarry, while the older women are less likely to do so. At the present time, just under 50 per cent of widowers and divorced men remarry, while for widows and divorced women the figure is just under 25 per cent. In recent years, however, the number of people who decided to cohabit rather than marry has risen considerably, particularly among the young and those who have been divorced. In 1986, 24 per cent of the women and 28 per cent of the men aged 16–59 were cohabiting.

Stepfamilies

As has already been indicated, until the twentieth century, because divorce was very rare, the majority of stepfamilies were created by remarriage following the death of one spouse, or the marriage of the hitherto unmarried mother of an illegitimate child, as was the legal definition of such children, or a repartnering which was more or less accepted by the local community. There is relatively little known about the actual family life of stepfamilies in the past, and most sources of information have been drawn from folklore and from myths, which in the western world consistently reflect a popular fear of wicked step-parents, particularly stepmothers. There is, however, another source, that of personal documents such as letters, diaries and autobiographies, though little use has been made of them to throw light on the privacy of stepfamily life. Recent historical research in which 400 people born in the late nineteenth or early twentieth century were interviewed found that almost a quarter had not grown up in intact families and they spoke vividly of their memories of stepfamily life (Thompson 1975). Stepfathers were chiefly remembered for the ability to bring improvement to the family's material circumstances, while stepmothers consistently provoked strong emotions, positive or negative in equal proportion. Sibling relationships often remained close, even among those living in different households. Older siblings frequently developed protective relationships with their younger brothers and sisters; and those of same sex often acted as role models for younger children.

Several issues emerge from the research referred to above, in which old people were looking at their childhoods in stepfamilies. It is apparent that the same stepfamily is perceived differently depending on the standpoint of the person interviewed, that a distinction needs to be made not only between parents and children and according to gender, but also according to the child's position in the family. The experience of living in a stepfamily was also perceived and evaluated differently at different stages of life – the greater the distance, the more understanding of the past (Burchardt 1989).

Modern stepfamilies

Nowadays most stepfamilies are created by the marriage or cohabitation of two adults, of whom one is the biological (or natural) parent of children and the other an adult who becomes a member of the family household. What might be described as 'committed cohabitation' has recently become more prevalent, not only among younger men and women (11 per cent), many of whom may subsequently marry, but also among once-married and divorced women (22 per cent of those with dependent children and 25 per cent of those without), and at present these seem less likely to remarry, although they may well do so eventually.

There are therefore four major groupings of what might be called stepfamilies: the formerly single mother now cohabiting or married; those where the previous spouse of the natural parent of the children has died; those where the natural parents have divorced and one or both have remarried; and those who have made a commitment to one another but for many reasons have not married. Within the first three of these four groupings there are varoius ways of distinguishing a typology of stepfamilies, one of which is based on the marital and legal status of the natural parent (Robinson 1980):

- The 'legitimating' stepfamily is one where the natural parent (usually the mother), previously unmarried, marries either the parent of the child or another unrelated adult. Now that the stigma of illegitimacy has been legally abandoned as well as being more socially acceptable, such families are hardly considered as stepfamilies, though this depends on the age of the child at the time the mother marries or enters a committed cohabitation.
- In the 'revitalised' stepfamily the widow or widower has remarried following the death of the previous partner; either or both may have children from the first marriage.
- The 're-assembled' stepfamily is one where the step-parent, who is childless, marries a divorced parent with a child or children.
- In the 'combination' stepfamily both parents, either divorced or widowed and each with children, remarry and join forces with both sets of children.

It is, however, apparent that there are many stepfamilies who do not consider themselves as such; and these can roughly be divided into three subgroups. Some are families where the step-parent, usually a stepfather, joins the family while the children are very young and effectively becomes a psychological parent to the children; these are families who regard themselves 'as if' they are nuclear families and indeed are often perceived as such. A second subgroup consists of those families in which the parents are often the most unstable and damaged individuals, who find it difficult to sustain relationships and therefore often move rapidly to new partners (Adcock 1992). Such families are often those who repeatedly attract the attention and concern of social-services departments, who may try buttress the single parent in a usually maternally headed household. The third grouping contains families in which one or both parents have remarried after their children have become adults and which therefore continue as virtually two separate families connected only by the marriage of their parents, who meet on rare occasions, rather than a family of stepkin (which includes stepbrothers, stepsisters) who have a shared childhood history together.

Some of the other ways in which stepfamilies can be distinguished according to a more detailed typology will be considered in the next chapter.

Summary

This chapter has given a brief history of marriage and its ending through separation or divorce and the repartnering or remarriage which often results. It seems clear that the changing attitudes towards marriage, separation, divorce and remarriage were very much influenced by conditions at any given time, particularly the relationships between the Church and the state, the prevailing economic conditions and the expectations of men and women of themselves, and one another and their attitudes towards parenting. The ways in which marriage can be ended through divorce and how these have changed, as well as the rapid increase in divorces since the Second World War, have been discussed, as have also the proposals for a new divorce law. We have shown that the stepfamily is not a new phenomenon but has been a familiar variant of family form, although viewed differently by society over the years. One typology of distinguishing forms of the stepfamily has been discussed; other typologies will be explored in future chapters.

CHAPTER TWO

Individual and family life cycles

Before continuing our preoccupation with stepfamilies, their individual origins and their development, it might be useful to focus on the evolution of a person, as an individual, as part of a couple and as a member of a family.

Individual and family development

One way of trying to understand personal development, whether of a separate individual or of members of families, is to think in terms of life cycles, that is, the biological, physical and social development which begins in our mother's womb and ends when we eventually die, usually in our seventh or eighth decade. It has been persuasively argued that as well as a biological life cycle we also have an accompanying emotional and social life cycle, partly because of the challenges which our biological development sets us, but also because these are accompanied by social expectations, according to the society in which we live. These social expectations confront us with psychological tasks in which we need to confront and to make sense of the relational, physical and moral world in which we live and our developing inner world, which forms the basis of our identity. Each stage of development therefore presents us with a series of psychosocial tasks and dilemmas which we need to confront and resolve sufficiently so as to cope with the next stage when it arrives (Erikson 1950, pp. 219–34). While there is by no means unanimity about such an individual-development theory, nevertheless the practical application of it seems to have been convincing enough for a number of differing schools of psychological theory to have been based upon it. However, more recently there has been criticism of the stages of the individual life cycle which do not reflect the importance of the interactional nature of our development. Developmental theory has traditionally described the infant as undifferentiated from mother and moving step by step towards individual autonomy. Feminist re-evaluation has led to a new social-learning explanation in which the traditional view only applies to boys, who, though primarily raised by their mothers in early life, forge their identity through separation. Girls, on the other hand, develop autonomy in the context of an ongoing relationship with their mothers, thus fusing attachment with the process of forging their identity (Chodorow 1978). Some of this re-evaluation of the theory of gender development will be incorporated into the following discussion of the individual life cycle.

Individual life cycles

It is postulated that there are eight stages of development, each presenting the evolving identity with a series of contradictory psychological alternatives which the child (and later the adult) has to resolve sufficiently in order for his or her development to proceed. There are two important and general criticisms of this concept: firstly, that the unique capacity of human beings to communicate through speech, which develops between the ages of one and three, are not mentioned nor specifically included; and secondly, that some of the gender-specific characteristics are excluded or implicitly denigrated and that this leads to a picture of human development which is biased towards the masculine perspective. A third criticism is that the stages of moral development as distinguished by Kohlberg (1976) have not been conceptually integrated with the stages of psychosocial development, so will merely be referred to below at what seems to be an appropriate stage.

The dilemmas at the very first stage are described as those of trustfulness or mistrust, which are said to be dependent on the quality of the early care-giving that the infant receives. These dilemmas include the element of connectedness between the infant and others, a crucial aspect of all human relationships. Infants who have not been able to trust sufficiently in their mother (or caretaker) seem to have found it more difficult to find sufficient faith in the trustworthiness of others at later stages of their development. For instance, in the last twenty years or so Bowlby (1979, 1988) has described the ways that the baby needs to become attached to his or her parent, initially usually the mother (or other caretaker), who reciprocally needs to bond with her baby. Of course, the conditions need to be good enough for them to develop this first exclusive relationship, and most manage it well enough. It is also important to point out that for infants who have not been given sufficiently consistent care-giving, so long as this is provided at a later stage then this early deprivation can be ameliorated. Recent research on mother–child interaction (Stern 1985) describes the infant as actively distinguishing itself from others from the very beginning of life. This led to the idea of 'dynamic autonomy' (Keller 1985), which recognises the possibility for both men and women to be both separate and related, in other words to be both separate and connected. This also changes their concept of both the self and the other.

The second stage of development is considered to be about the time when the young child is beginning to experience a distinct sense of self; this is characterised by holding on and letting go and by struggles with shame and self-doubt. For instance, young children discover that they have some control over bodily functions, but that this is somewhat uncertain. The toddler learns that by expressing individuality in ways which may not be acceptable to the loved parent(s), then the security of bonding, hitherto taken for granted, may be experienced as in doubt. The dilemma is that young children have, on the one hand, to become sufficiently confident in their own goodness and, on the other, to be re-assured from outside that their behaviour will be acceptable to the parents. If the child's actions and products are approved by the parent, then they can also be regarded with approval by the developing self; if they are not, then the child's self-censure is accompanied by feelings of shame. The earliest stage of moral development is said to be that the young child operates in reaction to fear and punishment.

The third stage is often described as being one which involves initiative and guilt and follows quite quickly from the 'terrible twos'. A child is now considered to have a sense of individual identity, is beginning to be aware of the differences between the self and others and also that others may have relationships and interests from which s/he is excluded. This is the age of early enthusiasms and imagination, but also the one at which the child needs to learn to share, to give up the exclusiveness which has hitherto been sought and taken for granted. Jealousies and rivalries have their roots at this stage, as the autonomy that was shakily established earlier now becomes focused on keeping rivals out, and the jealousy which results from the experience of younger siblings who also have claims on the loved parent leads to subsequent feelings of guilt. There are various differing views as to the level of development of the child's conscience, as there are also about when the young child ceases to be dominated by egoism. There is some agreement that if the child's parenting and development has been good enough at the first two stages, then by the ages of four or five the child has some capacity to feel guilt for misbehaviour, whether real or imagined. However, the child may experience deep conflict over the behaviour of a parent when the parent is experienced as betraying inconsistencies by failing to practise beliefs which that same parent has upheld to the child. The feminist revisionists have criticised the inclusion of guilt. They have also challenged the idea that the characteristics of doubt, shame, inferiority and role confusion in later stages are indicative of failure. These are frequently associated with female characteristics, which implies that these characteristics are not associated with healthy development for males. Such a view therefore appears to explain the limited capacities of many men who find it difficult to acknowledge their vulnerability, doubt and imperfection, which seems to lead to an impaired capacity for intimacy. Recent work (Sheinberg and Penn 1991) points out that if active autonomy is the ultimate goal, then balanced and reciprocal subjectivity replaces the more traditional gender dichotomy; and that therefore increased complexity in relatedness replaces individuation and separation as the basis of development.

The fourth stage is regarded as a struggle between industriousness and feelings of inferiority. The growing child discovers through use of manual dexterity with tools (for instance, ball games) and various skill developments (such as skipping or riding a bicycle) that there is a world outside the home which can be explored and enjoyed. This is the age at which the child usually begins school, and here, often for the first time, the child learns that s/he may not be regarded as, or consider herself or himself to be, as competent as another child. Earlier family life may not have prepared the child with sufficient self-esteem to weather these early disappointments in the outside world and this inferiority needs to be recognised and the child's attempts at industry re-affirmed. Again the criticism condemns such an individualised description which excludes and thus diminishes the value of children's interactions with others, for it is through peer-group pressures that they learn to apply themselves and develop a recognised, if uncertain, moral sense. Gender differences and expectations are also of increasing emphasis at this stage.

The fifth stage is that of identity versus role diffusion and is generally considered to be the time of dawning sexual maturity. There is rapid body growth and the pubertal child emerges into an adolescent. Young people become actively and intensely engaged with themselves and what sort of person they are and would like to become. Their peers, both men and women, assume central importance as it is within this group that they wish to evaluate themselves and be judged as acceptable. This is also the age at which young people begin to show interest in the opposite sex and to experiment with sexual ideas and behaviour in fantasy and reality. This often begins in an attempt to demonstrate to their own gender peer group that they are as good as anyone else, but then moves into patterns of more dyadic attachments, usually with young people of the opposite sex.

The sixth stage is the search for intimacy simultaneous with the struggle for some isolation or independence. As young people emerge from their uncertainties about who they are or might become, they move into a phase of experimenting with partnerships in an attempt to explore issues of distance and closeness. Young adults seek a relationship which is unique, allows them to receive intimate care and sexual gratification and yet also leaves sufficient space in which to continue some independent existence. This is the time of building a dyadic relationship which allows the recognition of 'us, our, we' (rather than just 'I' or 'me'), thus expressing beliefs, behaviour and feelings as a pair and in ways which demonstrate sharing our lives with one another. But such a relationship must also allow each of the partners to retain their individuality, to remain 'I', thus expressing their own identity particularly as woman or man (and later as mother or father), at work and with their original family and close friends. The description of this stage is criticised on the grounds that it implies that a healthy adult who is autonomous and industrious, who can take initiative and has an identity apart from her or his family, is a seriously imbalanced human being. This stage of moral development is linked with recourse to rules and law, although these may not always be compatible with those generally accepted in society. Recent work indicates that while the development of such characteristics forms aspects of the tasks of the young adult, such individual aspirations have to be balanced against the relational ones of mutual commitment and a capacity for intimacy.

The seventh stage has been described in terms of generativity as distinct from stagnation. This is perhaps a somewhat extreme way of expressing the need of young adults to expand their horizons and enrich themselves and their partner emotionally, physically and materially by establishing a home and a family. In this way the partners have an opportunity to express their belief in the possibility of becoming good enough partners and parents and thus ensuring their own place in the future through the expression of parental affection and responsibility towards each other and their children. An ability to contract and negotiate adult to adult as well as across the generations is morally characteristic of this stage. The alternative has been described as individual stagnation and interpersonal impoverishment, but restriction and disillusion might be a more appropriate way to describe the dilemmas which many adults struggle to resolve both in their intimate and family life and in society at the present time. This description is criticised on the grounds that such generativity is placed *after* that of young adulthood which therefore seems to place it in mid life as part of what is often described as the 'mid-life crisis' (Jacques 1965).

The eighth and final stage of the individual life cycle is known as the struggle for integrity as against despair. This is described as the ability of the mature adult to accept the limitations of life and living enough to tolerate limitations, disappointments and losses, including the inevitability of death, and yet manage to retain personal integrity and the hope of an ideal.

In describing the individual life cycle, it is therefore evident that by focusing on an evolving picture of the person while virtually ignoring their mutually reciprocal effects with those closest to them, particularly the members of their family, we fail to give a complete interactional view of the individual, the couple or family life. While individuality and its development throughout the life cycle is, of course, important, as has already been made clear, it is the checks and balances of the individual within her or his partnership and intimate circle which shape and enrich not only the life of the individual but also that of the family. For those individuals for whom the breakdown of their marriage may at least partially relate to their inability to form or manage the interdependency which marriage requires, they may develop sufficiently through the crisis which results from separation and divorce to be able to make a subsequent partnership a more mutual one.

Marital and partnership development

Skynner and Cleese, in their book, *Families and How to Survive Them* (1983), give a humerous and witty account in everyday language of why couples choose one another. Their argument is essentially that having failed to resolve certain of the dilemmas which are related to specific stages of individual development and which we have screened out, we usually choose a partner who has similar difficulties. Some couples appear to have an implicit agreement to avoid certain dilemmas which neither have resolved, while others seem to develop a kind of complementarity in which the other will confront them with aspects of themselves which they have long chosen to deny and ignore. Their interactions seem to lead to difficulties for which they often blame one another, and yet at the same time give a sign of hope in that this time the original failure can be faced and perhaps resolved. As the discussion of the individual and family life cycles shows, the process of the life cycle of the couple as partners is constantly affected by these other life cycles which will heighten or diminish their dilemmas as a couple.

Family life cycles

Family life cycles are usually described in terms of circular interactions and relationships within the family, but as these are ongoing there are also spirals of familial development. The circularity of family life involves processes of development which, it is argued, require a reflexivity of thinking in order to understand them. This kind of circular thinking, as it is known (Bateson 1979), allows us to describe the ways in which we acquire the beliefs on which our knowledge and behaviour are developed, and which through reactions and interactions with one another in ongoing and circular processes we live, move and have our being day by day. There is an argument that since communication is the way through which we influence one another, it is therefore through intersubjective conversation that we influence one another. Such discourse includes non-verbal communication, which is an important factor and one which can change the meaning of what we say. For instance, if a mother says to her child 'I could kill you' in a loving, if slightly exasperated, way, it has a different meaning for the child than if she says the same thing through clenched teeth while shaking the child. An additional factor in this exchange would be the influence of the past history between mother and child, so that, for instance, a stepmother who has only recently joined the family and who had the same exchange with her stepchild would be more likely to be misinterpreted by that child because there has not been the shared history since birth, nor may there have been enough time to allow the development of a mutually trustful relationship between them. There have been various attempts to distinguish stages of family life cycles in the way that individual life cycles have been described, but perhaps the most useful one is that based on six stages, which is to some extent based on the eight-stage cycle of individual life (Carter and McGoldrick 1980). As the early stages of the individual's life are usually spent with the family of origin, when the child is dependent on the parents some of the stages can be combined so as to reflect this interdependency. Like the individual life cycle, each stage of the family life cycle involves a crucial process of transition for which the family needs to evolve principles in order to manage that particular phase. At each stage there are major changes in family status which need to be negotiated and achieved by the family members, leading to new roles, in order for the family unit to proceed developmentally towards the next stage. These irreversible changes involve a total re-organisation of the family's patterns of beliefs and ways of being, which in themselves also result in further repercussions both within the family and outside it.

As the family life cycle is perceived as a series of circular interactions, it is perhaps more appropriate to consider it as a spiral which, if one includes three generations, eventually becomes an ongoing extended and continuing family, as the study of family dynasties shows. If we consider that most families begin when the parents have their first child and their parents become grandparents, then when that child in turn becomes a parent, thus resulting in the original parents becoming grandparents, their parents become great-grandparents. By this time the original parents are likely to be elderly, and by the time their child becomes a grandparent it is probable that they will have died or soon will do so. At each stage of the family life cycle there are both familial and societal expectations as to the way that the family members should interact and carry out their roles as child, parent or grandparent. In this way 'time present and time past, are both perhaps present in time future and time future contained in time past' (T.S. Eliot, *Four Quartets*, 'Burnt Norton').

While the family life cycle is, of course, also a circular one, the first stage is often considered to be that of single young adults navigating their way to leave home in order to begin their individual lives. This involves them in the process of accepting emotional and financial responsibility for themselves, without cutting themselves off or running to another emotional refuge to replace the original family. It also involves reviewing and sorting out what the young person will take along from the family of origin, nowadays a particularly demanding task for both young women and young men because of the relatively recent changes in the definition of gender roles which are now often very different from those of their parents. Their parents too will need to develop less hierarchical ways of relating to the young person, who is no longer a child. The major irreversible changes which accrue from this stage require the young person to differentiate the self from the family or origin, nowadays to develop intimate peer relationships and to begin to establish financial independence and work; and for the family of origin to reciprocate and adapt to these changes.

The second stage is the joining of families, through partnership or marriage, as a young couple. The key process is that of commitment to a new unit. These irreversible changes entail forming a partnership or marriage as a first priority which (at least at the time) is intended to be the beginning of the rest of their lives (Mansfield and Collard 1988). This implies a re-alignment of relationships within the extended family and friendship network to include the partner or spouse.

The third stage is the addition of young children, which entails the transition of accepting new members into the dyadic relationship. The irreversible changes which result include adjusting the partnership or marriage in order to make space for the first child and later children, finding new ways to share in childrearing, carry out household tasks and manage the finances. Another change is the re-alignment of relationships within the extended family, so as to include parenting for the young couple and grandparenting roles for the original parents.

The fourth stage is when the children of the family become adolescent; and the accompanying transition necessitates a greater flexibility of the boundaries of the family, so as to allow the children's independence, changes for parents and the possibility of grandparental frailties. The irreversible changes involve a shift in parent–child relationships so as to allow the adolescent to move in and out of the family unit or system, for the parents to review and refocus on mid-life issues connected with their marriage and carers; and a shift towards caring jointly for the older generation. The couple in mid-life therefore could be described as being in a 'dependency squeeze' (McGoldrick 1989), frequently torn between the needs of their adolescent children and of their elderly parents, who may be in failing health.

The fifth stage is that of launching the children and moving on. At this time the emotional transition is the need to accept many departures from and entries into the family system. The changes require the parents to renegotiate their partnership as dyadic again, but differently from their original paired relationship. It is necessary to develop adult-to-adult relationships between the adult children and their parents; and the relationships need to be further re-aligned so as to include the children's partners or in-laws and grandchildren. Further major changes at this stage entail managing the disabilities and dealing with the death of the parents' parents (grandparents).

The sixth stage is that of families in later life, in which the transition entails an acceptance of the shifting of generational roles. The irreversible changes involve maintaining individual and couple functioning in the face of physiological decline, and the exploration of new familial and social roles; as well as support for a more central role for the middle generation. Further major changes entail making room in the family system for the wisdom and experience of the elderly and giving them support without overfunctioning for them. The ultimate change is that of beginning life review and integration so as commence the preparation which enables one to deal with loss of spouse, siblings and other peers and to anticipate one's own death.

Stepfamilies and life cycles

It will now have become apparent that the stage of the individual life cycle at which step-parents join a stepfamily will have a considerable influence on their ability to link with that family. So also, from the point of view of the step-parent, will the stage of the family life cycle which s/he has reached. For instance, if someone who has never married, nor yet become a parent, joins a partner who already has children, then they are likely to find themselves catapulted into other stages of development both as an individual and as a member of a family, with all their challenges, yet without having done the groundwork, so to speak. Furthermore, they will also be faced with, and expected to share in, the family life of an ongoing family who already have a history together, of which they are not a part nor have they shared (see the case of Kevin and Jenny below). In addition, as particular families have their own belief systems as to how families ought to live together, they are likely to have established patterns of behaviour in which the step-parent has no part as yet. Furthermore, it is unlikely that either step-parent or family would understand what these patterns are, as they are not usually matters for day-to-day conversation but are often, though not always, deeply unconscious and lived out rather than talked about. Perhaps the example of the Albany family would help to demonstrate this dilemma.

Anne Albany married her husband Bill after meeting him at the local tennis club of the small country town where they both lived. She had heard that his wife, Joan, had died as the result of a car accident some eighteen months before she and Bill met, and that he had two young school-age children, Sally (six) and David (eight), who were being looked after by Bill's mother, a widow who had moved into the family home. Anne, an only child whose parents lived some distance away, was a nurse who had her own flat and was working as a staff nurse on the paediatric ward at the hospital in the nearby large town. Anne and Bill were instantly attracted to one another and soon realised that they wished to make a commitment to one another, so they began planning for the future. They had many discussions about these plans as there seemed various options open to them. Anne, who was twenty-eight, thought she would like to give up her career and move in to live with Bill and his children, though she wanted to keep the option open to work in the future, perhaps part-time. Bill in turn welcomed this possibility as Joan had given up her career when the children were born and he had always thought mothers should stay home when the children were little, as his own mother had done. Anne, on the other hand, had always been used to her mother, a teacher, being at work. One of the early dilemmas, then, is whether or not Mrs Alice Albany, who has given up her own home to care for Bill and his children, will remain in the home. Bill feels very torn about this as his mother has always made considerable sacrifices for him and since his father died has been to some extent dependent on him, both emotionally and financially, and especially since his sister emigrated to Australia.

The tasks which lie ahead for this newly created stepfamily in their attempts to become a family are many, and will be influenced by the beliefs which each member has about what a family should be. These in turn will be governed by long-standing family patterns of behaviour and also by the stage of the family life cycle which the individuals and family members will have reached. For example, Bill is enthusiastic about Anne's work and feels it would be wrong for her to give up her independence totally, but is used to women staying at home rather than working, as this is what his mother and his first wife did. Anne, on the other hand, is used to a demanding job, to which she is committed, as was her mother before her, but has often longed for more time to be at home and for children, and thinks this would be an opportunity to be part of a family, which she has always [illegible]ed. Therefore, while as individuals they both subscribe to the belief that adults should have their own careers, their experiences of the role of the woman in the family are different. The children for their part are used to their mother and their grandmother being at home and therefore available to them. They are also likely to have been affected by the loss of their mother, which in turn will have made them vulnerable in ways which are likely to be influenced by their ages at the time their mother died. Nor are they likely to welcome the entrance of a new adult woman into the family, who is likely to bring changes, one of which will be to make demands on their father's time and attention. As an only child, Anne has not had the experience of brothers and sisters and so the sibling relationships between Bill's children are likely to be a new experience for her. The entry of another daughter-in-law to the family is also a threat to Mrs Alice Albany, who has a long-standing close relationship with her son. As she sees it, she has given up her own home in order to care for her son and his family and she is likely to find that her son's remarriage and a stepmother for her grandchildren jeopardises her own sense of value.

Another example is the stepfamily of Jenny and Kevin, who married two years ago, after living together for two years. Jenny's first husband had been the headmaster of a junior boarding school for children with learning difficulties, although they and their four children had lived very separately and in the headmaster's house. The marriage was not happy and Jenny felt very downtrodden and neglected; it is not known how her first husband experienced this marriage. When the eldest child, John, went to university, the twins Rebecca and Rachel were at boarding school and Tim was boarding at a preparatory school run by a friend of his father's, she left the family and moved into a flat in another town. She and her husband, Tom, shared the children during the holidays fairly equally and the divorce was relatively conflict-free. Jenny built up a successful career for herself. She felt very guilty about leaving her family home, indeed feeling that she had failed the children. After about eighteen months, during which time the twins had left school and gone to university and Tim to a boarding secondary school, Jenny met Kevin. Kevin, from a working-class background, had not experienced a happy family life as his parents had been unhappily married and his father had bullied both Kevin and his mother. He too had made a successful career for himself, although his own first marriage had not been happy and he was seeking a divorce. Kevin and Jenny lived together for two years, eventually buying a house and getting married. By this time John had graduated and was undertaking professional training, Rebecca and Rachel had dropped out of university and were working overseas and Tim was taking 'A'-levels with a view to going to university. Although Kevin had been married previously, he had not been a parent and found it difficult to share Jenny with her adolescent children. On leaving school, Tim went to live with them, intending to find work then travel before taking up his place at polytechnic. The other young people regularly visited both their father and his new cohabitee and their mother and Kevin. Kevin found their 'adolescent' behaviour most difficult and attempted to assert his authority by making rules about table manners, setting curfews and so on, which led to the young people behaving in a surly manner towards him. Jenny found herself torn between her new husband and her children, who were in fact behaving in ways which many adolescent people do. Threatened by their stepfather's criticisms and what they saw as his attempt to control their lives, they retreated into talking in a kind of 'flip' code to one another, as they had often done when much younger. They included allusions to their stepfather in this kind of mutual and critical shorthand as a way of expressing their resentment towards him. This infuriated him as much because he could not follow it as because of what they actually said; and it upset their mother even more because she could! She telephoned the Stepfamily Telephone Counselling service and at the counsellor's suggestion Jenny and Kevin were referred to one of us

(M.R.) who saw them in an attempt to help. Jenny was very upset during the interview, feeling guilty and distressed about her children, and torn between them and her husband. Kevin, though concerned about his wife's distress, was inclined to the view that now her children were grown up they should get on with their own lives and not bother them. What then emerged was that now she had a comfortable home of her own, she hoped she could make up to her children for what she felt they had missed. The therapist offered to see all Jenny's children, but as the three older young people were all away from home, eventually saw them together. Although ambivalent about coming for an early morning session (the only one the therapist had free), they arrived punctually and it became clear to her that they now wanted to get on with their own lives. They were fond of both their parents, glad they were happy and wanted relationships with them which were adult to adult, rather than parent to child. They had indeed been hurt by their divorce, but felt that as both parents were now happy in new relationships they were therefore free to get on with their own lives. They loved their mother but wanted their stepfather to get off their backs yet also to take an interest in *them*. They quite understood that their mother and stepfather had household rules about tidiness, for example, but felt that it was their mother's place to tell them off, not their stepfather's.

Not all stepfamilies will solve the problems with which they will be presented in the same way. As has been shown, every stepfamily will be influenced by the stage which has been reached by each of its individual members, as well as collectively by the group which stems from the original nuclear family; and also by the long-standing family patterns of behaviour based on beliefs about families of both parent and step-parent. As with individuals and nuclear families, one way of attempting to clarify the complexities of stepfamily development is by distinguishing various stages of the stepfamily life cycle. These will, of course, be additional to those of nuclear family development and will be described and discussed later (Chapters 5 and 8). If the stepfamily is one which has been created post-divorce, then there are additional life-cycle stages which need to be faced and resolved during the divorce process, as unresolved difficulties relating to the ending of a relationship are likely to be carried forward into the formation of the stepfamily (see Robinson 1991).

The stepfamily life cycle

Each of the seven stages of the stepfamily life cycle entail the resolution of certain tasks so that attachment and bonding between the stepfamily members can take place. As with nuclear families there are certain irreversible changes which are necessary for the integration and development of a good enough stepfamily. These include the acceptance of the present situation as permanent.

The first stage has been described as new beginnings. Although some formerly married people appear to move to new relationships with confidence, the self-esteem of others has been so damaged by the failure of their first marriage and the subsequent divorce that they are cautious about risking a further commitment. In either case this entails the recognition by the remarrying couple of the myths and fantasies which abound relating to stepfamilies. Some of these are contained in the folklore and myths (which will be explored in Chapter 4) relating to wicked stepmothers and sexual attraction between step-parents and stepchildren. Others are more present-day, for instance the fantasy that the children need to be rescued from a depriving and unloving parent. Another is that along with remarriage comes instant love, the belief being that because we love one another and our children, so shall we each love the other's children as they will also love her/him. These myths will inevitably accompany their stepfamily life cycle. One of the first tasks a remarrying couple needs to face is to recognise and begin to find ways of managing these for themselves and their stepfamily. As has already been indicated, children do not divorce their parents, and therefore there is a need to find ways in which the formerly married couple can share the parenting of their children although they are divorced and one (or both) has remarried. There are many different kinds of shared parenting post-divorce, ranging from a close sharing both of time and decision making through to one in which the parents remain very separate, barely communicating about the children (and perhaps one seeing them only rarely), with various versions in between. Shared parenting which gives at least some priority to the needs of the stepchildren is sometimes hard for the step-parent, who, unlike the adoptive parent, did not choose the children, but chose their parent. It is nevertheless important at this stage for everyone involved, both parents and step-parent(s) to recognise that there is a need for the parents to find ways of coparenting the children. Because the parent–child bonds precede that of the remarriage, and because becoming a parent involves responsibilities as well as affectional bonds, the newest relationship, that of the remarried partners, is also vulnerable and as yet has no rooted shared history.

Dick and Lucy married after his first wife left both him and their children to live with a former boyfriend. Their daughters were then aged two and a few months. Lucy gave up her job and moved in with Dick and looked after the girls, who until then had been cared for by their grandmother and a number of 'mother's helps'. After a few years both the girls became very attached to Lucy, regarding her as their mother; indeed, the younger had no memory of her mother. Then their mother, Ellen, suddenly sent a Christmas card to her daughters signed 'from your mother'. Dick and Lucy explained to the elder daughter who the card was from, and the younger, who had thought that Lucy was indeed her mother, became most upset and fearful that 'the lady on the card' would come and take her away. Dick's anger with his first wife resurfaced, and it was Lucy who was left to try to console her husband and step-daughters and also to manage her own feelings of uncertainty.

The second stage involves the stepfamily's efforts to assimilate and become a family in their own right, not a nuclear family, but a different kind of family, with its own patterns of communication and rules for behaviour. This involves giving the step-parent the time and space, both psychological and physical, to develop her or his own relationships with the stepchildren. For a stepmother it is all too often expected, by both her husband and herself, that she will become an alternative mother, taking on maternal responsibilities and duties, including discipline. For stepfathers, it is often a *fait accompli* that they are expected and expect themselves to take on financial and disciplinary responsibilities from the word go. This is the stage when unresolved grief about the loss of the previous family is likely to be re-awakened for the children, as well as loyalty conflicts between each of their parents. If they and their stepchild(ren) are beginning to develop a positive relationship with one another in their own right, then it is likely that this will cause the children some conflict of loyalties as regards their affectional bonds with their out-of-house parent.

John and Judy had at one time worked together, although Judy had at that time thought John was somewhat overbearing. Both of them had unhappy marriages, each left their spouse and Judy, who had no children, sought a divorce. John felt very guilty about his daughter, then aged eight, and his son, then six. After a few years of single life, they remet, found that they were attracted to each other and moved in to live together. John's wife, Betty, was very angry when he sought a divorce, and there followed a good deal of acrimony over money and his wish to see the children regularly. Eventually it was agreed that they should spend every other weekend with John and Judy, who had by then been married five years. Johns occupation took him overseas for about a week every month, and Judy started a new and demanding job as well as an Open University degree course, which would lead to promotion for her. Judy found being a weekend stepmother extremely difficult, especially to her stepson, a silent and uncommunicative boy who seemed to behave as if she were not there. She could manage to relate to her stepdaughter, by then a teenager, as they had interests in common. John felt torn between the two of them and did not know which way to turn. He and his son built model aeroplanes together and watched the football on television. This drove Judy frantic, as they were invariably late for meals and dominated the sitting room at the weekend, when she wanted to do her Open University studies. Eventually she felt so guilty about her hatred of her stepson that she sought help, and both she and John came for marital therapy to try to sort out what was in effect a typical stepfamily issue.

The third stage is that of awareness, the time when someone in the new stepfamily, usually a woman and often the stepmother, recognises that all is not well with the stepfamily. What sparks this unease may be the advent of a perfectly ordinary family difficulty, such as are common during adolescence but which are often seen as specifically stepfamily problems and may be complicated by the structures and processes of stepfamily life. For instance, a common feature of stepfamilies is that the biological parent and her or his children may be at a different stage of the family life cycle than is the step-parent, particularly if s/he has not previously been a parent. Not only do they share a history together in which the step-parent has (usually) had no part but the step-parent has not yet acquired the knowledge and experience which accompany that period of the family life cycle. In other words s/he may not have yet been confronted with the dilemmas of that particular period. Another aspect of dawning awareness of stepfamily life is the issue of boundaries. These often emerge as the remarried parent and step-parent quite naturally attempt to define their family life around the boundary of their own household. For stepfamilies, and particularly those where the children and stepchildren move between households, this is just not possible.

All families have their own rules, not only household rules for day-to-day living, but also as regards ways of interacting, including communication (see Chapter 8). Such family patterns are usually deeply unconscious expectations and pressures to behave and communicate in particular ways. These family patterns are unique to every family and inevitably have to change when entering a new household. The difficulties arise because these differences are not recognised and confronted by the members of the developing stepfamily until things begin to go wrong. Often the stepfamily is confronted with such boundary issues just at the time when society and they themselves expect that their family solidarity will be reinforced. Family celebrations, rituals such as Christmas, weddings, christenings (and even funerals) are typical occasions when families regroup and re-affirm their affection and attachment to one another, as well as being the time when old rivalries and jealousies may resurface! For stepfamilies, such celebratory occasions often prove to be just those when the outsider status of the step-parent is highlighted. This stage of awareness is most often the one in which members of stepfamilies seek some kind of therapy.

Matthew, aged sixteen, was referred to one of us (M.R.) by his mother, Jill, who was a trainer in the higher-education field. Matthew had precipitately left school and was said to be lying in bed all day until late in the evenings, then going out and mixing with undesirable friends. He was also involved in drug taking. Jill and Matthew's father, Peter, had been divorced when Matthew was three and his sister six. Peter was still contributing to Matthew's maintenance and they met regularly. When seen with his mother, Matthew presented as a not untypical teenager: somewhat grubby, spikey hair and apparently inarticulate. However, in response to the therapist's interest and attempt to engage him, he was able to talk about his situation. His mother was always on at him about his schoolwork and he had hated school. He got on all right with his mother's cohabitee, Dick, and in general kept out of his way. One of Dick's children from his previous marriage, Sam, was at school with him and in the same class and they seemed to have a kind of love–hate relationship with one another. Dick was in touch with his children, though there was no other contact between him and his first family. Matthew saw his own father when he wanted, usually when he asked him for money; and in fact had lived with Peter and his second wife, Sally, and her children for a time, but it did not work out so he returned to Mum. When asked about this, he said he did not like the rules in that household; Sally was too strict. His anger was reserved for his headmaster, who he said had encouraged him to be open about the marijuana which he and Sam had smoked, promising him that he would not reveal the information to anyone; but he had informed the police, who had given Matthew a warning about drugs. Matthew was so angry he had left school at once. A week later, Matthew was seen by the therapist together with his father, because his mother, although in telephone contact with Peter, had told the therapist that she would prefer not to be seen together with him. Peter had collected him from his mother's household and as he did so mother had put a can of beer into Matthew's hand. Peter was furious about this and had said to Matthew that he would not be allowed to behave like that if he lived with him. By this session, Matthew had had his hair cut, was dressed in relatively clean clothes and was generally more talkative. He had also got himself a temporary job, which he enjoyed. He and his father talked about his future and Peter agreed that if he got himself some qualifications he would consider taking him into his relatively successful building business. His mother later wrote to give the therapist a progress report, saying that Matthew had done just this and was now working in his father's firm and doing well. She concluded by saying 'and we have got our old Matthew back, now older and wiser'. This stepfamily situation illustrates what is a not unusual adolescent rebellion in which Matthew was expressing his anger with both his parents and at the same time asking for limits to be set.

Another family which came for help to one of us (M.R.) as the result of the stepmother's desperate appeal to the Stepfamily Telephone Counselling Service was the following. Kate, a woman in her forties had lost her first husband after a long illness, soon after her daughter Isobel (now thirteen) was born. She had met Derek (also in his forties), the father of three children, Miranda (now at university), Paul (seventeen and at school) and Carol (ten), whose first wife had suddenly died after Carol was born, and they had fallen in love. They had prepared for their forthcoming stepfamily life with great care and involved all the children in their planning. Kate gave up her job, and after a short period in Derek's house they had bought a new home with a considerable mortgage because they needed a rather large house for so many children. Kate put enormous thought and care into becoming a stepmother, and Derek, who had been a lone father for so long, took considerable trouble in becoming stepfather to Isobel, who had never really known her own father. What Kate had not anticipated was the resentment and disappointment she would feel in her stepchildren, and in particular about the behaviour of Carol, who seemed to tell pointless lies about everything. She could get on well with Miranda as she understood about adolescent girls and young women but found it difficult to reach Paul who was a somewhat withdrawn lad and who also told lies when in a corner. Kate found Carol impossible to understand or even like and it always seemed to her that just when it seemed possible for them to get a bit closer, Carol would spoil it all with her pointless lies about such silly things. Derek himself could not understand it, and was himself at a loss to understand what had happened to Carol.

During the early years he had had to work hard to keep the family together and they had had a series of au pairs, although he had always been home in time to put the children to bed. Although Derek was not idealistic, he had thought that when he met and married Kate and they brought the two families together they would work things out between them.

In a family session all the children talked about their hopes and fears 'when we got married', which was how they put it. Isobel said that she had wanted to have a dad and a brother and sister, but she had found it difficult to share her Mum and sometimes she resented them, especially when Carol was naughty and upset her Mum so. Paul said that he had been glad when his father remarried and he too liked having another sister, but it had meant a lot of changes and things were not so casual about the house as they had been when it was 'just them'. Carol wept and said she did not know why she told so many lies. She had longed for a mother; no-one talked about her own mother and although Miranda and Paul had known her, they had not told her what her mother was really like. She wanted to be like Isobel, whom she admired, but she felt so bad she did not think she ever would and anyway Mum (i.e. Kate) loved her much more than she did her (i.e. Carol). This sad state of affairs was as much related to the unresolved mourning for the loss of Kate's first husband, Derek's first wife and the effects of these losses on the families left behind as it was to the attempts to combine the two families together into one stepfamily household. This family session in which all the members were encouraged by the therapist to share with one another their perceptions and feelings about the present situation enabled the parents to make the decision to separate for three months in order to take stock of what they now wanted to do. Derek and his children moved to a three-month tenancy nearby and he sought help for Carol at the local child-guidance clinic. Kate and Derek had previously been offered help with Relate (marriage guidance) but had been told they would have to wait; but now this was made available to them. During their planned separation they intended to meet frequently on their own and sometimes with the children, so that both generations had time to reflect on their own relationships, the remarriage of the couple, the children's relationships with their parent, as well as with their step-parent and with each other. The therapist offered them occasional family sessions.

As this case demonstrates, these first three stages – new beginnings, attempts at assimilation and awareness – may need to be repeated after the stepfamily have begun to face and tackle the fourth and subsequent stages together.

The fourth stage has been described as restructuring. It is at this stage that someone, usually the step-parent, and especially a stepmother, realises that it is necessary for some changes to occur. Often s/he attempts to initiate them by some degree of confrontation with the partner (or even directly with the stepchildren), for instance a stepfather might consider it necessary to introduce a degree of discipline in a situation where he considers his wife to be somewhat overindulgent with her children. Stepmothers, on the other hand, may try to move into a maternal role too soon; indeed, given the expectations of society, it is difficult not to do so (Smith 1990). These confrontations may lead to tensions between the parent and step-parent, and/or problems within the stepfamily. The restructuring phase entails sorting out where the power actually lies in the re-formed extended family, and who has power of decision making and about what. This involves setting up structures and procedures which relate to rules for the children according to one stepfamily household and respecting those with prevail in the other household. If the children are old enough, it probably also involves setting up some way of consulting and negotiating with them, so that they can take part as well as understand the necessity for some rules.

In any stepfamily household, space is often at a premium and requires careful discussion and rules about territorial rights. For a stepfamily living in the original family home of some of the stepfamily members, this can become a particularly difficult issue. Psychological space is also a delicate issue, in that children who are used to an almost exclusive relationship with a parent find it difficult to give up some of that parent's time to the incoming step-parent. Younger children are often particularly demanding in anxious situations, and becoming a stepfamily is just such a situation, one with few guidelines for any family member.

Becoming a stepfamily also raises sexual anxieties, particularly for adolesent children. Newly remarried partners are often very sexually active and in their excitement at finding one another may be physically demonstrative with one another around the house. This sexual ambience may stir up both sexual anxieties and jealousies for the stepchildren, especially if they are already grappling with their own emergent sexuality.

Jim and Maggie, both in their early forties, had been married for two years, they had no children living with them and were doubtful whether they would embark on parenthood even if they were able to conceive a child. Jim had been married before and had two daughters, Shirley (sixteen) and Jackie (twelve). He and his first wife had had a stormy relationship, which ended in her throwing him out, and they were divorced some years later. His first wife did not remarry, although she had a series of men friends, some of whom lived with her and the girls, although these also were often stormy relationships. Jim had always made the girls and their mother an allowance and saw the girls regularly once a month. Maggie, although she had never married, had had several serious affairs, and had lived in the United States for some years. She returned to this country when her father was terminally ill, and met Jim soon after her father's death. Their friendship ripened into a deep and enriching affection which was particularly precious to them both as they felt that neither had previously had such a mutual and loving relationship. Maggie was determined to build a good relationship with Jim's children and did not try to become a substitute mother to them. She felt that she and the younger daughter (Jackie) had begun to build a friendship, but was shocked to find herself resentful and jealous of Shirley. Jim too found Shirley difficult as she not only looked like her mother but was as volatile and irritating to him as her mother had been. Both Jim and Maggie well realised that some of Shirley's behaviour was as the result of an unhappy adolescence, and they determined to continue to try to help her. Shirley was thrown out several times by her mother, but returned home usually as the result of Jim alerting his brother who lived nearby and mediated with Jim's first wife. During these times Shirley would make transfer charges on her father's telephone at work, complaining about her mother and asking for money. Jim and Maggie thought she was probably dabbling in drug taking, though Shirley denied it.

When she stayed with them, she also stayed in bed much of the time and did seem very exhausted. She helped herself to food from the fridge, to Maggie's make-up and clothing, though was not otherwise unpleasant, as it seemed that she was at her mother's house. She was, however, particularly demanding with her father, usually wanting to sit beside him on the sofa, or walking with him when the four of them went out. Maggie found herself deeply resentful of this behaviour, although she was well aware that it was the result of Shirley's distress at what was happening between her and her mother. Jim and Maggie found it enormously difficult to draw the boundaries between what they could and could not do to help Shirley when she was not living with them and also to make limits about her behaviour when in their home. Maggie was terrified that Jim would want the girls to come and live with them as she was fearful of the effect this would have on their cosy life together. Jim in his turn felt that they ought to offer Shirley a home, yet dreaded doing so and felt guilty about not making such an offer. They used the session with the therapist they contacted (M.R.) to work out what they each thought would be reasonable protection for their own life together, what they could and could not offer to the girls, particularly Shirley, and to set some limits for her when she was staying with them.

The fifth stage is going into action, in which the whole stepfamily begins to relate to one another and work together in a new way. This is the stage at which the remarried couple, often by now married for a number of years, together begin to take stock of their situation, consider possible options and take steps to explore what might be workable solutions, as Jim and Maggie did in the example given above. This is likely to be the stage when the parent and step-parent may resume contact with former partner(s) so as to negotiate new arrangements, particularly as regards custody and access. It is not unusual for parents who are in acrimony and bitterness over the ending of their marriage to have been unable to agree and set out what are workable arrangements for their children so that they can be in regular contact with both of their parents. Two researchers who explored ongoing relationships in stepfamilies (Burgoyne and Clark 1984) found that it was often the step-parent who was most resentful of the non-custodial parent intruding into their family life. They distinguished three ways in which stepfamilies attempted to solve such conflicts. A common one is that because the parents have not been able to make some shared sense of the failure of their marriage they are unable to develop a co-operative relationship, and the non-custodial parent finally withdraws. Their child, deprived in this manner, may try to bring them together in an attempt to resolve the situation for her or him (as Matthew did in the example given earlier). In other families, because of practical difficulties, often geographical distance, and because of the stepfamily's attempts to draw tight boundaries around their household, the contact with the non-custodial parent becomes less and less, eventually often dwindling only to contact as family festivals or none at all.

When the parents are able to create flexible access and to separate the arrangements for these from any ongoing conflict which they may be having, for instance about maintenance payment, another solution is possible. Such flexible solutions may involve the whole of the re-formed extended family. For example, the grandparents might offer to provide a picking-up point so that the former partners do not have to meet. Even if formerly married parents cannot develop a sufficiently positive relationship that allows them to share the parenting of their children, a difficult task and one not made easier by either (or both) finding a new partner, they may be able to create a sufficiently comfortable situation for their children. Something children find particularly painful and difficult is to hear one parent criticising or making negative comments about the other.

The sixth stage is that of integrating and is one in which contact and intimacy are beginning to be achieved within the stepfamily. This takes some years and a rough guide is that these include the length of marriage, plus the age of the youngest child at the time of the remarriage.

Mark and Alison have been married for ten years, they have two sons, Richard, aged eight, and Michael, six, and live in the south of England. Mark has previously been married and has two teenage daughters from his first marriage. He and his first wife amicably agreed to part and she has a new partner, who lives in London with her and the girls, with whom he gets on well. Mark's daughters, when younger, visited him and Alison every month and spent some part of every holiday with them. They spend alternate Christmases with each parent and visits are arranged either near or on their birthdays. The girls have been involved with Richard and Michael from birth and are looked up to and loved by them, the girls in their turn being affectionately bossy elder sisters. Now that they are older, the girls arrange their own visits according to their school and social activities, and there are frequent telephone calls. Mark and Alison are not well off, but payment for visits from the girls as well as treats for them have always been an integral part of their budget (see Chapter 6). When they were younger, Mark and his first wife would share the journeying, one fetching the girls and the other returning them, or they would meet at some mutually convenient half-way point. Now the girls make the journey on their own, usually by coach, which is cheaper than the train. The elder of the two girls is now at university, reading the same subject as Alison had done many years earlier. When asked about this, she told her stepmother, 'Well you set me a good example, so I thought I'd do what you do.'

The seventh stage is characterised by the ultimate acceptance throughout the whole family that the stepfamily is 'good enough'. There are advantages in being a stepfamily. Parenting is very hard work and step-parents can, by agreement of all, take over some tasks, thus lightening the burden. Some of the advantages include the relative objectivity which a step-parent can bring as well as additional personal interests. There may also be the availability of additional grandparents, and the description 're-formed extended family' also includes the various kin, whether affinal, biological or former partners and their new partners. This stage may take years and may never really be achieved, although most stepfamilies, like most families, learn to rub along together well enough. Thus the final resolution involves the stepfamily in an ultimate recognition and acceptance that stepfamilies are not and never can be nuclear families and that many of the problems they have experienced on the way are similar to those which are faced and resolved by all families. As therapists, we do not usually see families at this stage, and though the same issues may re-arise, the families will be able to manage for themselves and get over them quickly enough.

Typologies of stepfamilies

There are various ways in which stepfamilies can be described so as to summarise the complexities which stepfamilies encompass. A classification based on the marital status of the remarried parent(s) has already been referred to (Robinson 1980), but does not include the custody and access arrangements or whereabouts of the children, for instance full-time or part-time stepfamilies. Another typology which is based on different levels of the stepfamily's complexity has a ninefold classification, demonstrating the diversity of stepfamilies. The classification relates to the remarried couple and the children of either, or in common, and moves from the simple to the complex stepfamily structure, which also includes children from both previous marriages as well as children born of the remarriage who are half-siblings of the stepchildren (Ihinger Tallman and Pasley 1987).

1. Couples where neither partner has children, although one partner has previously been married.
2. Both have previously been married and have a child in common.
3. One or both have an adult child from a previous partnership.
4. The couple have a child in common and one or both have a child from a previous marriage who does not live with the stepfamily.
5. There is no child in common, but one or both have children of a previous partnership who do not live in the family and may or may not visit the stepfamily.
6. At least one had a child from a previous relationship who now lives with them.
7. Both have a child or children from a previous relationship now living with them.
8. Both have a child or children from a previous relationship living with them plus a child in common.
9. Both have a child or children from a previous relationship, at least one of whom lives with them, while others reside elsewhere, plus a child in common.

Many stepfamilies are part-time ones, where children of one or both partners' previous relationships come for weekend and holiday visits. A common part-time stepfamily is one in which the stepfather's children primarily live with their biological mother, but come for regular contact visits, while the stepmother's children live with them and visit their biological father. This will also be a stepfamily household which may include children from the new relationship. These structures dictate the nature of interaction within the stepfamily, which are complex indeed, as will be discussed later.

Summary

In this chapter we have looked at individual, couple and family life cycles, the periods of transition and the dilemmas which are posed at each stage. We have mentioned that divorce is also a period of transition, and this will be discussed more fully in the next chapter. Unless these individual, couple and family life-cycle stages are sufficiently confronted, the stepfamily is likely to be faced with difficulties from previous stages of development. The stages of the stepfamily life cycle and their accompanying dilemmas have also been explored and another typology for describing different types of stepfamily discussed.

CHAPTER THREE

Betwixt and between

All families go through a difficult and distressing period following the death of a parent, a permanent separation or a divorce, during which they try to confront and come to terms with what has happened. For families where one (or both) parents remarry following a death or divorce, the phase between these events is an important period which allows for the necessary mourning. During this time the expression of grief can both assuage the loss and permit the contemplation of a future which will be different for each and every member of the family, as well as for the family as a whole. When one partner dies, there are various cultural, religious and familial traditions related to funerals in which the grief is shared and which can be healing; but the only ritual following divorce is the legal pronouncement of the decree in open court, the only public recognition of the ending of their marriage. In fact, this is rarely heard by either partner, so for each of them the recognition that their marriage is ended is a telephone call with their solicitor or a letter which comes to their door. For spouses who have been bereaved following death of a partner, the funeral marks the beginning of widowhood or becoming a widower, words which symbolise for all their state of aloneness. For those bereaved as the result of a divorce, the term divorcee is the only name which is given to each of the divorcing partners; there is no word which symbolises the state of becoming unmarried after a marriage. For families bereaved as the result of a death or a divorce, a phase of lone parenthood follows and the phrase 'one-parent family' often both denies and conceals the presence of another parent who may not only be alive, but may also wish to continue to be an involved and responsible parent.

We have already emphasised that by far the majority of stepfamilies are created from a family situation which has involved such a loss, and this chapter will focus on this painful, distressing and sometimes bitter background history, because if the losses are not sufficiently mourned and accepted then they are likely to intrude upon the life of the developing stepfamily at the most vulnerable early stages. It is important to recognise that these losses are threefold and at a number of different levels. At one level there is either the absolute loss of a parent who has died or the partial loss of a parent as the result of separation and divorce, both of which result in a radical change in family relationships. For the couple there is also the loss of a spouse or partner, whether through death, separation or divorce.

At another level, that of the nuclear family as a unit and the extended family network, there is also the loss of the family as it was prior to the death or parental separation. This tripartite loss, of parent, spouse and family, is experienced at different but interconnected levels and, initially at least, underlies many aspects of stepfamily life, although it may be denied, disguised and thus often not consciously recognised. Therefore, the most crucial issue for any stepfamily is whether those members of the original family unit have sufficiently come to terms with the experience of loss and their feelings connected with it. This is a necessary healing process which needs to be resolved both individually and collectively, so that the family can begin to regard the future as a challenge to be faced with hope. It is easy to make such a statement, but when it is explored as part of day-to-day family life, it is a good deal more complex, even confusing.

As has already been described, individuals and families go through life cycles, the stages of which are usually linked with the biological and psychosocial developments common to all families. If the family has been functioning well enough, then the needs of any particular family are likely to have been met sufficiently for the members both individually and collectively, to enable them to cope with the usual hazards which accompany a particular stage. Since there is no such thing as an ideal family, most families, as has already been indicated, are described as being 'good enough' families if they can be considered to meet the needs of their individual members sufficiently. If they have not met these needs, then those families who have not been good enough will remain vulnerable and at risk following any losses which they might experience, whether they be minor losses or the major loss which the death or departure of a parent entails.

Each aspect or level of the tripartite loss will be considered in turn, although, of course, they are all interconnected and the experiences at one level will be mirrored by and will influence each of the others, both at the time of the actual loss and subsequently. For instance, the loss of a parent in childhood will affect a person's own experience not only of family life in childhood but also, later on, of their relationships as a spouse and as a parent. Each individual will experience a particular loss in terms of her or his age and level of development at the time, as well as the effect on their own individual identity. The loss of a parent, a husband, wife or partner, whether through death or the failure of the marital relationship, while having some similarities, also has major differences and these will be considered at each level of loss.

Effect on the child of the loss of a parent

Death of a parent

Although the experience of loss for adults is well known to be immensely distressing, the experience of such loss for children is none the less intense, though it is experienced somewhat differently from adults. Research into the effects of the loss of a parent during childhood, whether as the result of parental death or divorce, has shown that the subsequent development is related to the age and stage of development of that child at the time that the loss occurred. The stages of the individual life cycle (as described in Chapter 2) give some indication of the likely effect on a child of the loss of a parent. For those infants and children up to the age of about two who lose a parent through death there is little likelihood of actual memories of that parent. They are, however, likely to have feelings which relate to that experience and which effect their development. So, for example, a two-year-old who loses a parent, particularly her or his mother, will have a different experience than had this occurred at the age of fourteen.

The loss of a parent at the stage of the individual life cycle when the young child is at the stage of self-centredness (approximately two to five years) and believes that everything that happens has a direct relationship with her or him, can bring problems often unsuspected by those who care for such young children. Very young children have limited comprehension and their thinking is both concrete and infused with magical ideas. This makes it difficult for them to grasp the idea of death being final and not infrequently they expect that their lost parent may return some day. Whether a parent dies or leaves home, then, a young child is likely to believe that Dad or Mum has left because the child has driven them away by their naughtiness or badness. All too often the parent who remains either explicitly or implicitly discourages questions about what has happened. The child may react by being particularly demanding towards the remaining parent or regress to an earlier stage of development, perhaps by bed-wetting or having temper tantrums. This may be partly due to a fear that this parent will leave them too if they are difficult, which sometimes lead them to test this out. Loss at this early stage can affect the child's sense of trust as well as their capacity for attachment in later life. It should be pointed out that the examples which are given later in this section are mostly from children who were not helped to grieve and therefore sought or were referred for help later for problems which had their roots in earlier bereavements and were not mourned at the time.

Bob's mother was pregnant with him when his father was killed in the Second World War; and for his first two years, his depressed mother and he had a very close relationship indeed. When he was two his mother remarried and one of his first memories is of his 'losing' her when she went away (presumably on her honeymoon), leaving him with his grandmother, and came back with his stepfather. Bob never really got on with his stepfather; the family were poor and Bob was educated at a school for the children of servicemen killed in the war. He left home as soon as he could and, being ambitious, became a very successful professional. He found it difficult to speak of his feelings and when he married, chose a wife for whom, because of her own childhood experiences, it was extremely important that she be reassured of her self-value. The marriage ran into difficulties and Bob's wife 'threw him out' for a period of six months, during which they both had individual and marital therapy. Bob discovered that there were two sides of him: one was the apparently self-contained hard-working man of few words who was a devoted husband and father; the other side, in apparent contradiction, was an ambitious competitive perfectionist, determined to make a lot of money and to live up to the fantasy image of his own father which he had created in his own mind and who was everything which his stepfather was not.

Charles, on the other hand, had a relatively happy childhood in a stepfamily. His mother died when he was born and his father remarried some months later. Although his stepmother looked after him, she was not a very demonstrative person and he missed the warmth of his grandmother, who had cared for him during his early months. His father and stepmother did not keep his true parentage secret from him, but neither did they talk about his mother openly. It was therefore many years before he felt he had permission to ask questions about her openly, although secretly he found out all that he could. He had no internal picture of his mother, and all that he knew of her was derived from photographs and much later conversations with members of his family other than his father. Charles did well both socially and at school. He was also successful in his chosen career and had many girlfriends; but, unlike his contemporaries, he did not marry until he was in his mid thirties. His wife was exceptionally outgoing and warm, they had a mutually strong relationship and wanted children. Sadly, he and his wife found that she was unable to have any and it was this which led them into therapy. After sharing their grief about their inability to conceive, they adopted children and had a happy and fulfilling family life.

For children who are of early school age, the loss of a parent is experienced differently. As they are old enough to have some capacity for abstract thinking, they are able to have some idea of the concept of death. They are also at the stage when socialisation amongst peers and conceptual ability and skill development become important for them. Depending on the circumstances of their early history and their relationship with the parent who has died, with sensitivity and understanding children can often be helped to grieve for the parent, let them go, thus becoming freed to make new attachments.

Sam's father died when he was six. His parents had divorced, but were still living acrimoniously in the family home, a cottage on the farm where Sam's father was employed. Sam's father had a heart attack in Sam's presence, from which he never recovered and almost at once he died at home. Sam's mother, always a heavy drinker, constantly denigrated her deceased husband, so that by the age of eight Sam was caring for his mother, by now an alcoholic, who neglected him. He was received into care and in order to prepare him for adoption for a number of years had therapy in order to help him to come to terms with what had happened to him. By now aged twelve, his destructive outbursts of anger made living in a family difficult for him. After one such occasion, when one of us (M.R.) as his therapist was trying to help him to understand and control his anger and encouraged him to talk about his father, whom he had loved, he burst out 'How would you feel if D. (the therapist's husband) had died and left you?'

Mary was ten years old when her father was drowned on a business trip abroad. An adopted child, she had never been close to her mother, but adored her father. There was no funeral and Mary's mother, shocked and withdrawn herself, sent Mary to boarding school and took herself abroad for several months to come to terms with her widowhood. For many years Mary half expected her father to return and never grieved his loss, until she entered therapy many years later. She married early and had a child, whom she abandoned with her first husband when she left her marriage. She subsequently remarried and had two children, and it was when there were also difficulties in this marriage that she sought help for herself.

Young people in adolescence are moving towards independence and can usually begin to recognise their own struggles and weaknesses. In some ways adolescence is a second chance to resolve issues which were not dealt with at earlier stages of development. The death of a parent at this age, while still a terrible blow, is less likely to shape the young person's whole personality, as it can with a younger child. Young persons of this age are becoming very aware of their own sexuality and gender identity and therefore their experience of such a loss will be influenced by whether the parent is of the same sex as themselves or not. For instance, a girl of fourteen whose mother dies is likely to be particularly angry, as she is at the stage when she is quite rivalrous with her mother, whereas a boy would be likely to be more angry than sad with his father. Of course, these are oversimplifications of the feelings which follow such a loss, but nevertheless give some indication of differences. There are also the cumulative effects of the loss of a parent, which may be followed by other losses, which then, instead of allowing or enabling the child to deal with the loss at a later stage of development, reinforce the feelings of abandonment and loneliness.

Jane was the eldest of three children, and the only girl. When she was three, with one younger brother, her father developed cancer, which for some years was controlled by medication. Her mother had a third pregnancy, during which she was hospitalised for some months because of a threatened miscarriage, and Jane and her younger brother were cared for by her somewhat distant grandmother with daily help. Throughout her early school years the health of Jane's father deteriorated and he died when she was eleven, leaving her feeling that she hardly knew him. A bright child, she had flung herself into her school life and the friendships which this offered. Half aware of what she was doing, she attached herself to the family of her best friend, particularly to her friend's father; when she was sixteen he also died. She grew to become an extremely competent and apparently successful woman, but had very low self-esteem and dealt with her own need for dependency by 'taking care' of everyone (though some experienced this as overcontrolling!), yet letting no-one get really close to her. During mid life, a career failure led her to seek help, and at this time, by now in a good enough marriage and family life, she was able to make sense of what had happened to her in her earliest years.

When a child loses a parent through death, it is relevant whether that death was expected or was sudden. If the parent becomes terminally ill, this can allow the family, and also the children, if the family permit them, the opportunity and time to mourn the impending death. The family can draw closer together to grieve and support one another, as will be discussed later. However, when the death is unexpected and sudden, the results are shock and disbelief, which must be assimilated before the normal mourning processes can begin. The child is no exception to such severe shock and may well be virtually ignored in a family where a parent's death leads to temporary collapse of the remaining parent, as happened to Jane.

The loss of a parent during childhood is therefore affected not only by the age and stage of development of a child, but also by the quality of that child's relationship with the parent prior to the death. This will be an important factor in that child's ability to grieve and to 'let go' of the parent who has died, and to form a different kind of relationship with the remaining parent. The remaining years of childhood subsequent to the loss are also an important factor, including how a child experiences the behaviour of the remaining parent following the loss. The young child of a widow who has been bereaved by the death of her husband will be aware of her or his mother's depression as if it were taking her away, as she too may seem to have gone away, although to older children she may seem fragile and preoccupied or may even be particularly irritable. Older children, too, often deal with their own feelings of grief by looking after the parent who remains, or caring for their siblings at the expense of their own feelings and needs, as Jane did.

When the remaining parent remarries after the death of a first spouse, the children need to be allowed opportunities to ask questions and to talk about their biological or birth parent, so that they are able to recognise and value this relationship. This is important, even when the child is very small at the time of the remarriage. For instance, in some families parents who have remarried sometimes allow the child to believe (either deliberately or implicitly) that the step-parent is in fact a biological parent. While there is always the danger that someone else who knows the facts may reveal it to the child, whose trust in the truthfulness of their parent then becomes jeopardised, there may also be unexplained gaps of knowledge relating to the family of the child, which raise questions for her or him. Even if the child is informed as to the true state of its parenthood, there will be many questions about what sort of person their natural parent was, and often a general sense of uncertainty about their own identity.

It will be apparent that the gender of the lost parent is significant, as the loss of a mother, particularly during the early years, is different from the loss of a father in terms of physical presence, the actual relationship and its meaning to the child concerned. But the gender of the child is another important factor: to lose the parent of the same sex means the loss of someone on whom one can choose to model oneself, whereas the loss of the parent of the opposite sex has implications for one's close relationships with all men or all women. The loss of a parent can also mean the loss of knowledge and one's place in the family history of that parent.

Parental divorce

Losing a parent through parental divorce does not have to lead to a loss as absolute as if that parent had died. While the relationships of both parents with a child are irrevocably changed by divorce and this does involve some loss, in that the parenting relationships for the child are separated, usually becoming diadic rather than triadic, it is not necessary that this becomes such a total one as that of the death of a parent. It has to be acknowledged that many parents (usually fathers) who leave home prior to a divorce *do* lose touch with their children; but this does not have to be the case. It is now known that, given sufficient contact with the parent who lives in another household, after a period of distress the children of divorce can recover and resume their developmental path. This is particularly so if the divorced parents have a sufficiently co-operative parental relationship.

Too many divorcing parents do not prepare their children for the departure of one parent from the family home and this comes as a sudden shocking realisation, perhaps even some time after the actual separation. Many children are aware that all is not well between their parents, but cannot bear to contemplate that it is possible that one of them may leave the family home, or are too fearful to check out their fantasies. Indeed, often parents themselves have great difficulty in facing up to the end of their marriage and the implications that one partner will ultimately have to leave the matrimonial home. It is an added burden for them to contemplate informing their children and this is sometimes left till the last moment or even after the departure. Some part, get back together again, only to part later, and it is only in retrospect that they are able to recognise when their psychological separation or emotional divorce actually occurred. Emily, aged twelve, and John, eight, were aware that their parents were 'having a lot of talks and not so much time for them' and one day John asked Emily if they were getting a divorce. Emily responded 'of course not', but as she later confessed to her mother who had found her crying in bed one night, she had heard telephone conversations which she had found very worrying. Their parents had not yet made up their minds what they were going to do about their marriage and had been reluctant to tell their children and uncertain what to say. However, they decided to talk with their children and to tell them that they were in a muddle and that they did not yet know what they were going to do about staying together or getting a divorce. They also stressed that this was nothing to do with what Emily and John had done or not done, and that they would both always be their parents, whatever happened. Emily and John said they would rather be told that their parents had worries and what they were thinking than wonder what was wrong and have a decision sprung on them.

As with those children who lose a parent through death, the effects of divorce on children are related to their age and stage of development, the quality of their relationship with that parent and, of course, their lives subsequent to the divorce. For very young children the possible effects of the loss of a parent through divorce are very similar to those for young children whose parents have died, although the fact that somewhere there is a living biological parent puts the loss in a different context. Most young children will easily become attached to a step-parent, although much depends on how this is handled by both their biological parents.

Mark's mother had lost a previous child at birth and this had seemed to sour her relationship with his father. When he was a few months old, she took him on holiday to her parents in her country of origin overseas. While there, she decided not to return to her marriage and subsequently married a friend of her former husband, with whom she had two more children. Mark was brought up believing that his stepfather was his biological father until, when he was five, his natural father, who lived overseas, wanted to come back into his life. Mark became confused, mistrustful and isolated, wondering who he really was and where and to whom he belonged.

Young children of school age, as has already been mentioned, have a capacity to understand divorce and, providing this is carefully explained to them, can make their own sense of the fact that their parents no longer love one another, as long as they are reassured that both parents still love them. They are usually involved at school and with friends, in developing their skills and conceptual abilities. Unfortunately, as a result of divorce many children have to leave their home and move schools, an additional uprooting which requires careful handling by both their parents.

Susan was aged seven when, after several unhappy years, her parents parted. Susan's father was very attached to her and for a few months, by arrangement with her mother, came regularly to see Susan while her mother was at work. These times were important to Susan, although she was often quite difficult with her mother afterwards. When Susan's father acquired a woman friend who was separated from her husband and with children of her own, he did not see Susan for some weeks and she became fretful and depressed. At the request of her mother, he resumed contact with Susan, but, to her dismay, these other children (of whose relationships with her father she was jealous) were included in their outings, which were also quite irregular. However, she and her mother were able to talk about this, and after a while she grew to like the other children, who were about her own age. After a year or two Susan's father ended this relationship and Susan saw him once a month on her own. When asked by a family friend how her father was, Susan told her matter-of-factly, 'Oh he's fine. I don't live with him you know', and showed the friend his most recent gift as if to convince both the friend and herself that her father did care about her.

Adolescent children often find the parental death or divorce particularly difficult to manage, partly because this is the time when they are trying to differentiate themselves from their parents and to discover for themselves who they would like to become. It is also the stage when they are very aware of their own sexuality and are often surprisingly moralistic about their parents' sexual behaviour.

Stephen was fourteen when his parents separated and divorced, his father remarrying quite soon. His stepmother had been a friend of his mother's and she felt she had not only lost her marriage and her husband, but also a confidante to whom she had confided her troubles. As Stephen's father had run his garden centre from their home, it was decided that his mother, his sister (twelve) and he would move to a new house near their old home and that the children would go to boarding school. Stephen's mother became very depressed and Stephen became her comforter and protector, a role which he felt was forced on him by his father's behaviour. At the same time he felt very angry towards his father, whom he felt had not only abandoned them, but had 'gone off' with his stepmother only because she had entrapped him sexually. Despite his own interest in the family business, he refused to visit his father and stepmother there. He bitterly resented the fact that his stepbrothers now lived in his old family home and spoke of them with contempt. During the year following his father's remarriage, Stephen went to boarding school partly with relief and partly with misgivings, worried about his mother, and so, perhaps not surprisingly, he did not do well. The one good thing in his life was his developing relationship with Carla, who lived nearby, and she became his girlfriend and support. Yet in this relationship too his distress as well as his fears about his developing sexuality threatened to overwhelm him. With the passing of the years, Stephen, like many children, was able to come to terms with the loss, to forgive his father and to begin to form a relatively good relationship with his stepmother.

In summary, then: while children do not necessarily lose a parent as the result of a divorce, their relationship with both their parents is nevertheless radically changed as a result. If both parents are able to support the child through the initial distress at the change in circumstances and to rebuild separate but mutually beneficial relationships with their children post-divorce, then, although the children's family life will be different, it can also be rewarding and fulfilling.

Becoming a stepfamily is another transition for children and this will be considered in much more detail in a later chapter. It is, however, important to note that whatever age the child was when the biological parent either died or left the family home, the child's age and stage of development when a step-parent joins the family is also a relevant factor, as will be the quality of relationship that the step-parent is able to force.

Loss of spouse/partner

For the individual adult the loss of a partner entails a multitude of losses, physical, psychosocial and often economic. The intensity experienced would depend on the quality of the relationship which the individual had had with the lost person and how closely intertwined their lives had been. For the person who is left alone, whether as the result of death or of divorce, much will depend on their capacity to manage that loss. As has already been indicated, their age and stage in the individual life cycle will be relevant as well as personal strengths. Losses, whether the result of death or of divorce, also involve a change of role: for instance, a man who loses his wife through her death becomes a widower, a singleton rather than one of a pair, and this has implications for his role as a member of society and of the community in which he and his wife live. As a general rule, the community network of the couple are sympathetic to those bereaved as the result of the death of their partner; indeed, such a bereavement is recognised and regarded as respectable by society, which provides supportive structures, including financial support, at least for a time. There are no such rituals for those bereaved as the result of a divorce who also become 'singletons'; and it is less likely that those around them will look on their situation sympathetically. While many of the other aspects of the loss of a partner are similar to those which will be described later, the fact that the partner has died rather than left or been left gives a more respectable ambience to the bereavement and generally the remaining partner receives respect and sympathy, which are not always accorded to those who divorce. Those bereaved as the result of the death of a partner can find some comfort in the knowledge that the relationship was a predominantly mutual and fulfilling one, but those who are bereaved as the result of divorce usually emphasise in recall the negative aspects of the relationship and therefore are often unable to reflect on the positive aspects of the relationship, initially anyway, and this of itself may make it difficult to embark upon the mourning process which is necessary in order to detach from the previous spouse.

Death of the spouse
For the widow or widower who is bereaved as the result of the death of a spouse the many changes which result emphasise his or her aloneness in what is a new situation, one which may or may not be unexpected but is almost certainly unwanted.

- The partner or spouse is no longer physically present, nor available to the bereaved person.
- The person who has usually been the most intimate companion, sexual partner and friend has gone, leaving the surviving partner socially and sexually deprived.
- The partner or spouse who has been a helpmate in practical terms is no longer available, which leaves the widow or widower to cope with numerous practical household and managerial tasks alone.
- As parents either the father or mother has been deprived of a coparent and in future will have to care for the children on his or her own.
- It is likely that there will be some immediate financial insecurity and income will be reduced.

The impact on the partner who is left following the death depends on a number of factors, and among the most significant is the quality of the couple's relationship prior to the death, whether the death was unexpected or anticipated, as well as the circumstances in which it occurred. If the partnership was a negative or ambivalent one, then this is likely to affect the process of grieving. In circumstances where the partner was killed as the result of an accident, for which responsibility or blame could be attributed, then the anger of the remaining partner is likely to be intense and is usually directed at those considered responsible. Similarly, where the death is the result of suicide, then a similar intense anger is more likely to be repressed or directed elsewhere. If the partner has suddenly died as the result of a physical condition hitherto unrecognised, the initial shock is likely to add to the impact of the death. Where the illness is recognised to be a terminal one, then although the couple may not overtly share their grief at the inevitability of the death, they may each individually be mourning in private.

For the individual who is facing her or his own death and trying to cope with the inevitability of an illness which is known to be terminal this is an experience which is almost impossible for another to comprehend, let alone understand. During this process five stages have been distinguished (Kubler Ross 1970).

1. The dying often deny that this will in reality happen, and this sometimes leads to the withdrawal and isolation of the terminally ill person.
2. The denial gives way to anger, 'Why should this happen to me?', to resentment towards others or blaming those who have attempted and failed to help.
3. A stage of bargaining, for those who seek spirituality by making a pact of faith, usually privately or with a priest; or by attempting to postpone the inevitable, for instance by determining to remain alive for a particular event.
4. As the terminally ill begin to realise the inevitability of death, they begin to cope with the myriad losses which this entails and they become depressed.
5. The final stage is the acceptance of the imminent death, which it is hoped will be pain-free, calm and peaceful.

The patterns of the mourning process for the other partner are likely to be similar, although not necessarily synchronous. For those whose personal strengths as well as the strengths of their relationship may allow them to grieve together for the impending loss, there can be comfort for both. This period will provide them with opportunities for anticipatory grieving as well as occasions of shared closeness, the memories of which the bereaved partner can subsequently draw upon for comfort.

In a similar process there are four phases of mourning a lost partner, and although the bereaved may move backwards and forwards through time they are usually distinguishable (Bowlby 1980).

- In the first place there is usually a period of numbed disbelief, which may be interrupted by bursts of intense distress or anger. Anger is one of the elements of any loss, and this is one of the reasons why the experience is often so confusing to those who are left. How can one be angry with someone whom one loved and who has died? Such feelings are not acceptable to most of us and we may repress them, thereby adding to our distress by finding ways of expressing our anger which are acceptable.

- The second and usually much longer phase is that of pining for the lost spouse, yearning for their presence. The bereaved person is preoccupied with thoughts and images of the lost partner, searching for him or her and becoming generally depressed (Murray Parkes 1986).
- The second phase gives way to a third one of disorganisation, when the person who is bereaved experiences intense despair.
- A final and later phase of more or less reorganisation follows.

One of the ways of helping to manage loss of a partner through death is for the bereaved spouse to maximise the partner's good qualities. This process, known as idealisation, is usually comforting.

If the loss is sudden and as the result of a traumatic accident in which the survivors were also involved, those who are left may initially block out all memories of what has happened to them, as the survivors of the *Herald of Free Enterprise* recounted. There also may be guilt that they have survived and their partner has not. If the loss was anticipated, because the spouse had been ill, then the possibility of such a loss would be anticipated at least to some degree; some grieving would perhaps have begun before the death and therefore perhaps the stress of the impact would be to some extent ameliorated. However, as already indicated, the degree of stress will be affected by whether the death was unanticipated, conflicted or results in chronic grief, as it did for Queen Victoria (Murray Parkes and Weiss 1983).

Robert and his wife Penny were married for thirty years; it was the second marriage for each of them, and they put a great deal into making their relationship successful. They became parents for the first time during their forties. Robert was a successful and innovative professional and Penny gave up her career to devote herself to Robert and her children. When their children were considered old enough, and at his suggestion Penny joined Robert in his practice. Rather to her surprise, though not to his, she became more than a helpmeet, a professional in her own right, and this gave pleasure to them both. She developed cancer and after an operation was considered to be cured. However, eight years later she developed another cancer and it was discovered that this was a secondary to the earlier primary cancer. Although Penny had further operations and chemotherapy, it became evident that her condition was a terminal one. The family all drew together and faced this inevitability with courage. During Penny's last two years, although Robert and her children continued with their lives, they were all able to share their lives with Penny and openly to talk of their love for one another. From time to time, when things were particularly bad, Penny would admit herself to a hospice, but most of the time she remained at home, as she had done earlier in their lives, and family and friends dropped in to see her. She died as she had lived – amidst her family. Some years later Robert found a new partner, who became very important to him and a friend to his now grown-up children. She never discouraged the family conversation when it turned to Penny and subsequently was able to take part, actively listening and at times asking questions as if to get to know Penny for herself.

Loss through divorce

When a marriage is not going well, at least one of the partners gradually becomes aware of this. All marriages have some disappointments which most partners accept and gradually come to terms with or, after confronting their partner, negotiate their differences in some way which makes them tolerable to live with. When a marriage or relationship breaks down, the loss is also one of magnitude and multiplicity:

- For one partner the separation is usually unwanted and may even be sudden and unexpected.
- There is the loss of a sexual partner.
- There is the loss of being a couple and sharing domestic and social activities and together.
- There is very likely to be the loss of their home, at least for one partner and perhaps eventually for both.
- There is the loss of day-to-day contact with their child(ren) at least for one parent, and the need to change their parental roles both as regards their children and *vis-à-vis* one another.

- There is also the loss of being a couple which is also part of an extended family and a community network.
- There will be the threat of eventual financial losses and for some partners these will be considerable. For many women following divorce their income is half what it was previously.

As with bereavement following the death of a partner, research now shows that there are stages of uncoupling which may eventually result in a divorce (Vaughan 1987). This begins at a stage prior to that in which one of the partners begins to think of opting out of the marriage, as they begin to keep small dissatisfactions secret from the partner and sometimes also from themselves. At the same time, the dissatisfied partner also begins to develop a private life which is not shared with their partner (Vaughan 1987). At one level, this may be quite harmless, such as a sport or business activities; at another, it is the importance and the secrecy with which it is endowed that detracts from the marriage.

If not recognised, confronted and dealt with, this may result in a gradual emotional disinvestment in the marriage, and a redefinition of the self. This partner, who may eventually become the initiator of the divorce process, begins to display discontent with the marital relationship, thus setting in motion a social process of mourning. During this phase the initiating partner is likely to form an important relationship with a transitional person, who becomes a confidante and assists in bridging the old life and the new. This relationship is not necessarily a sexual one and could be with a close friend, lawyer or therapist.

Although the 'other' partner may recognise that something is wrong, they receive mixed messages from the partner who becomes the initiator; together they both collude and collaborate in maintaining the relationship and ways of thinking which they have constructed together. Eventually this 'cover-up' begins to collapse, as the couple spend less time together and the initiator begins to contemplate how to leave the relationship. The ultimate confrontation may be carefully planned, for example a family milestone, or be triggered by some often minor event. This confrontation creates a situation in which the couple can begin to work on their difficulties together, or to negotiate about how they can separate. Even so, the initiator retains the balance of power, as the partner is both vulnerable and at a disadvantage, as well as usually being unprepared for the situation.

There comes a time when the couple's private sorrows inevitably become a public issue and this is when one partner, often not the initiating one and usually it is the wife, decides to seek legal advice (Robinson 1991). It may be only at this point that the couple recognise together that the stage which their marital difficulties have reached is a very serious one which has major implications for the future. If the couple eventually decide to separate, then each will need to grieve for the loss of the relationship, the initiator usually commencing her or his mourning process earlier than the partner, whose grief is exacerbated by the knowledge of the rejection. The ultimate home-leaving is a public statement and may or may not be planned. This act of 'going public' itself makes it more difficult for the partners to negotiate with a view to reconciliation, because the social alignments which are created may serve to reinforce the separation, particularly if the couple have children.

There are a number of particular aspects related to the pain of such a loss:

1. It will be affected by the history and quality of the relationship between the partners prior to the loss.
2. Such a loss will be affected by whether the spouse suddenly departs, agrees to leave the home they have shared together or, as is often the case, particularly in lower-income groups, tries to stick it out and force the other to leave the matrimonial home.
3. Even in these days, when there is less stigma attached to divorce, for the couples themselves, or at least one of them, there is a sense of shame regarding the failure of the marriage and there is considerable guilt in relation to their children.
4. The pain of separation will be influenced by which partner it is who has decided to end the relationship. It is rare that both spouses want to leave the relationship simultaneously and there is usually one that wants to end the partnership and the other, at least initially, who does not.
5. If the initiator wants to end the marriage because they have

found someone else with whom they would rather live, this is likely to provoke feelings of jealousy which will become intertwined with the feelings of grief and anger which accompany the loss.

Pauline and Dick had been married for twenty-five years and had two young adult children. Their daughter, who lived at home, was working as a nurse, and their son, also living at home, was attending a local technical college. The family had moved south some years previously, had few friends either collectively or individually and they 'did everything together'. On moving south Dick had obtained promotion to become the manager of a transport company. Suddenly and inexplicably, to him, to Pauline and the children, he became friendly with a woman who worked in his company and who was twenty-five years older than himself. Pauline became frantic and she and their son followed him after work to find out where the woman lived. Dick refused to talk about what was happening, and eventually left home, apparently to live with the other woman. Pauline harassed him at work and informed his boss, so that the woman was sacked. Pauline and one or other of their children would often drive over to where Dick seemed to be living and drive up and down the street looking for him. On one occasion Pauline sprayed the word 'Whore' on the woman's front door, and when recounting this incident her shock and shame at this uncharacteristic behaviour was evident. Eventually, Dick agreed to return home providing he could spend two nights a week with his 'lady friend'. This uneasy truce is likely to break down, and should Dick decide to live with his woman friend this will place his children in a stepfamily situation which they are unlikely to accept.

The experience of loss of a partner is therefore comprehensive, confusing and complex: and whether the partner dies or departs from the home, it is a bereavement and the feelings which accompany it are intense. They will include disbelief that such a thing can be happening and will be accompanied by physical experiences of emptiness and confusion, followed by feelings of immense sadness and yearning, sudden outbursts of crying, often when least expected, preoccupation with the partner, anger at being left, perhaps bitterness and fury. The importance of the funeral as a healing ritual cannot be underestimated. The processes of bereavement which follow a death are more or less recognised by care-givers in society (particularly by the organisation Cruse and the clergy), but such understanding is not easily available to those who are bereaved as the result of divorce. In such a situation, which arouses guilt as well as anger, both partners attempt to maximise their own self-esteem, which has been lowered at the failure of their marriage, by blaming the other for its failure, and in doing so may enlist partisans in support. Unfortunately, our present divorce laws assist in this blaming process. Some whose spouse leaves for another manage their angry feelings by putting them onto the third party, whom they believe led their partner astray. The fact that they are thereby diminishing their former partner usually remains unrecognised by them.

The effect on the family of the loss of a spouse/parent

The third level of loss, which results from the death of a parent or parental divorce, is that of the family as a unit or system. In both loss situations it will be clear that the stage of the family life cycle which the family has reached is as relevant as those of the life cycles of the individuals, whether parents or children. Family life cycles have already been discussed (in Chapter 2), and particularly significant is the way in which the couple have been able to manage becoming parents during the stage at which they move from being a couple to become a family. It has been found that couples need to maintain a boundary between their own relationship as husband and wife or as parents in order to manage their parental responsibilities with regard to their children. When a couple have their first child, they are essentially moving into a three-person relationship, perhaps for the first time since their own childhood, and this means negotiating and reworking old issues of sharing and competitiveness. In family life, although each parent has an individualised dyadic relationship with each of their children, these are inevitably placed against a background of the other relationships of the family, including that of the parental couple, which may be affected by each and every interaction within the family unit. The stage of the family life cycle at which a parent either dies or leaves the family is therefore likely to be the most relevant aspect to their ability to manage that loss.

For young families where a parent dies or leaves, their attachments and development as a family unit are likely to be at a more vulnerable stage than, for instance, for a family in later life, when many of the children have already embarked on their adult lives and perhaps also their own families, which will sustain and support them. As has already been described, the loss, whether through death or because of divorce, will have an effect on the remaining parent, as will their capacities to deal with that loss. This in turn will affect the way they are able to support and care for their children in their loss; the examples given in the section describing the effects of such losses on children show how important these are for them. What is not always realised is that there is also a need to grieve for the family as it used to be, because subsequent to a death or a divorce it will never be the same again. Although the remaining parent and their children can eventually come to terms with the departure of the other parent and rebuild a satisfactory family life, the family as it once was cannot be recreated. Even in family situations where the parents are able to rebuild separate and co-operative relationships as regards their children and they are able to have access to the parent who no longer lives with the family, the reality is that the family itself will never be the same again. This too needs to be mourned, so that the family in a new form can emerge and ways found to minimise the angry bitterness which often remains between parents and to maximise the attachments between the children and both their parents. This sort of family is often described as a binuclear family (Ahrons 1980). When the need for mourning has been faced and sufficiently completed and the family is able to find itself again, albeit in a new form, then there can be hope and even enthusiasm for the future.

For families where the children are of school age the children's conceptual abilities, their development of skills and their own peer support group will be important factors in helping them to manage the loss, as has already been discussed. In families where there are several children the siblings have their own attachments as between siblings and in many families these relationships often become stronger and more mutually supportive following a death. This seems to be less likely during the divorce process, although it is not clear exactly why this might be. But the children will also be concerned about the parent who is left, whether as the result of a death or a separation. If it is possible for the remaining parent to help the children talk about their own grief at the loss of a parent, then a bereaved family can grieve together and support one another during the process.

This is more difficult when there has been a separation and divorce, as the children will find it difficult to understand why their mother or father has left the family home and, while they may be angry with them for going, they are also likely to be angry with the remaining parent for driving them away or allowing them to go. Also, the children are likely to see the parent who has left and to be confused and puzzled at least in the early stages as to why they too have been abandoned. The divided loyalties which often result from parents' failure to manage their own and their children's distress can make the children's day-to-day lives more difficult. Parents often become very confused, as each of them appears to have been given a different perception of how their children feel about the divorce or separation. What often happens is that the children, in an attempt both to comfort each parent in their distress and to maintain their own attachment to that parent, tell the parents what they think they might want to hear.

Where the parents are in the early stages of contemplating separation and perhaps divorce, it is usually very difficult to discuss this with one another without becoming angry and distressed. This makes it difficult for them to make plans together and these may become formulated only subsequent to the departure of one partner, often via their solicitors. Often they neither tell their children what is happening nor discuss their future plans with them. There are a number of reasons for this:

1. Most parents who separate and divorce are extremely guilty about their children. It is relatively rare, even for the parent who wants to end the marriage, not to feel deeply concerned about the effect of divorce on the children and her or his relationship with them.
2. Parents who are separating are commonly so preoccupied

with their own grieving processes relating to the ending of their relationship that they find it difficult also to contemplate the fact that their children too will be affected by this loss.
3. Parents who are grieving often find that they can barely manage to cope with the day-to-day practical activities of running a household and managing a job, so have little emotional energy left to cope with grieving processes other than their own, and so cannot help their children confront what has happened and grieve in their own way. While this may be a temporary stage of the bereavement process, it is a very important aspect of their children's lives.

For parents who are separating with a view to divorce it is also helpful for their children if they talk to them – together if they can manage this – and explain to them what is happening and, if they know what their future plans are, discuss these with their children. Although children may be consulted about where they would prefer to live and the amount of time they will spend with each parent, and possible proposals may be discussed with them, they should *not* be given the responsibility of deciding which parent they will primarily live with. Such a decision confronts them with a conflict of loyalties between their parents and is a burden which no child should be asked to bear. Adolescent children in particular often have very definite ideas about short-term and long-term plans, and it is helpful to include them in the decision-making process. The ultimate decision is best made by their parents, though the implications of them being unable to do so will be discussed later.

Both types of loss also affect the extended family. For one set of grandparents the death of a partner also means for them the death of their child. This is a particularly distressing consequence of the death of a young or relatively young parent. Most parents expect to die themselves before any of their children, and to lose a child in this way awakens deep fears for them.

A divorce not only tends to change the family into a binuclear family (Ahrons 1980) but it also separates the extended family; this is why a more accurate description of the post-divorce family is that of a re-formed extended family (Robinson 1991). In view of the distress felt by the couple who are parting and the helplessness often experienced by their children, it may be difficult for the extended family to avoid taking sides; and they tend to line up with the partner who is of their own kin. Yet this is the phase when the children of the divorcing partners, who are most likely also to be the grandchildren of their partners' parents, most need the support and attention of someone who cares about them and what they are likely to be going through.

Katie and Gavin met at university and married soon after they both graduated. Gavin was very ambitious and though sometimes very successful, at other times seemed to land in financial difficulties. This was not helped by his extravagant lifestyle. Katie herself had had a demanding occupation until they had Mike, when she gave up full-time work, though she worked part-time until their daughter was born. Gavin found the restrictions and responsibilities of family life too constraining and he began to have affairs. Katie, on discovering this, threw him out, although they were reconciled and parted several times. As the result of one such reconciliation, they had a third child, Caroline. Gavin's parents lived overseas, but Katie came from a very close family who were quite well off, and her parents and siblings were deeply concerned about what was happening to her and the children. They struggled to be impartial, bailed the family out financially and did their best not to be too critical, believing that there must be faults on both sides. However, they eventually found Gavin's financial irresponsibility and casualness towards his children intolerable and they refused any further financial help when the couple got back together for yet one more reconciliation, which eventually failed. Gavin later remarried and Katie struggled with herself to encourage their children to remain in contact with their father; but her parents, the children's grandparents, to whom they were very close, undermined these attempts and contacts, albeit unwittingly, because of their own disillusion, anger and distress.

Beginning again

For the single-parent household, following the death of a partner, the completion of the mourning process merges with the stage of beginning again. Inside the family, the children and their remaining parent need time to settle into a new day-to-day family life in which, with one parental role remaining unfilled, the tasks which were carried out by the deceased parent need to be redistributed. The family which is bereft of a parent also must learn to cope with being seen differently by the rest of society, and this is often a painful and continuous experience.

Beginning again is inevitably more complicated for the post-divorce family. This is partly because, quite often, one of the partners may have already embarked on a new life prior to the divorce; indeed, this might be the cause of the actual separation. This phase of beginning again post-divorce often re-awakens the pain of the loss, this time stimulated by jealousy over both the new social life and the sexual partners of the formerly married spouses. For the children this means becoming used to the family in its new form and accepting their own changed relationships with both their parents.

Summary

After the ending of a marriage the individuals – parents and children – and the family need to go through a process of mourning at all levels, each of which interact with one another, during which they try to accept and come to terms with their loss. The loss of a spouse through death is a grievous blow to a family, both to the widow or widower and the children, whose age and stage of development are particularly relevant. However, such a loss is recognised by the family network and community and there are family rituals which help towards alleviating such a loss. On the other hand, the loss experienced through divorce by the former partners and their children is marked by no healing rituals. In many cases the whole extended family joins and supports the perceptions of only one of the former partners and all too often the needs of the children go unrecognised and they are not given sufficient opportunity and support to make their own sense of what has happened to them and to their family. Bohannon (1971) sums what he describes as the six stations of the divorce process as follows: the emotional divorce and grief; the psychic divorce and the problem of autonomy; the legal divorce and the problem of grounds; the coparental divorce and the problem of custody; the economic divorce and the problem of property; the community divorce and the problem of loneliness. However, these are different strands rather than stages of the divorce process.

Guidelines

Bereavement, as the result either of a death or of divorce, is a complex and multi-level process to which it takes time for the family to adjust, whether as individuals or as a whole group. It is therefore important to recognise and attend to individual patterns of mourning, as they are likely to proceed at different paces. After a divorce many children keep hoping that their parents will re-unite and often it is only when one or both remarry that the children may begin to grieve for what has been lost or changed irrevocably. Becoming a stepfamily is a further transition which requires major adjustments on the part of the whole re-formed extended family. It is not always possible to wait until the grief which follows the death of a parent or a divorce has been 'worked through' before remarriage, this is a critical double transition and any unresolved mourning is likely to interfere with the process of becoming a stepfamily, although this may be disguised, for example in the form of anger or bad behaviour.

Children need to re-address and understand the loss of a parent and family changes at each level of their development. As their cognitive abilities develop they need to be able to understand and make their own sense of what has happened to them; and as adolescents or young adults they can, and often do, seek out the parent whom they had once thought lost to them as the result of divorce so as to discover for themselves what their 'lost' parent is really like.

CHAPTER FOUR

Myths and realities

Stepfamilies, although a familiar family form throughout human history, are surrounded by myths, fantasies and misunderstandings. In most societies there is a deep suspicion that the stepfamily exists because of wrongdoing, and that the children in a stepfamily inevitably will be harmed. It would be false and not appropriate to the purposes of this book to suggest a rosy picture of stepfamilies in an attempt to counter such negative expectations. It cannot be denied that stepfamily life is difficult and very few children are happy about becoming part of one, at least in the beginning. Some stepfamilies fail the children badly, and we need to understand more about the factors which make that happen. In this chapter the myths stepfamilies must live with are explored, with the suggestion that these mistaken beliefs contribute to the problems and complexities of creating a satisfactory stepfamily life.

Stepfamilies are tainted because they cannot fulfil the cultural dream, especially prevalent in the Anglo-European world, of two adults married for the first (and only) time with their children, linked by love and biology, and supported by a loving family network. The myth of a 'perfect family' affects every family, and every family falls short in its own or someone else's estimation: we are all subjected to the demands of the ideal. To be sure, there are many good things to be had in an affectionate family; this is not in question. There is no question either about stepfamilies being able to provide the nurturing, caring and sense of belonging that human beings require. But stepfamilies, with their awkward shapes, with extra sets of parents and grandparents, have a greater challenge in meeting the needs of their members at their beginning. There is often a high degree of tension and disagreement in a stepfamily, certainly at first, about who really belongs to it, usually accompanied by conflict and confusions of loyalty. Also, they cannot fit the model assumed to be the only right one. The reaction to the suspicion that a stepfamily is an inferior, even dangerous kind of family may lead to ignoring the facts and pretending that a stepfamily is not different from the traditional nuclear family of two parents and their children. On the other hand, it may lead to investing the stepfamily with a mythology – a set of unexamined beliefs – because it is different.

Myths are inventions. The traditional myth is a legend, usually embodying primitive beliefs in the supernatural, although the subject of myth is not always magical. For example, the myth of Sisyphus does not employ magic to tell of Sisyphus forever pushing a stone uphill which rolls back down as soon as he nears the top, a myth which is a reference for unending labour at tasks which can never be finished. Myths which deal with the passage of time, with the cyclic nature of seasons, or rebirth and renewal, use stories and ceremonies and perhaps belief in re-incarnation. A myth may be used to explain the sun appearing and disappearing, or the human psyche, but above all, myth is a social phenomenon, 'embedded in society and requiring explanation with reference to social structures and social functions' (*The New Encyclopaedia Britannica* 1989). Myths are expressions of popular ideas or beliefs about natural or social phenomena, subscribed to uncritically (*Oxford English Dictionary* 1982; *Longman Dictionary of Contemporary English* 1982), with origins often unknown or lost in time, but their function is to explain some institution or practice and to protect cherished values. The myth of the American West, a modern myth perpetuated through films and books, portrays the native Indians as morally inferior to the European settlers. The function of this myth is to protect the belief that the taking over of native lands was justified. In recent years there has been a challenge to this belief, resulting in a (partial) demythologising of the events and practices of a period of human history. Other examples of the social uses of myth are found in beliefs having to do with racial or gender superiority.

Myths about stepfamilies explain the belief, arising from religious and cultural systems, that they are a deviant family form – not 'right', nor 'ordinary' or 'natural' – because they do not conform to the ideal for families. Therefore the myths about them protect the family of two parents and their biological children and maintain a belief that no other family form can successfully rear children. The reality of stepfamilies does contain sad and contradictory elements. First and foremost, stepfamilies result from the death of a parent or a divorce between parents and therefore their beginnings are predicated upon painful changes, in contrast to the celebrations of renewal which a first marriage symbolises. Yet a stepfamily is also a renewal. The cultural myths about stepfamilies powerfully reflect such inherent contradictions. An example is the one mentioned above, that stepfamilies are inferior to a traditional biological family, yet can and should duplicate one. Another is that stepmothers are wicked, but love should spring up instantly between them and their stepchildren, and what is more, they should love their stepchildren in the same way as they love their own children. This myth applies to stepfathers as well, of course, but may be less powerful for a man's self-esteem than for a woman's, because men are often less directly involved in family life than are women, although this seems to be changing amongst younger couples as women and men attempt to develop a way of sharing family responsibilities. Against the myth that a stepfather or stepmother can quickly understand and love a stepchild is the belief that stepchildren are always forlorn children, used as scapegoats and permanently damaged by having a step-parent.

Members of stepfamilies also hold fantasies about themselves – dreams and illusions and sometimes fears – and about the new life which begins with the stepfamily (Papernow 1984). Some of these fantasies are linked to the myths about stepfamilies which exist in the outside world; the pressure to be the same as a traditional family comes from both within and without. Adults try to create an instant family and behave as if it had always existed; they hold fantasies about being a 'perfect parent' and putting right for a new partner and the stepchildren all that had gone wrong in the past. Children in stepfamilies usually have fantasies about their two parents re-uniting. They frequently do not know which adult to trust and fear losing both their parents, one to the new partner and the other, the one they no longer live with, to the world beyond the family and possibly a new partner with that parent as well. In the early stages of a stepfamily, the children inevitably will resent a step-parent, and perhaps a stepmother especially. A stepmother arrives on the scene encumbered with the unlovely attributes of the stories about them which children from an early age have heard or seen in films. Stepmothers are familiar as figures representing cruelty the world over. Their image in folk and fairy tale is synonymous with the confusions of relating and trusting which are inherent at the outset of life in a stepfamily. In the tradition of folk literature, the stepmother is a symbol of abuse, sometimes of murder, always withholding kindness and affection from helpless children, and often of actively creating friction between others because of jealousy and greed. In the classic tales of childhood and especially in ones made familiar by the Walt Disney films – Cinderella, Snow White, Hansel and Gretel – no other family member appears more often as an abusing one than the stepmother (Thompson 1946).

Stepfathers do not have such a place in the tradition of tales told to children, but there are some stunning examples of evil stepfathers in adult classics. One is in Sophocles' *Elektra* and another is the murderous stepfather in *Hamlet*. Both are examples of stepfathers hated by stepchildren who want revenge for a father's death. (Is it possible that many stepchildren feel their absent parent has been somehow killed and their other parent stolen by the step-parent?) Hamlet's stepfather was first his uncle. Motivated by desire for power and status to the extent of murdering his brother, the King and Hamlet's father, he married the Queen, Hamlet's mother, and plotted Hamlet's death as well. The ghost of Hamlet's father gives him information but does not protect him (unlike the fairy godmother and other supernatural phenomena in folk and fairy tales). Hamlet dies, and we have a legacy of poetry and a tradition of literary conjecture about the meaning of Hamlet's behaviour. There is no mystery about the person of the evil, unscrupulous stepfather–King, however.

In fairy tales the abused children are rescued from the wicked stepmother by magic, usually a representative of the mother who has died (just as the ghost in *Hamlet* is his dead father). No such aid exists in the real world for children caught in situations of abuse unless it comes in the form of other adults in the family or society's agents. Those cases, widely publicised, in which the help was too little or too late, often feature a stepfather as the abusing adult. In the world presented in newspapers there is now a picture of stepfathers as terrifying as any stepmother in folk and fairy tales; and it is fact, not myth. But what is important is that the reaction to the fact of stepfather abuse is fuelled by the myth that all step-parents are abusers. In three of the four most widely publicised cases of child abuse and death in Britain in the 1980s the perpetrator and murderer was the child's stepfather (Kimberley Carlisle in 1986, Jasmine Beckford in 1985 and Heidi Koseda in 1984 were all killed by their stepfathers. The fourth case was Tyra Henry, killed by her father in 1984.) The word 'stepfather' appears in the headline of many reports.

As the newspapers searched for explanations for these horrific crimes, the steprelationship appeared to be the most readily available. Social workers who failed to rescue the child were next to be blamed: for example, the *Daily Star* on 16 May 1987, referring to the social worker in the case of Kimberley Carlisle, reads, 'HE Let Her Die'. The inquiry also cited the social worker's failure to act decisively, which was covered in the *Daily Telegraph* on 12 December 1987 amongst others. Some papers explored the scapegoating phenomena in families; how one child is singled out for abuse (*Today*, 10 May 1987). Every newspaper report, however, pointedly made reference to the identity of the child's abuser as a stepfather. In the *Independent* on 10 March 1990, a headline on page 8 reads 'Stepfather "tortured girl for bed wetting"'. A young man of twenty-one abused both the child and her mother, but it was his status as a stepfather that was featured in the headline. The report states that the child fortunately was recovering, but by implication the steprelationship is the reason the child was hurt. When a man who is in a stepfather position hurts his stepchild it is rightly appalling, but the steprelationship may be only one of many factors which contributed to the situation in which violence occurred. The *Sunday Times* on 17 May 1987 explored the four child-death cases cited above in some depth and made the point that all four were from poor, ill-housed backgrounds. When environmental pressures accumulate and combine with innate vulnerabilities, frustrations become unbearable. The step-relationship is a fertile ground for misplaced anger, and mistreatment of the worst kind easily follows. On a larger scale, society's attitude towards stepfamilies *per se* can make them the target of undeserved blame, treated as scapegoats for the struggles and failings of all families. It is as if the very existence of stepfamilies explains many of society's casualties, just as other groups can be singled out for blame and become targets of fear and resentment, for example black workers blamed for white unemployment.

Scapegoats inside and outside

A scapegoat is a person or animal – or even thing – which bears the blame and takes the punishment for the ills or sufferings or wrongdoings of others. The origin of the word 'scapegoat' is found in Jewish antiquity in the ritual of Yom Kippur, which involved symbolically burdening a goat with the sins of the people. It was then released into the wilderness, taking away the sins and thus freeing the people of their burden for the year to come. The ritual and its requirements is described in the Old Testament, Leviticus 16, in the law relating to the Day of Atonement: two goats were to be chosen by lot, one sacrificed and the other, allotted to bear the sins away, was allowed to escape – hence, scapegoat.

Other cultures also used animals to absolve wrongs and placate punitive gods, and some used human sacrifices. At a rite of spring celebrated in the Greek religion, Thargelia, the Ancient Athenians chose a man and a woman to represent the deity, but also to act as scapegoats for community guilt. They were first paraded around the town and then driven out and perhaps killed, thereby cleansing the wrongs of the past year and protecting the city from harm for the new year (*The New Encyclopaedia Britannica* 1989, vols 10 and 11). In early Roman law an innocent person could choose to assume the punishment of another who had confessed guilt. Christian belief reflects this in the doctrine of Jesus Christ dying to atone for the sins of all humanity.

A story set in the seventeenth-century Puritan colonies of New England by Shirley Jackson, *The Lottery* (1950), uses a ritual of scapegoating to explore themes of blind obedience to tradition and the price of rebellion. In this story, which is fictional but with factual antecedents, the entire community gathers on one day of the year, in June, to draw lots to determine who will bear the guilt of all. A refrain is chanted by the people to justify the ritual: 'Lottery in June, corn will come soon.' The person who draws the paper on which there is a black spot is stoned to death by the rest of the community. This is a tale of human sacrifice which can be linked to the Biblical source for the meaning of scapegoat, save that the two goats have become one human for whom there is no escape.

By extension, the scapegoat is one who is innocent of the offence for which she or he is made responsible, but the blaming serves a purpose, or even a set of purposes, for others. Unlike the ritualistic scapegoating of earlier times, however, the purpose or reason is obscure and probably beyond consciousness. The person who becomes the scapegoat might have a purpose too, conscious or unconscious, in attracting blame for the sufferings of someone else. One person, for example, may attract blame in order to protect the guilty party. Usually, however, the scapegoat does not realise what is happening until the effects are felt, and perhaps not then. The child who is treated as a scapegoat has no understanding of why the rejection is happening (Skynner 1976). The perpetrators of the scapegoating process probably have little or no awareness of what is happening either. It is simply that where there is a collective stress one person can be singled out as being the cause. In families with relationship difficulties one member is often identified as the problem and the family seems to say 'We are all right except for that one.' Frequently the scapegoated member is behaving in a way which is frowned upon by a given family's set of beliefs and values, in other words, behaving in a way which is disloyal to the family, although there may not be a conscious awareness of the source of discomfort everyone experiences as a result. In group situations, not family groups but other groups, for example in work or training settings and especially in therapy groups, the members are prone to become apathetic and blame the leader, thus making the leader a scapegoat for the discomfort and doubt about the group's value. The most controlling and directive member may serve as the group's scapegoat also because that person will garner resentment (Klein 1956). Being active and being different may produce hostility.

It often appears that society treats the stepfamily as a scapegoat through a similar set of processes. Marriage as an institution is highly valued and receives huge social approval; divorce is tolerated as a necessary means to end an unhappy marriage. It is accepted that people should not be condemned to suffer for a lifetime in a miserable relationship; at the same time there is great uneasiness and ambivalence about the stepfamily which follows separation and divorce (Visher 1984). As one man, a stepfather, put it in a letter to the *Newsletter* of the National Stepfamily Association: 'Our society hustles people into marriage, is embarrassed by divorce and completely ignores the likely hazards of second marriage' (no. 22, spring 1990). Is this because stepfamilies by their very existence threaten the social ideal of the family and what it should be – one sexual union for life? Divorce may be sanctioned, but trying to be more successful in a second marriage is regarded narrowly or ignored. The ideal of the family is seldom questioned; families which do not conform to it are treated as scapegoats, carrying 'sins' which relate to an ideal of perfection. Their difference is at fault, therefore stepfamilies must be disguised or ignored; and when they cannot be ignored, they must be blamed for their own difficulties. In individual families, as already suggested, the scapegoated member often acts in a way which challenges the ideals of the family unit. It seems that the stepfamily challenges cultural ideals in a similar way. Thus stepfamily life begins without blessing, with a burden of potential disapproval and with a set of highly complex and ambiguous relationships.

Two case examples follow, one in which the step-parent is a stepfather, and one which features a stepmother. In both cases a woman made the first contact, as is usual and familiar to all agencies offering counselling or therapy. It is by and large women who take care of others at an emotional level and ask for help when things are not going well.

One of us (D.S.) was contacted by a woman, Lynne, who described the problem she wanted help with as a difficulty between her husband and her children by a previous marriage. She has two children, a girl aged nine and a boy of six at the time of referral. She had been married for five months to a man with sons of ten and six living with their mother. She said her husband was rejecting her children, withholding affection from them and criticising her parenting. In turn she was trying to protect her children, as she saw it, and becoming resentful and angry with her husband. An appointment was arranged for the two adults. It seemed inappropriate to involve the children in the first instance and in any case Lynne asked to come with her husband only.

The couple had been together for over three years and each had previously been in marriages of many years' duration. The husband, Greg, was living alone when he met Lynne, seeing his two children regularly and frequently. He said at the first meeting that he had left his first marriage because of rows which he felt were damaging for the children to witness. It was for their sake, in his view, that the separation and then the divorce had taken place, and he had always wanted to make up to them for not having a 'normal family'. He revealed that his father had died when he was a little boy. His mother had never remarried because of her belief in a lifetime commitment to one marriage, a belief which was deeply held by Greg as well. Greg's mother had come to his and Lynne's wedding, although he had not expected this gesture of support from her. Not surprisingly, Lynne described Greg's mother as 'distant' and somewhat disapproving.

Lynne was still living with her previous husband when she met Greg. The marriage was unfulfilling and Lynne had tried to find other channels to a satisfactory life, and had been partially successful. She had work which stimulated her and she had her children plus a circle of friends. But when she and Greg met they were immediately attracted to one another and began to live together as soon as Lynne separated from her previous husband. Her mother approved of her new partner and marriage. Her father had died shortly before she met Greg. That loss may have been significant in her being unable to continue to tolerate an empty marriage.

At the time Lynne telephoned for a meeting with a family therapist, there had been another set of changes. Greg had a new job and they – Greg, Lynne and her two children – had moved from the town where Greg's two children still lived. Lynne had given up her job, glad not to have to juggle the hard work of home, children and full-time employment but missing the work itself and her colleagues. She was lonely in the new town, and because of difficulties in finding a house there had been several temporary moves. Then at almost the final minute of the first meeting, when coats were being collected, Lynne said she was pregnant, and in a tone of light-heartedness which sounded false she said that Greg did not really believe her. The therapist warmly acknowledged the information and made a mental note of the way it had come – at the end of the meeting and in such a way as to suggest that Lynne was not certain Greg welcomed the pregnancy.

Their attachment and affection for one another was obvious, but Lynne was clearly trying hard to match Greg's rather teasing and dismissive manner. Often when she spoke seriously and sounded as if tears were close, Greg would tease her, especially when she spoke of missing her work and of feeling lonely. On the other hand, he sat with an arm round her and they looked at one another frequently. They each described the satisfaction they experienced in their marriage. Greg's words were: 'I wish I had met Lynne years ago and the children were all ours.' But that was not a sufficient answer for Lynne, who saw what seemed to her to be Greg's rejection of her son and daughter, and when that happened, she felt rejected also. Her words were 'I want Greg to love my children the way I do.'

Greg's pattern of contact with his two children had been altered by the move to another town. He missed them, and his feelings of guilt were increasing. He felt torn about giving attention and affection to his stepchildren on a daily basis and to his own children on a twice-monthly basis. His conflict became acute when his children were present and his stepchildren competed with them for his attention. His desire was for time alone with his children, an extension of the sort of relationship he had developed with them when he had lived alone following separation from their mother. Lynne had agreed to try a weekend when she would take her children and stay away, leaving Greg to have undivided time with his children, but secretly expecting that Greg would not see this as a solution once he had tried it. To her dismay, he had enjoyed the weekend very much indeed. She then felt that the family he really wanted was his children and that she and hers were merely poor substitutes. To complicate matters, both were in agreement that Lynne's previous husband was an indifferent father. Contact between him and the children was irregular and infrequent. He did not press for it and often made cancellations. The habit of being together was being lost. The older child was loyal to her father; for example, she never called Greg 'Daddy' and corrected her younger brother, who sometimes did so, and would ask for visits while the younger child sometimes wanted to stay with his mother and stepfather rather than go to his father. Lynne wanted her children to have the kind of fathering she saw Greg providing to his own children, but withholding, in her eyes, from his stepchildren.

In stepfamilies there may be parenting issues and difficulties which go on for many years and in spite of this source of tension, the marital relationship can be satisfying and sustaining (Anderson and White 1986). This information was offered to Greg and Lynne, but Lynne said that rows between them were occurring and getting worse. Greg denied the two could be divided and used his teasing defence until the therapist pointed out that he was unable to see how distressed Lynne was, but that from where the therapist sat (literally and figuratively) it was very obvious. He became more thoughtful and receptive as they talked about the expectations each had had about stepfamily life, and about their fantasies of creating one family of their combined children. They discussed too, the ideal of one marriage with which Greg had grown up and his deeply held feeling that he was in the wrong no matter what. In part of themselves they wanted to annihilate the previous family history and become an 'ordinary' family. Lynne talked of asking Greg's two children if they wanted to live with her and Greg, one way she saw to try to resolve the uneven fathering. Greg also had this fantasy of winning his children away from their mother and sharing daily living with them once again. He tried to convince himself that he would then feel the same way about all four children. When these fantasies were explored aloud in the context of the therapist's questions and comments, both recognised them for what they were. Lynne said, 'But my children are scapegoats for what we haven't worked out.' She was also beginning to feel that she and the unborn child were scapegoats too, innocently carrying the blame for the attitudes and failures of others.

That Greg and Lynne had a strong affection was without doubt and this was the resource and basis for work with them to help them to be more open about the issues, to accept the structure of their unique family with both its strengths and weaknesses and to work together in supporting one another as the parent to their own children. Greg had to acknowledge and respect Lynne's skills with her children. He had come suggesting that she was indulgent and not firm enough. Lynne had to allow Greg to be sad about his children from time to time and support his need to have them to himself sometimes without feeling she and her children were then rejected. In terms of what we know about stages of development in stepfamilies (Papernow 1984; Robinson 1991; and see Chapter 3) Greg and Lynne were in the early stages, experiencing difficulties as they moved beyond fantasies about living 'happily ever after' and being perfect parents to one another's children. But they were trying to substitute another fantasy to solve the problems, the fantasy of 'one' family. They were trying to convince themselves that the children would fare better in one unit and without contact with their other biological parents. They were, in fact, rather close to promoting less and less contact between Lynne's two children and their father. Since he was rather unreliable in his contact and changed the arrangements frequently, it was tempting to allow these visits to slip into abeyance. The older of the two was more attached to her father than the younger child because she had known her father longer. She asked about him, telephoned him and was sad when visits were cancelled. The younger one was attached to Greg, seeking his attention and approval and showing his feelings of jealousy when Greg's own children were present. At these times Greg resented the little boy's appeals for attention as they distracted him from the total attention he wanted to give his two children.

At the time of writing the couple are trying to find flexible ways to arrange contact visits for both sets of children so that Greg does have his children alone from time to time and also so that Lynne's children do not lose contact with their father. Greg has come to realise how important he is to the younger of Lynne's children and is trying not to reject him at times when he, Greg, feels torn between all the children. Greg's feelings of loss arising from his first marriage are an issue he has yet to confront fully.

One of the societal myths influencing stepfamilies is that the children will adjust to the stepfamily more easily if the other parent withdraws (Visher 1984). It is wishful thinking, and Lynne and Greg were tempted to apply it, but Greg's devotion to his children prevented their going very far with it. Some fathers, however, suffering the pain of separation anew every time they see their children, withdraw themselves and try to believe that it is for the sake of the children that they do so. Stepfamilies may be given advice by family and friends and others outside the family suggesting the children benefit if a parent gives up contact rights. Even counsellors without specialist knowledge, using a conventional-wisdom approach, may offer such a recommendation. However, everything we know about children whose parents have divorced is that they make a better adjustment if they have not *lost* one parent. As Visher puts it, 'It appears that an important principle in post divorce parent–child relationships should be: "No parent is disposable"' (1984: 5).

Lund (1984) compared groups of children whose divorced parents were continuing to act as parents in a reasonably co-operative way, a second group whose parents were both still involved but where conflict between them occurred, and a third group in which were children who had no contact with one parent. The children in all three groups were of a similar age, although the study does not compare age at divorce. The results clearly show that children with both parents still active in their lives were far better adjusted and confident about themselves than those whose one parent had dropped out. Even when there was a fairly high degree of conflict the children showed better adjustment, and the group with parents who co-operated showed not only no difference from children in first families, but even seemed better adjusted in some ways. Wallerstein and Kelly (1980) also found in their study that the most disturbed children in their sample were those who had little or no contact with one of their parents. Children fear abandonment, and when it seems to have taken place, they often assume they are the cause of it themselves (Visher and Visher 1979). There can be no good case made for a 'clean break' between a parent and child unless there is definite and destructive damage to the child through abuse or neglect. Even an annual contact from a parent to indicate continuing interest and concern can give a child the feeling of being valued.

The second case example involves a stepmother. In this instance one of us (D.S.) had two telephone contacts while on duty as a telephone counsellor. A woman rang one evening rather late in the session. She began to speak rapidly and urgently about her feelings towards an eight-year-old stepson. She had not been married for long to the child's father, but had lived with the two of them for several years. The mother had died in childbirth.

One more myth is highlighted by this case. A stepfamily which results from death, it is often said, has fewer difficulties and integrates more readily than those which result from divorce (Visher 1984). This myth appears to arise from the powerful one already discussed, that a stepfamily can and should duplicate a first family. A belief which is linked to this myth, underlying it, is that a stepfamily is successful to the extent that it most clearly resembles a first family of two parents and their children. Many people reason from this starting point that stepfamily life is less complex and fraught if there are no extra parents and no potential for conflicts and jealousies over contacts with former partners. Indeed, distraught adults in stepfamilies sometimes wish for the death of former partners when there seems no end to conflicts and their divisive, destructive effect on a new partnership. Death does not end loyalty, however, nor resolve disappointment and anger. Children whose parents have died do not always accept a replacement and they tend instead to idealise the dead parent. The step-parent can ony fail by comparison. And that person may live with unresolved fantasies about the qualities of the parent who has died, leading to miserable jealousy and resentment of the child who embodies them. This is what the counsellor heard from the woman who telephoned about her problem.

She did not want to give her name, but for simplicity we will call her Sarah. Sarah began by saying that she had finally confided in her husband, having tried to disguise her feelings for over five years, and she warmly said that he had been responsive to her. She had told him of her resentment of his child and her jealousy of his first wife. She felt not second in his affections, but third or fourth, coming after his memory of his first wife, his affection for his child and his obligation to his first wife's parents. She resented having to share her home with her stepson and every evening and weekend she shared her husband with the child as well. She asked for time for the two of them to be alone; he agreed, and they had just had a weekend together, the first for a very long time. The trouble was that Sarah felt the same anger and resentment towards the child after the weekend and the talk with her husband as she had before, and she was afraid of her feelings. They were becoming violent. She had hit the child almost within minutes of collecting him from his grandmother's, where he had spent the weekend. This grandmother is the deceased mother's mother, and she had cared for her grandson for the first two or three years of his life. Sarah felt a degree of support from the grandmother, but also a feeling of being an intruder, a stranger who was watched and criticised.

As the story unfolded, Sarah began to describe her anger and lack of control. She felt she would forever be an outsider, her hopes of closeness in a happy marriage and family were destroyed, and although she recognised her irrational and unjust resentment, her stepchild seemed to her to be the cause of her sufferings. The child was a scapegoat, burdened with the sorrows and wrongs which were certainly not his own, and being punished for them. Sarah did not describe her stepson as a difficult child but one whose existence diminished her own. Although she cared for the child, took him to school and extra lessons and activities, discussed his progress with teachers and in every way did what she and others expected of a mother, she could not love the little boy. This failure made Sarah hate herself and the child for causing her pain. Sarah wanted to stop this happening but how was she to be helped?

The life Sarah was leading was one of isolation. Her husband had a demanding job which kept him working long hours and had required several house moves. His expectation, Sarah believed, was that she would look after his home and child and make few demands on him. Indeed, Sarah expected this of herself. Whatever her husband's first marriage had been, he was uncritically loyal to his first wife, which had become a brooding preoccupation for Sarah. Sarah's marriage had included a child from the beginning. The jealousy she felt was of the years without children in her husband's first marriage as well as jealousy of an idealised predecessor she believed was better loved than her. Her stepson symbolised all this. Her dream of marriage and what it should be was shattered, and she needed help to relinquish her dream (Visher and Visher 1979) as well as help to value herself. Both she and her husband needed help to work out a different arrangement for caring for the child.

After more than an hour Sarah disclosed that she was pregnant and was acutely fearful that having her own child would only exacerbate her negative feelings towards her step-child. She added that when she told her husband of her fears and her continuing resentment towards the child following their weekend alone, he had become angry and rejecting. She would give no information that would enable anyone to contact her, but a promise was extracted from her to telephone again when the counsellor would have information about help in her area. She rang again the next day, earlier than the appointed time, to say that her husband had asked for a divorce.

She was even more isolated than had been apparent, with no close family. This could well have been a factor in her forming and remaining in a marriage which appeared to offer her less affection than she needed and in which she felt she had a low status. When she asked for help it was inadequate and too late; the problem had become entrenched and there may have been deep-seated issues which were not apparent in a telephone contact. The point is that Sarah's story is not a story of her failure, but of the challenges inherent in step-parenting which the individual can seldom cope with in isolation. If, as Visher says, 'Children need to learn, and be shown, that a new stepparent is *not* a replacement for a dead parent or for a parent living in another household' (1984: 7), it must also be true that frequently the step-parent has the same need. Sarah needed to learn that she was someone of value in the life of her stepson, providing for the child in many vitally important ways and adding a dimension different from that of a mother, but that she was not a replacement and that she was not failing by having feelings of mixed affection and resentment. She was failing by hitting and hurting the child, a fact of which she was acutely aware.

For women especially, socialised to assume the nurturing and the entire responsibility for the emotional wellbeing of everyone in the family (Walters *et al.* 1988), being a stepmother means trying to do the impossible. How can she provide nurturing and emotional care for children who may be virtual strangers to her, and whose mother may be providing this sort of care in any case (Carter and McGoldrick 1989)? Women who have satisfactions in other areas of their lives, in work, friendships, as mothers to their own or adopted children, may yet find themselves feeling depressed and confused by the role of stepmother (Morrison and Thompson-Guppy 1985). They expect to love their stepchildren immediately; they expect to be able to facilitate the family integration quickly. Men also expect the stepfamily to mesh quickly and they also feel inadequate and angry when this mythical expectation comes to grief. It is unlikely, however, that men suffer the same undermining of self and self-esteem that women do in this context. The 'failure' to be 'successful' as a stepmother strikes at a woman's fundamental sense of having value in the world. At the same time, the name 'stepmother' calls forth every image of failed mothering (Smith 1990). When a woman begins to perceive that her feelings for a stepchild are not what she wanted or expected them to be, she feels she has become the wicked stepmother.

Divided loyalties

To be loyal is to honour an allegiance – to a person or place, a group or code of behaviour or to a family. By far the deepest and most complex loyalties are to family. Loyalty usually refers to deep feelings of attachment, of wanting to demonstrate it, show affection and have it returned. It can also mean remaining obedient to certain standards and traditions, to the unwritten rules which are part of the requirements of membership in a group or family. Family membership is different from membership in any other group because it is not chosen, except as marriage (Carter and McGoldrick 1980). When two people marry for the first time they are expected to leave behind a primary loyalty to their family of origin and create a new system of belonging; the marriage ceremony symbolises this transfer of allegiance (see Chapter 8 for a description of the significance of the marriage ceremony in the family life cycle).

The actual experience is a staged process; creating the new unit of family bonds and family loyalty takes time, and furthermore, some of the new will contain elements of the old. In families where change and growth with all the associated transitional requirements is going reasonably well, developing loyalty to the new couple and family identity is not blocked by conflicts about loyalty to the families in which each grew up. There will be periods of adjustment with associated stress, a normal part of any change. This will be followed by a new stage of development with new forms of security and familiarity until the next change, when the transition will be eased by the safe passage of the previous one. Alternatively, if each transition is marked by increasing strain which is not sufficiently resolved, the couple may not stay together. It must be remembered that in some cultures, and in some sections of the multi-cultural society in contemporary Britain, primary family loyalty is expected to remain with one's parents. Conflicts can arise if one generation is less loyal to the traditions of the previous one and absorbs features of the adopted culture by, for example, establishing a separate home and rejecting the domination of parents. Those who become involved in cultural displacement have an experience which is not unlike the loyalty conflicts inherent in stepfamilies.

When a stepfamily is created it is in the context of allegiances to several previous families, including the family of origin of each of the adults, the family that each might have formed with a previous partner and a lone-parent family also, at least for one of them. The two adults are attempting to form a new family which might include children who feel they are members of another family, to which they are loyal. Their feelings towards a step-parent are at best mixed or may be openly hostile. The step-parent is an intruder and a symbol of changes the children find too painful and confusing to accept. It can be seen how the step-parent may be a scapegoat for the children's feelings and fears of losing parents all over again. Or the new family may exclude children who are psychologically and emotionally deeply attached to one of the adults. Grandparents in stepfamilies are faced with loyalty conflicts too. In remaining active as grandparents when their own child, the parent of their grandchildren, is no longer living with the children, are they being disloyal, that is, to their own child?

Children in stepfamilies have to conform to the requirements of the new family before they have a sense of belonging to it. A step-parent, wanting to make the family come together quickly, all too often imposes discipline before the children are ready to accept it. 'You can't tell me what to do! You are not my father!' is a statement of loyalty to the parent inside the child and to the family as it used to be. It is highly likely that loyalty conflict is at the root of most of the stress suffered by individuals in stepfamilies and others in their family network. The societal myth which fuels such conflict is the one about stepfamilies being able to integrate quickly, because it encourages adults to ignore the loyalty issues.

A researcher who examined stress levels for adolescents in stepfamilies discovered that the most significant factor causing stress was the one associated with loyalty conflict (Lutz 1983). The adolescents in this study did not find it particularly difficult to live in two households or to explain their stepfamily to others. What they did find painful and confusing was to hear one parent and a step-parent criticise the other parent. When that happens the child feels criticised as well, because a child is part of both parents (Visher and Visher 1979) and wants to love them both. It is that love – and love is synonymous with loyalty – which is challenged and abused by hearing separated parents criticise one another, particularly when the new step-parent participates in the criticism. If children can be allowed to go on loving both parents, living or dead, they will suffer less distress in the complicated changes and can more easily accept and develop loyalty to a step-parent.

Loyalty conflicts for adults in stepfamilies have their major origins in issues of parenting. Being a parent and also involved in a new partnership causes tension. Who comes first? Romantic love for a new partner can seem incompatible with loving and caring for children. In a first family the couple relationship will have grown past the first stage of intense sexual and emotional involvement by the time a child is added. (If that does not happen, the transition from being a couple to becoming parents will be marked by serious conflict. Becoming a parent is perhaps the most profound change any of us have to make.) In a sense, then, the stepfamily is 'off time' in the family life cycle (see Chapter 2). The pattern of development in a first family from being a couple to a couple of parents with a child is convoluted. This means the two adults have little time alone or have to become an instant family on occasions when children are present. More than anything else, it seems, there are relationships with children which began before the couple relationship began, and at times the parent and child bond will take precedence. It is older and stronger and, of course, different. When children come first a step-parent can feel neglected and suddenly displaced. The other person, the parent, feels pulled in two directions, wanting to respond to opposing demands for time and attention. The new couple has not reached the stage of being able to share and complement each other as parents, while their own opportunities for intimacy are reduced.

This is not to suggest that the adjustment to being parents works automatically in first families simply because there has been time to be a couple before parenting begins. Divorce rates for couples with children appear to demonstrate that marital satisfaction goes down when children are added. Of course, many childless couples divorce also, but it must be noted that increasing numbers of children whose parents divorce are in their early childhood when the divorce occurs. Children are not responsible for their parents' divorce, but their presence makes parents of two people who might find the adjustment impossible and the effects on their life as a couple intolerable. They may become distant, less emotionally nurturing for one another. The mother almost always is wholly involved with the child and the father usually is less so, creating tension and resentment in both directions – in her because he is not as tied as she or does not help enough, in him because she is less attentive, the baby is demanding or he feels less an integral part of the household. Many possibilities exist for transitional crisis when a child is added. 'A baby makes the mother and father; otherwise they are just ordinary people', a child once said (Krauss 1960). That the baby makes the mother is an inescapable fact for a woman; whether the baby makes the father in terms of direct care is a matter of choice for a man. Some of the lowered satisfaction in their relationship which couples often experience following the addition of a child often results from a lack of sharing between the two, but even when they do work together there may still be stresses which threaten their stability. There may be changes in their standard of living as family expenses rise, for example. In any case, looking after small children means the parents simply have less time together and for each other. This is where the couple in a stepfamily begins. No matter how emotionally mature the two adults are and try to be, the step-parent feels supplanted by the children at times, and the parent, loving his or her children and being in love, has to balance the practical demands of child care with the time available to enjoy and develop a love affair. This is true whether the children visit or live with the parent and step-parent.

In the example which follows, a father was caught in a conflict of loyalty between his new wife and his two small children. The children lived with their mother and had weekend visits with their father. The new couple had known each other for several years and been friends while each had another partner. Their close relationship followed the ending of their previous partnerships and both thought they were well prepared for the realities their marriage would bring. She, Irene, had been a nurse specialising in the care of children and felt confident she knew what demands children make and how to meet them. He, Tom, was determined that he would not lose contact with his children. The children were included in the wedding day and Irene's parents accepted them and treated them with gifts and attention. When Tom moved into Irene's home, together they made a bedroom for the children to accommodate them on weekend visits. They knew there would be adjustments to make, among which was Irene's having to share her home and make it Tom's as well, and sometimes his children's. But they seemed to have thought and planned well.

Yet Irene became desperate after about a year. During one weekend visit she became so resentful of the children's demands on Tom and his reactions, which seemed to her to ignore her completely, that there was a major and bitter argument between them. Irene was incredulous that she could have such powerful feelings of anger and resentment towards children – any children, and especially children to whom she had dreamed of being a good substitute parent. In the end she had felt she was nothing whatever to them except 'in the way' when they visited their father. She felt distanced from Tom when the children were present, her efforts to care for them seemed unappreciated and even resented and she began to dread the weekends when the children were to come. Tom was determined that he and the children would have good times together and that he would make up to them for being absent from their lives on a day-to-day basis. 'I left their mother, not them', he said. Tom and Irene disagreed about some issues concerning the children's behaviour, Irene taking the position that she was expert in matters of food and health and thus was critical of much that Tom allowed. He took the position that his feelings for the children made him the expert. Irene began to doubt that their marriage would survive. She wished to have children herself and was beginning to feel that the atmosphere she and Tom had created was wrong for any more children to live in. Both were hurt, sad and needed help to begin to work together, to stop criticising one another and to relinquish the fantasies each had been cherishing about what their marriage would be like. Irene had to accept that Tom's children had a prior claim on him, but that that did not negate her or make her less important to him. Tom had to fulfil his responsibility for his children without excluding Irene.

Another major conflict of loyalty for adults in stepfamilies also is concerned with parenting. Someone who is both a parent and step-parent usually experiences a painful emotional dilemma about having differing feelings for their own children and their stepchildren, with guilt as the almost inevitable result (Visher and Visher 1988). Most step-parents hold an ideal of loving their children and stepchildren equally and feel guilty if they do not; they also feel guilt, that is, a deep sense of being disloyal to their own children, for trying to love all the children in the same way. For parents who live with their stepchildren but see their own on a visiting basis, and usually this will be fathers, the conflict can be especially poignant. If they enjoy their stepchildren it almost seems that they are depriving their own children of the affection which is rightfully theirs and then when the stepfather's own children are present the attention and affection has to be shared between all of them. It can seem that there is not enough affection to go around, but that is not the issue. The issue is really one of loyalty and guilt – loyalty to the children one helped to bring into the world and guilt at not being part of the daily life of those children. The conflict of loyalty then arises because of being part of the daily life of other children.

Greg, in the example described earlier in this chapter, experienced this conflict. His answer was either to have time with his children when his stepchildren were not present, or to persuade his former wife to change the children's residence to his with his present wife and her children, creating 'one big, happy family'. This fantasy, and it is a fantasy, because the stepfamily structure with its additional parents and grandparents continues to exist whether all the children live in one household or not, might have provided relief for Greg's loyalty dilemma, but would have introduced other tensions. Lynne, Greg's present wife, would have had daily care of a large family of children and her differing feelings for her children and stepchildren, a matter which she at first denied was any problem, would have been highlighted and might have reached breaking point. This would have been an even greater difficulty for her than Greg's were for him since she would have been in the role of mother to all four children all of the time. The children would continue to leave and return in order to have contact with their other parent. This procedure seldom works smoothly or in the same way in stepfamilies with children from two previous families. One parent will have a better relationship with a previous partner than the other; visits with non-custodial parents will not be synchronised or go as well as with the other and so on. Greg's first solution, to have time with his children without the presence of his stepchildren, was hard for Lynne to accept. She felt her children were being rejected and her loyalty to them, her powerful protective feelings towards them, came to the fore. Her fantasy, that Greg would 'become' the father to her children, had to be dispelled before she could accept his need to have his children to himself for some of their visits.

In another stepfamily, the conflict between a father's commitment to the children of his first marriage and to his second wife caused extreme tension in his new marriage, to the extent that contact with one of his two sons ended. This child felt criticised and unsupported by his father and stepmother and was distressed by the condemnation of his mother which he heard them express. The older of the two sons was living independently of both parents but was his father's ally in the conflict. The younger son lost both his father and brother for a time in the schism which resulted. The previous family was split in two, with the mother and younger boy on one side and the older boy, father and stepmother on the other. Contact between the mother and her older son was strained and between the brothers it was non-existent, as it was also between the father and his younger son. Loyalty conflict in this instance was resolved by sacrificing important and irreplaceable relationships. It is possible that in time there will be a healing of this rupture, a reparation from all sides, as both sons mature, the pain of the divorce heals and recedes and the new marriage stabilises.

The stepfamily is a unique family form and can never be the same as any other family structure. While there are stresses which are inevitable, stepfamilies have strengths too, and these will be apparent when the stepfamily uniqueness is accepted. In the examples above, Greg and Lynne each have something special to give to their stepchildren which enriches their own lives and those of the children. It is possible to enjoy this while at the same time supporting and honouring the right of the children to remain loyal to both their parents. In the second example, the younger son experienced intolerable conflict of his loyalties and resolved it by cutting himself off from the father he loved. The losses for everyone are great. Fortunately, in many stepfamilies a better and less extreme resolution is found.

Summary

Myths which have an influence on stepfamily integration have been discussed in this chapter. Visher (1984) listed seven: stepmothers are wicked; love happens instantly; a stepfamily can replicate a biological family; children of divorce and remarriage are permanently damaged; children adjust more easily if their non-resident parent withdraws from contact; stepfamilies which follow death are easier to integrate than those which follow divorce; and stepfamilies can integrate quickly. To these can be added an eighth myth, which is that of the 'perfect family'. All families face difficult adjustments, and they grow and change and experience shocks from, for example, illness, deaths or economic circumstances. All living requires compromise; relationships which survive are a record of more or less successful and balanced adaptations. The 'ideal' of trouble-free family life is as burdensome a myth as the ones listed.

Scapegoating, the process by which an individual or group can be blamed and punished for ills and struggles everyone shares has been described as it applies to the stepfamily. The particular stresses in bringing together children from previous partnerships can lead members of stepfamilies to blame one for the confusion and ambiguity all are experiencing.

Loyalty conflicts are inherent in stepfamilies and these have been described, with case examples.

CHAPTER FIVE

The law and stepfamilies: help or hindrance?

The law and stepfamilies

In view of the long-standing societal attitudes and even folklore regarding stepfamilies, it is perhaps not surprising that the law has failed to keep abreast of the current trends whereby stepfamilies are frequently created through divorce followed by remarriage and cohabitation. The law in relation to stepfamilies is as complex as stepfamilies themselves, and it does not appear that the Children Act 1989, as recently implemented, confronts the relevant issues and may even have added confusion. The Child Support Act, passed in July 1991 and due to be implemented in 1993, seems to compound the situation even further. Neither of the authors has legal training, and although we shall try to highlight some of the legal issues in this brief chapter, readers are advised to consult a family lawyer (such as a member of the Solicitors' Family Law Association, Box 302, Keston, Kent BR2 6EZ) for appropriate advice on any particular situation. This is particularly important, as it seems likely that this is an area where some individual cases may go to appeal, and through what is known as case law, some of the confusions will be clarified and thereby affect subsequent decisions.

The Children Act 1989

The Children Act 1989 is proactive in that it attempts to change societal attitudes to the family. It brings together for the first time what is known as private law – that is, the law relating to families, for instance those who are divorcing – with public law, which relates to the involvement of local authorities with children and families, particularly the making of care and supervision orders. There are three essential principles on which the law in relation to children is now based:

1. That the welfare of the child is paramount. This includes the recognition that delay in decision making regarding children is prejudicial to their welfare.
2. Continuing parental responsibility for children.
3. That orders should only be made when the court is satisfied that this would be better than making no order at all.

Each of these will be considered separately, although of course they are all interlinked. The Act also includes the court structures which have been reformed so as to give various courts the discretion to make orders (under Sec. 8 which is discussed below) in a variety of situations in what are termed 'family proceedings'. There are many day-to-day guidelines governing the functioning of the courts which are currently being worked out, and these have been recently issued as court rules or judicial directions. These envisage the consolidation of proceedings as being desirable, as distinct from the previous situation whereby proceedings concerning the same family could be (and sometimes were) heard in different courts. It is, however, important to remember that at each level, whether magistrates court, county court or high court, those who have the responsibility for decision making have a certain amount of discretion as regards both procedures and judgment.

The Act retains the present principle that the child's welfare is the paramount consideration, and sets out a checklist of matters which a court must take into account before making a decision. These are as follows:

> The ascertainable wishes and feelings of the child concerned (considered in the light of his age and understanding).
> His physical and educational needs.
> The likely effect on him of any change in his circumstances.
> His age, sex, background and any characteristics of his which the court considers relevant.
> Any harm which he has suffered or is at risk of suffering.
> How capable each of his parents, and any other person in relation to

> whom the court considers the question to be relevant, is of meeting his needs.
> The range of powers available to the court under this Act in the proceedings in question. (Children Act 1989: Sec. 1.3)

(Sec. 1.3 of the Children Act 1989 puts this list solely in the masculine gender, although it is of course intended that it should also apply to female children!)

The second principle, that of parental responsibility, is that 'parents should have all the rights, duties, powers, responsibilities and authority which by law a parent of a child has in relation to that child and his property' (Children Act 1989, Sec. 3). If the parents are unmarried then the mother has parental responsibility, although, with her agreement or through application to the court, the father may be included. Subsequent to a divorce, there will be the assumption that the *parents will continue to share the responsibilities of parenting*. But, as has been pointed out (Eekelaar and Dingwall 1990), the definition of what constitutes parental rights has never been laid down clearly, except in terms of what could be described more appropriately as privileges such as naming the child, the religious persuasion in which the child is to be brought up and the choice of a school. The Act does not use the term step-parent, nor are they given special rights or responsibilities. Unless they have parental responsibility, step-parents can only take actions which would be considered 'reasonable' by any other adult having temporary care of a child, such as a visit to casualty department or consent to emergency treatment. However, the Act does also provide (Sec. 2.(9)) that a person who has parental responsibility for a child may arrange for some or all of it to be met by one or more persons acting on her or his behalf (e.g. a step-parent) although s/he may not surrender or transfer any part of that responsibility to another and would still remain liable for any failure to meet any part of her or his parental responsibility. The Act retains the concept of 'child of the family', which comes from the earlier Matrimonial Causes Act (1973, Sec. 52). A child of the family is one who has been treated as such, and the fact that a child is a child of the family has legal implications relating to the rights of the non-biological step-parent to make an application to the court. It also has implications in relation to the step-parent's financial support of the child (though see the section on the Child Support Act 1991 below, and on money as an expression of rights and responsibilities in Chapter 6). However, the fact that a child is a child of the family does not give the step-parent parental responsibility for that child; a further court order would be necessary before parental responsibility could be acquired.

One of the new principles (under Sec. 1.5) is that the court should not intervene in family life unless it can be proved that such intervention will be better for the child than if the court had not been involved at all. With regard to Section 8 orders (see below) the court can make such an order if it considers that to do so would be better for the child than not making an order, for instance, making a residence order in favour of a step-parent if it considered that it was in the child's best interests to do so. The court can only become involved in making a care or supervision order (under Sec. 31) for a child if it considers that she or he is suffering or is at risk of suffering significant harm, and that this is attributable to the care being given which is not what a reasonable parent would be expected to give, or that the child is considered to be beyond parental control. At present what a court might define as constituting significant harm remains somewhat unclear, as it is specified as 'ill treatment' or the 'impairment of health or development' (though see Adcock *et al.* 1991). The health of the child includes both physical and mental health. Development includes physical, intellectual emotional, social or behavioural development (Sec. 31.9). There have, of course, been considerable precedents which have been established under our present child-care law, and these are likely to provide initial guidance for the social workers and family solicitors who would be likely to consider bringing proceedings in relation to a child under the Act. However, there is also question of what could be considered reasonable parental care, and the guiding principle of a child's basic right to a certain standard of care would appear to override any excuses or justifications which a parent could offer, such as his or her own physical or mental disability. For instance, according to Bentovim a 'good enough parent' provides the following:

- Adequate verbal communication to give information and intellectual stimulation.

- Sufficient physical freedom to encourage the development of the child's sensory and motor abilities.
- Adequate responsiveness which balances the child's need for attention to his or her behaviour, and the needs of the parent.
- Positive warmth and a loving framework. (1991: 36)

Such principles imply a presumption that the parents themselves have adequate resources, psychological, financial and housing.

If there should be concern regarding the care and arrangements for the children, or parental conflict about these, the court may consider it necessary in the interests of the child for an order to be made. Lawyers traditionally give legal advice to their clients, not only from their knowledge of the present law, but also based on what the courts would be likely to award should the case go to court. While case law sets various precedents, the Court of Appeal has consistently been at pains to indicate that children's cases *always turn on the particular facts of that individual*. It is difficult to predict what norms will now influence this kind of legal advice given to divorcing parents: and, indeed, there are many who would now question whether lawyers are competent to give advice to parents other than that based on knowledge of the law. To advise parents adequately concerning their children's needs would ultimately require psychological expertise regarding child development post-divorce and the effects of stepfamily life. Nevertheless, it is still likely that some parents who are in dispute regarding their children will continue to attempt to seek their exclusive care and therefore to deny the child her or his right to contact with the other parent.

The new court rules under the Children Act 1989 suggest that divorcing parents who are in conflict should be asked if they are willing to be referred for conciliation, and this has now been made more definite, in that the Statement of Arrangements, which must be filled in on any application for a divorce where there are children of the family, specifically asks whether the parties are prepared to discuss matters with the other parent and a conciliator. This area of alternative dispute resolution in which parents voluntarily involve themselves and whereby they are assisted to reach decisions which are uniquely suited to their own family situation is likely to become the focus of interest for family policy in the immediate future.

The Law Commission (1990) has made proposals for a new divorce law through which the couple, either together or individually, can make a statement to the court stating that their marriage has irretrievably broken down and they wish to seek a divorce. This would only be granted eleven months later, following a period of negotiation during which they have reached agreement regarding (a) arrangements for the future of their children and (b) financial matters. Divorcing couples may already seek mediation (also known as conciliation) voluntarily in which they may be helped to reach their own agreement regarding their children, or comprehensive mediation in which they are helped to come to agreement regarding both their children and their finances (see Fisher 1990; Parkinson 1990; Robinson 1991, 1993; and others). The bill proposed by the Law Commission incorporates the possibility of conciliation and is on the Lord Chancellor's rolling programme of law reform (Hansard 4 March 1992). At the present time many of the services affiliated to the National Family Conciliation Council provide child-centred mediation cheaply, often under what is described as the 'green form scheme' (i.e. through the solicitors, with the cost being met by the Legal Aid Board). Some also provide comprehensive mediation, which includes the disposition of the matrimonial home, assets and maintenance. While such schemes are highly professional, they are usually run on a shoe-string. The Family Mediators' Association trains lawyers and counsellors to work together to provide comprehensive mediation, and, although inexpensive by the standard of legal fees, each individual still requires their own separate lawyer, which can prove too expensive for many.

With regard to the private law, a new network of legal provision has replaced the old one so that there is no longer the possibility of custody, care and control or access orders. As has already been mentioned, under the Children Act 1989 there are a number of possible orders which can be made, which are known as Section 8 Orders. One or more of these may be made either singly, or in varying combinations, such as the court might consider would be of benefit to the welfare of the child.

The first of these orders is a *residence order*, that is, where and with whom the child should live, but this does not cancel the rights and responsibilities of the other parent. As Masson writes (in her very lucid chapter of the book *A Step in Both Directions?*, 1992), 'parents and their lawyers will need to consider the purpose of having a residence order following divorce or separation and also what the terms of that order might be'. Specific conditions (see below) may also be included as an additional order, perhaps as a specific issue. Although it is not spelt out, there is a clear implication that parents will continue to have joint parental responsibility following divorce, and that they will not lose this even should a specific court order be made giving someone else a degree of responsibility. It is also clear that parents will still be able to exercise their responsibilities without having to consult one another and that neither will have the right of veto over the other as regards their child (White *et al.* 1989). For instance, should a residence order be made specifying mother and stepfather, parental responsibility other than the residence of the child would be shared between father, mother and stepfather. Furthermore, at present it appears that all three could exercise their responsibility independently of one another, at least when the child is in their household. It seems likely that this principle will have some implications for step-family development and solidarity. Fisher considers that

> mediation would seem to have an important role in helping parents and stepparents negotiate whether and how they are going to share parental responsibility and how they are going to make practical decisions about the day to day care of the children of the family . . . . Ample opportunity is therefore needed for mediation to help parents explore the possibilities for cooperation from the point of view of the children, especially where conflict is generated by transitions and connections. This may involve mediators in more work *preventing* disputes than they currently carry out in *resolving* them. (1992: 58)

However, it does appear that Section 2, under which a parent is given the legal right to delegate parental responsibility by arranging 'for some of or all of it to be met by one or more persons on his behalf', short of surrendering his (or her) responsibility, might enable a step-parent to take some responsibility. Although as yet this is by no means clear, it seems to imply that there may in effect be split-residence orders for children where it is in their best interests to share their time with both parents, as has already begun to happen in many post-divorce families. For instance, this would give each parent the right to take the child out of the jurisdiction of the court (e.g. on holiday abroad) for one month without the necessity to seek the consent of the other person with parental responsibility.

Where the child has been treated as a child of the family, step-parents who are married to a child's parent can make an application to the court for the award of a residence order, although if the step-parent is unmarried the child would need to have lived with them for three years before such an application could be made to the court. In such circumstances it seems likely that courts will need to be able to make an assessment of the quality of care given by the step-parent.

The second is a *contact order*, which specifies the child's contact with the other parent. This can be more detailed than the present access orders, as it might include contact by telephone or letter. As James (1991) has commented with regard to the checklist, 'there are likely to be significant unintended consequences' and in 'considering the possible effects on the lives of stepfamilies we are left with more questions than answers' (p. 21). For instance, in taking into account the wishes and feelings of the child, will the courts also try to take into account the 'children's views about new partners, or about contact with the non-resident parent', especially where the child refuses to have contact with the parent with whom they are not residing? This is not uncommon and is frequently related to a parent not giving explicit encouragement or even implicit discouragement to the child regarding visits to the other parent and/or to the child's own conflict of loyalties. It is at least possible that courts may make contact orders which include a requirement for supervised contact by a named adult or attendance at places currently known as access centres. Such centres, like the one run by the Thomas Coram Foundation in London, provide comfortable and homely surroundings and staff who enable non-residential parents to maintain their relationship with their children. Hitherto the making of access orders has not necessarily included step-parents, nor necessarily taken into account the way they perceive their role. Where parents are not able to make their own agreements regarding their children, courts may require an investigative inquiry by the Court Welfare Service and in future it is possible that in making these welfare reports court welfare officers will be more likely to include recommendations regarding contact with step-parents and to comment on their capacities to fulfil a step-parental role.

Third, there is what is known as the *prohibited steps order*, which applies, for instance, in a situation in which two parents of different religions divorce and live apart and no order is made as to residence. If one parent intimates to the other that s/he wishes the child to take steps (e.g. for a non-Sikh parent to indicate an intention that a child's hair will be cut) which would be in contravention of the religious beliefs of the other parent, then the only legal remedy would be for the other parent to seek a prohibited steps order. Another example would be that a child should not be allowed to come into contact with an abusing parent or step-parent.

Fourth, there is a *specific issues order*, which will give what is known as court directions in relation to a particular issue which has arisen. It would seem that it is this order which would clarify the question of parental responsibility should the need arise.

Step-parents would need to seek the leave of the court before they could apply for a specific issues or prohibited steps order.

There is also another order, the *family assistance order* (Sec. 16), which is a short-term order (six months) under which the court appoints a court welfare officer or social worker whose task would be to help the family during a period of turmoil, which is common following a divorce. Such an order can only be made with the agreement of every person named in the order. At the time of writing, the indications are that very few such orders are being made.

If the local authority or National Society for the Prevention of Cruelty to Children (NSPCC) seeks a supervision or care order (under Sec. 31) and the case is proved that a child (or children) is suffering or at risk of significant harm, then the court may decide that it is appropriate to make a supervision order (Sec. 31), which would be for one year in the first place, with an ultimate limit of three years. The role and duties of the supervisor are set out in the Act (Sec. 35), and these are as follows:

1. To advise, assist and befriend the supervised child.

2. To take such steps as are reasonably necessary to give effect to the order.
3. Where the order is not wholly complied with, or where the supervisor considers that the order may no longer be necessary, to consider whether or not to apply to the court for its variation or discharge.

Committing the child(ren) to the care of the local authority (similar to the present care order) does imply that a parent would lose some parental responsibility. (As Adcock (1992) comments: 'at present few social workers are likely to have had much teaching on the development of stepfamilies.') Where a child may be committed to the care of the local authority, the Act provides that while a care order is in force the local authority will have the power to determine the extent to which a parent or guardian of the child may meet his parental responsibility for him (Sec. 33.3). This power of the local authority is constrained in that they may only exercise parental responsibility if they are satisfied that it is necessary to do so in order to safeguard the child's welfare (Sec. 33.4) and in that nothing will prevent the parent or guardian of the child who has cared for him from doing what is reasonable in all the circumstances of the case (33.5) for the purpose of safeguarding or promoting his welfare. This seems to open the way for some legal uncertainties about the continuing role of parents whose children have been committed to the care of the local authority. In cases where a step-parent has parental responsibility for a child who is made the subject of a care order, this would immediately cease because the step-parent's parental responsibilities stem entirely from the making of a residence order. However, such a step-parent would have the right to apply to the court for orders as to contact with the child while in local-authority care, although may not make application to discharge the care order; this could only be made by those with parental responsibilty or the child herself or himself.

The Act clarifies the position of guardians who may be appointed to have parental responsibility on the death of a parent who has it. If a parent with parental responsibility makes a written, signed and dated declaration, then a step-parent can become the guardian of a child following the death of both parents. It is advisable to seek legal advice before taking such a step because this is the sort of technicality which could cause severe problems after someone's death, for such requirements tend to be rather strictly interpreted by the courts. If the parent who died had a residence order in her or his favour, then the guardianship would take effect on her or his death regardless of whether or not the other biological parent is still alive (Sec. 5). If there is no such residence order in effect, then the appointment of the guardian would not be effective until the death of the other parent with parental responsibility. Therefore the step-parent who either has a residence order in her or his favour or whose spouse had a residence order in her or his favour before their death and was nominated as a guardian by that spouse is in a different position from that of other bereaved step-parents. Where there was no residence order the only way step-parents could acquire parental responsibility following the death of the biological parent would be to apply to the court for a residence order in their favour.

In summary, then: step-parents do not automatically acquire parental responsibility through marrying a child's (or children's) parent, though they can do so upon being appointed that child's guardian, or through a residence or contact order. It will already be clear that there are considerable implications for the position of stepfamilies under the Children Act 1989, and in view of the present number of divorces and subsequent remarriages it seems a somewhat striking omission that there are few references to step-parents.

Adoption

Under the Children Act 1975 an attempt was made to discourage step-parent adoptions, and where this has seemed appropriate some parents were encouraged to return to the matrimonial court to apply for a custody order, though many courts in fact continued to make adoption orders. There have recently been three Department of Health discussion papers on the adoption law (1990, 1991), and we still await the results of the responses to the review, new court rules relating to adoption and possibly new legislation. It is, however, likely that step-parent adoptions will be much easier. However, a single mother who subsequently marries and together with the stepfather makes application to adopt her child by a previous cohabitee could find that the child's biological father will make application to the court for parental responsibility and seek contact as well as refusing to give consent to the adoption.

Such a family were Julie and her husband Martin, who applied to adopt her son David by a previous relationship, who was then aged six. David's father, Gordon, and Julie had lived together for a couple of years, both were doing well in their chosen careers and were earning good money. Gordon wanted to go on a world tour and Julie had gone along with this idea. When she became pregnant they discussed Julie having an abortion but decided against it, and indeed both looked forward to the baby. Gordon agreed to delay his world tour, although Julie lost interest in it, and they bought a house with a considerable mortgage. After the birth of David, at which Gordon was present, Julie gave up work. Although Gordon was a devoted father, they found their financial circumstances considerably straitened, and their relationship deteriorated. Eventually, Julie left with David after a particularly unpleasant row involving violence. Gordon continued to visit every other evening and to put David to bed. Their relationship continued to deteriorate, and Julie's motherhood had changed her attitude considerably so that she no longer wanted the high-spending social lifestyle that she had previously enjoyed. When David was fourteen months old his father decided to go on his world tour after all and he departed after leaving a sum of money to support Julie and David. While he was away, Julie met Martin and, after living together for a while, they married and had two daughters. David, who was two at the time they began cohabiting, became very attached to Martin and regarded him as his father. When Gordon returned from his trip eighteen months later, he asked to see David. Julie had kept in touch with Gordon's parents, and although she and Martin refused to accept Gordon's offer of maintenance for David, it was agreed that Gordon should see David once a month at Gordon's parents' home. Although Gordon had written to Julie once or twice, he had not sent cards or presents to David. Because

David no longer remembered his father and had to build a new relationship with him, Julie thought she should be present at these contact visits. Gordon, who had not anticipated this, was deeply hurt that his son did not seem to know him and indeed talked of another man as Daddy. He became somewhat blustering and because of the past violence Julie insisted that Martin should be present at the visits, which Gordon found even more difficult. He became unreliable about keeping to the arrangement and Julie and Martin were irritated when, after driving to Gordon's parents with David and their daughters, he failed to turn up; the arranged contact visits ceased. When David started school they changed his name by deed poll and decided to apply to adopt him. Gordon, by now in a relationship with another young woman and the father of a daughter himself, refused to give his consent and applied to the court for parental responsibility. A preliminary hearing was held at which all were represented by barristers. Julie and Martin had always explained to David that Martin was not his real Daddy. For this reason, and partly because of the birth of his sisters, he understood where babies came from; but because he had three sets of grandparents, at the age of six he realised that there was something different about him, even though he and his half-sisters had the same surname. David told the Guardian ad Litem who had been appointed under the Act to make a recommendation to the court that he wanted his Daddy to be his 'real, real Daddy'. After a short period of reflection and before the date of the hearing, Gordon withdrew his objection to the adoption and it was granted.

The Child Support Act 1991

Concerned at the increased demands on the public purse for maintaining the children of lone-parent families, at the rise in their numbers (over a million in 1986, 14 per cent of all families with children) and at the failure of many divorced fathers to pay child maintenance, the government produced a White Paper which proposed the creation of a Child Support Agency to be established under the Department of Social Security ('Children come first', vol. 1, Sec. 2.1, 1990). The stated intention is to ensure the following:

- Parents honour their responsibilities to their children whenever they can afford to do so.
- A fair and reasonable balance is struck between the liable parent's responsibilities for all the children he or she is liable to maintain.
- The system produces fair and consistent results.
- Maintenance payments are reviewed regularly to reflect changes in circumstances.
- Parents' incentives to work are maintained.
- The public receive an efficient and effective service.
- Dependence on Income Support is reduced.

It was proposed that a formula should be calculated whereby the liable parent (usually the father), while being allowed some exempt income for a personal allowance and housing costs, should be assessed for the remainder on a formula concerned with the needs of the children who reside with (usually) his former partner or wife, to be known as the 'caring parent'. The White Paper postulated that as

> perhaps 1 in 10 children live in stepfamilies, and while there is no doubt that stepfamilies aim to provide a secure and loving home for the children and that stepparents willingly accept many obligations towards their stepchildren . . . it is nevertheless right that a child should look first to his own natural parents for his maintenance. A parent's responsibilities towards a child are not in any way removed or reduced when the child becomes a member of a stepfamily (and) persist for as long as the child needs maintenance. (p. 97)

At the request of the Department of Social Security a two-year survey was carried out on lone-parent families (Bradshaw and Millar 1991), which found that only 29 per cent at any one time receive regular payments from the absent parent. The researchers concluded 'that income support is very important to lone mothers . . . [and that] lone parents are very dependent on public sector housing' (p. 97). Two-thirds of those receiving maintenance receive it only for their children: and only about a third of those receiving none thought that their previous partner could pay anything. The research estimated that among those who knew the circumstances of the absent parent 41 per cent of those paying nothing could pay something. Of the lone mothers 83 per cent were still relieved to be free of their former husbands or lovers and 64 per cent preferred to live alone rather than seek another partner. Indeed, their major difficulty was finding affordable child-care arrangements which would allow them to work and to improve their living conditions.

The eventual legislation, rushed through prior to the parliamentary recession in July 1991, removed the task of assessing child maintenance from the courts to the newly established Child Support Agency, which will operate from within the Department of Social Security. The Act, due to be implemented in 1993, emphasises the importance of parental responsibility for their biological children, whether the parents are married or not, rather than for those (other than those who have been adopted) who do not have two biological parents who have accepted financial responsibility for their care. Initially, the Act will be implemented in respect of those 'caring parents' who are on income support, while it is likely that the provisions relating to the use of the Child Support Agency by those not claiming income support will be enacted at a later date. The child-support officers will have responsibility for maintenance assessments for those 'persons with care' of their children who are in receipt of benefit and for those who are not but seek the assistance of the Child Support Agency in claiming maintenance from the 'absent parent' (Bird 1991). A person with care of a 'qualifying child' (i.e. one under sixteen) who is in receipt of prescribed benefit, for instance income support or family credit, must, if required to do so, authorise the secretary of state through the Child Support Agency to take action to recover child maintenance from the liable parent. As the result of the considerable public protest following the White Paper, particularly on behalf of those women with violent former partners or spouses, this authorisation may not be insisted upon if it is considered 'that there are reasonable grounds for believing that this might result in harm or undue distress being suffered by the person with care of any child living with her' (Bird 1991). The parent with care must supply such information as would be necessary to make the assessment, and sanctions are available if she fails to do so, including the child-support officer's discretion to give a 'reduced benefit direction'.

The maintenance benefit will be reached according to a formula which includes the maintenance requirement, calculated by aggregating the incoming support allowances for the children (variable according to age) with the adult income support allowance for the parent with care, the family premium and the lone-parent premium. The child benefit is deducted from this. The assessable income of the liable parent is calculated and a deduction rate is also calculated from the assessable income of both parties in order to meet the maintenance requirement. Once the maintenance requirement has been set, the absent parent will be expected to contribute a further proportion of her or his income by way of maintenance until a specified statutory maximum has been reached. The protected income of the absent parent is similar to that in the attachment of earnings regulations, which is the income below which no family of persons liable to maintain a child is allowed to fall. Where such a stepfamily contains an 'absent parent' from another family the regulations will specify an amount below which a stepfamily's income must not fall. However, any subsequent increase in earnings brought into that family by the step-parent will serve simply to free the absent parent's income to be made available for payment of maintenance calculated under the formula. For many families this will represent a new form of poverty trap. The most contentious feature at present is that absent parents will be expected to pay 50 per cent of their assessable income towards maintenance – that is, about 20 per cent of their gross income – until the standard maintenance requirement has been satisfied. A recent newspaper report (*Sunday Times*, 18 October 1992) indicates that while 'the average weekly award to single parents will double to £45 under the new system [they] will not necessarily be better off as they will lose £1 off state benefit for every extra £1 child maintenance they receive'. There are other issues which arise from these proposals. Once an assessment is made the amount will be collected and enforced by the agency, which may also collect other forms of maintenance, for example spousal maintenance or that for stepchildren. There will be a right of appeal, at first carried out by another child-support officer and ultimately to a Social Security Appeal Tribunal. The courts will retain jurisdiction in respect of children not covered by the Act, for instance stepchildren, those who are over eighteen and cases where one party is abroad.

It is thought that about 10 per cent of children are living with their natural mother and a stepfather, whether they are married or cohabiting (Family Policy Studies Centre 1991). According to Dimmock (1992):

> the position of stepchildren is affected in two ways. Firstly as children claiming support after the breakdown of a household including stepchildren, and secondly, as children who are members of a second family needing to be taken into account when assessing an absent parent's responsibility to meet a child support obligation to a first family; or to put it more simply, the financial balance between first and second families.

However, according to Eekelaar:

> No assessment can be made against stepparents. Nevertheless the fear that stepchildren who have been treated . . . as children of the family might lose their right to apply for a court order for support from their stepparent has not been realised. The Act only prevents the court from making child support orders . . . with respect to a qualifying child; their jurisdiction to deal with child support applications by stepchildren who are 'children of the family' remains untouched. (1991: 513)

During the discussions on the Act, it was argued that

> there would be little opportunity for trading child support payments against poverty settlements because the formula ensures that a parent who transfers the house to the caregiver will automatically pay less child support than he would otherwise do because his housing costs would rise. (ibid., p. 515)

However, this fails to take into account that the housing exemption will be made by officials according to the regulations; it will not be a bargain made by the couple at the time of their divorce. Also the couple may wish to trade an element of a period of child support for capital support other than housing; and transferring a house may not always leave the absent parent with increased housing costs. At the time of writing, much needs to be clarified, including the regulations. It is therefore suggested that, where relevant, readers acquaint themselves with up-to-date literature and, if possible, seek legal advice. In many cases the calculations will be quite complicated and many solicitors and advice agencies are likely to need the assistance of computer software to calculate a person's liability, as there will be little chance of people being able to do these calculations for themselves.

At the time of the third reading of the bill an amendment was introduced whereby the Lord Chancellor (or the Lord Advocate in Scotland) may decide to permit consent orders to include child-support provisions, 'obviating the necessity for a separate application to the agency' (Eekelaar 1991: 511). At present it seems clear that the Act's intention to treat child maintenance as an administration matter to be assessed by child-support officers, rather than the courts, will deprive the poorer families and those middle-class families whose only asset of any value is the former matrimonial home of the power to negotiate their own financial settlements. This fails to 'put children first' in the present government's stated aim of a classless society.

Summary

It is evident that the child-care legislation as well as that for child maintenance is primarily based on the model of the nuclear family of biological parents and their children, and tends to favour them. Burgoyne and Clarke (1984: 101) found 'that whilst family structures which deviate from the family norm will tend to experience closer public scrutiny and control the greater the material and interpersonal resources of the family the more its members are able to insulate themselves from public intervention and dependence on public institutions'.

Children Act 1989

The Children Act makes the welfare of the child paramount and this is evidently a prime injunction to the courts at all levels. It is also stated that courts should not intervene unless it can be proved that such intervention is better for a child. Despite the careful caution and the possibility of orders under Section 8, it remains unclear just how overstretched social workers in under-funded Social Services Departments can help families at risk.

Child Support legislation

According to the Family Policy Studies Centre, the issues arising from these proposals are as follows:

- The formula – the 50 per cent rate of deduction; the maintenance ceiling and minimum payment; the mother's personal allowance; children with disabilities; the nominal 5 per cent deduction; and the Community Charge.
- The obligation to name the absent parent.
- Second families and 'protected income'.
- Enforcement of maintenance payments.
- Work and benefit entitlement.
- Maintenance disregard.
- Housing.
- Appeals procedure.
- Obligation to use the Agency.
- Obligation to use the formula.

It will also be evident that stepfamilies are not and cannot ever be the same as nuclear families and that unless the children are very young at the time of the creation of the stepfamily, the hopes of parents and step-parents to re-create their family life with one (or more) new members is just not possible. Indeed, many of the difficulties in which stepfamilies can find themselves are the direct result of such unrealisable aspirations, and the law at present tends to make the confusion worse. It is not only that parents and step-parents hold inappropriate and unrealistic ideals for their family life; it is also that those whose occupations are directly related to the support and care of families make their assessments of stepfamilies based on the more or less generally accepted norms for nuclear families. Stepfamilies who are likely to be affected by any of the new legislation are advised to seek legal advice at an early stage.

Another area of difficulty at present is that not only general practitioners, health visitors, child psychiatrists, family therapists, marriage guidance and other counsellors and social-security officers, but also those within the legal profession as well as courts who are called upon to evaluate the functioning of stepfamilies are likely to do so by comparing them with the expected functioning of nuclear families, often making a deficit comparison. There is a great need for education and training of such care-giving professionals about the stages of stepfamily development and day-to-day life.

While there are generally accepted social, cultural and ethnic guidelines for nuclear families – although there are those who choose not to accept them – there have hitherto been none for stepfamilies. Each stepfamily has to find its own way by trial and error, often very slowly and painfully. As authors of this book we have tried to remedy this situation, but, as it stands at present, the law provides little assistance.

CHAPTER SIX

Money: more than finances

In this chapter the focus will be more upon stepfamilies which come about because of divorce and less on those which result from the death of a former partner, and the subject is money and its influence. While this chapter is not meant to be a financial guide for men and women going through the dismantling of a shared life – expert and individual advice is usually needed for that – there is some specific information about the ways in which settlements and maintenance agreements may be reached and the role of the state in supporting those who require it. Money has far-reaching significance which goes beyond weekly bills, however. The financial considerations during the divorce process have enormous potential for increasing whatever bitterness and acrimony already exists, even in instances where there is no shortage of money and both partners agree to the divorce.

Of course, there are also financial issues when death ends a marriage, and often terrible insecurity and hardship, especially for women – the forlorn widow is a familiar figure in fact and fiction. The disposition in a person's will is well known as the cause of suspicion and alienation in some families, and the question of wills and inheritance in stepfamilies will not be ignored here. For divorcing couples, however, financial assets or their lack assume symbolic significance as the two people try to extricate themselves from a life of joint emotional and financial interdependence. Two people living in one household with one income or two incomes combined have to become two households, each with an income. If there are children the situation becomes infinitely more complicated. The ways in which the two go about settling financial issues will probably replicate some of the struggles of their relationship. Money and power can become synonymous in the separation and divorce process, just as it may have been in the course of the marriage.

Such power can serve to punish a former partner, prolonging the legal divorce procedure and maintaining a high level of stress and conflict. Conversely, coming to financial terms can facilitate the separation and its completion at every level, practical and emotional. These possibilities will be explored in this chapter.

Marriage – its meaning and practice – is continually being redefined. For most people, it is the most intimate relationship of their lives, and this holds true for those who have more than one in a lifetime. While once marriage may have been primarily a means for the propertied classes to increase their holdings and therefore their wealth, it hardly could be said to function that way now. The procreation of children within a legally contracted marriage protected both women and children, but the concept has changed in relation to children also; women may have children and remain single by choice, or a couple may have children in a cohabiting union. Marriage is not now the only or major means for a woman to attain social status and economic stability. If marriage could be defined as a publicly sanctioned sexual relationship, many people do not feel the need to declare their sexual connection in a legal contract, and for homosexual couples, male or female, no public declaration is available. Still, we marry, and with enormous expectations that social acceptance, family approval and a romantic attachment will last a lifetime, providing for nearly every emotional need the two may have. What marriage is, the impact it has upon the lives of those who contract into it, the differences of the experiences of women and men within marriage, is frequently discussed and written about. The concept of marriage is challenged and redefined by legal changes and social practice. It is a social institution which has become an ideal none of us can escape whether we enter into it or not.

Since we are living longer and marrying younger, and early death through war, illness or childbirth is less frequent than it once was, a marriage for life can be a very long time, as much as sixty or seventy years. This places enormous expectations on individuals to choose the 'right' partner and survive various environmental pressures such as erratic employment, inflation and recession, social approval and disapproval, racial attitudes, war, accidents – to say nothing of the pressures on a couple which result from events inside the family, births, deaths or infertility, feuds and estrangements, and from their development as individuals, their values, ambitions and attainments. The list is endless and the compromises are numerous and complex when a couple maintains their relationship over many years. That many do not should be no surprise, yet, as every divorcing couple knows, divorce is a painful process and there is no general support for those going through it. It is hidden; no socially sanctioned ritual exists for marking the end of a marriage, formal or informal in its contraction. In the past and in some communities – for example, in Wales in the seventeenth and early eighteenth centuries – there were trial marriages, and if they did not succeed, commitment to them was ceremonially ended by jumping backwards over a broom (Parker 1991). In a time when many marriages end we do not have even that simple exercise, but then divorce threatens the marriage ideal, whereas trial marriages were accepted at one time. If death ends a marriage there are rituals for expressions of grief at the loss, the loss of a person, one half of a relationship which may or may not have been completely satisfying but was of enormous importance to the surviving partner. Divorce, however, is usually regarded as a failed relationship for which grief is not thought to be appropriate. The loss, and the stigma, often hang like moss on a tree to those who go through divorce, influencing decisions about children, money and property. (The reader is referred to Chapter 3 for a full exploration of the issue of loss and grief.)

What happens when a couple relinquish their choice of one another and become free to choose again, and what are the ways in which finance influences the process? The impact on the process of creating a new partnership of the decisions made or forced on a divorcing couple as to money and property adds to the pressures described in Chapters 4 and 5 which challenge the new, that is, the stepfamily, couple as they try to form a life together. The economic consequences of divorce are often far-reaching and differ for men and women, and this appears to be true whether or not there was significant wealth to dispose of between the two and their children, and even if there were no children.

Women and divorce

In the past marriage was expected to provide women with financial security as well as social status. Now, the notion of marriage as conferring a right to lifetime financial support has changed to one of marriage as a partnership in which both contribute and share assets (Cretney 1990). What might this mean when a marriage ends? It could mean that financial settlements may be made in the form of periodical payments over a period of time, or in one lump-sum payment rather than support payments over many years. Fixed periodical payments and lump-sum payments are provided for under the Matrimonial Causes Act 1973, Section 23. They are made in accordance with the needs of children, the length of the marriage and the wife's contribution to the couple's joint assets. If the marriage was brief and the wife is able to provide for herself, there may be very little in the way of financial settlement once the shared property has been divided. Even so, research indicates that a woman's living standard drops following divorce, with or without children, and does not rise to the previous level she enjoyed while married or sharing expenses in a two-income household. Childless divorced women who remain single are poorer than the general population (Eekelaar and Maclean 1986), due to the generally lower pay and tax benefit for women, but if a woman forms a new partnership her standard of living has a chance of rising again to the average pattern. (Social policy might thus be reasonably expected to support repartnering. However, the Child Support legislation, designed to prevent absent parents from avoiding paying for children of previous partnerships, could be construed as discouraging to stepfamilies, especially those with young children and low incomes. The woman looking after young children would be unlikely to be able to earn and if the man, usually the stepfather, is having to contribute from a small income to his children in another household, the stepfamily will remain at a poor level.)

The right to hold and retain assets as a married woman was hard fought and has a long history. It may seem that the relevance of this question is exclusive to propertied classes and it certainly is the control of wealth and property which motivated social change through several centuries, but every person is heir to changes which influence social attitudes as well as legislation. In the seventeenth and eighteenth centuries married women had some control of money or even separate property which was theirs by an agreed settlement, usually at the time a marriage was contracted (Staves 1990). However, women were not significantly empowered by these arrangements, since legal rules ensured that property was transferred from male to male. The ideal for women was virtue and gentility in the private sphere of domesticity, not activity in the public world. Women were thus subordinated even when they had some money of their own and the idea grew that they must be controlled and protected by men. According to Staves, while rules governing married women's property appeared to benefit women during the Restoration period, they were not basically different from the rules at the beginning of the nineteenth century, when women had to give up control of their own wealth to their husband. Public law, where it intervened on women's behalf, did so apparently to prevent women and children from becoming public charges.

Through a series of Acts, culminating in the Married Women's Property Act (MWPA) 1882, women were enabled to retain rights to property which was theirs at the time of marriage. Before this legislation reform any property a woman possessed or inherited became her husband's and part of his estate. 'In law husband and wife are one person, and the husband is that person' – a statement ascribed to an eighteenth-century jurist, Sir William Blackstone, which sums up social attitudes to women's status in marriage, vestiges of which are still with us but they are being challenged and diluted. Although the passage of the MWPA 1882 was a major step towards equal rights for women and justice in property law, it has little relevance for women divorcing in the late twentieth century if they have no property and no skills in the workforce. If they have children and have obeyed the cultural demand to stay at home and look after their children they may be ill-prepared to earn any money themselves, and society does little as yet to help with child care for the employed woman, or for that matter, the employed single parent whether man or woman. Even if 'the theory of marriage will no longer be based on the enslaving of one but on the equality of two' (Eliza Lynn Linton exulting in 1870 on the passage of the first Married Women's Property Act), the real situation of a woman with children will hardly appear to be equality in terms of her standard of living or her ability to improve it.

'The average wage for married women with dependent children is less than ⅓ of that for a man so that unless these women were to have improved their incomes substantially following separation, few would have been in a position to lift their families out of benefit' (Davies and McLeod 1983: 220). Thus women with dependent children are the worst off after divorce, with more than 50 per cent living on welfare payments, far below the average family income (Eekelaar and Maclean 1986). Many of these women will have worked and contributed income during their marriage when the husband shared in child care, at least to the extent that the wife was able to go out to work. Between the two of them the family may have had a reasonable standard of living and the children were looked after, but after separation many women cannot maintain a job, or find that they have a greater income from income support if they do not go out to work. Davis and McLeod found that 65 per cent of their sample of women with care of children after divorce had worked during marriage, but only 54.5 per cent after separation. The same did not apply to the men with care of children, 77 per cent of whom were working and continued to work after separation, reflecting the fact that a man's earning power is higher and also that the children who were in the care of fathers tended to be older than those who were with mothers.

Another reason for the application of lump-sum payments or fixed-term periodical payments rather than continuous support payments is the 'clean break' philosophy of divorce. This facilitates financial independence for both husband and wife at an early date after a divorce decree is granted. The 'clean break' philosophy applies to the divorcing couple and not to the children; obligations to support children continue, parenting being a responsibility which extends beyond those the two adults have for one another, a responsibility which encompasses the emotional and psychological needs of children to know and be in contact with both their parents. The 'clean break' is intended to sever links between the couple by releasing women from financial dependence on their former husbands and men from financial obligations to former wives. But neither periodical payments or continuous support payments means financial security will follow for women with children (Edwards *et al.* 1990).

Over half of all divorcing couples have children under sixteen, and in 1986, of all those with children under that age, nearly half were under five (*ibid.*). The parent with whom the children live, usually the mother, has great difficulty in working to supplement financial settlements because of limited child-care facilities, as mentioned above; and most maintenance orders or periodical payments are low in value and often in arrears. Edwards *et al.* state that approximately half of all periodical payments are registered in magistrates courts, implying their poor value in terms of financial security. Davis and his colleagues found that women who did receive maintenance were more likely to be employed than those not receiving maintenance, probably because they could lift the family income when their earnings were added to maintenance payments, even low amounts, whereas their earnings actually reduced their total income when earnings were deducted from income support. In the, broadly speaking, middle-class group, the women with job skills were more likely to be employed both during marriage and after divorce. They would gain more and lose less and be more able to pay for child care.

The position of divorced or never-married women with young children, especially unskilled women, is a poor one economically. If divorced or separated, their standard of living inevitably is lower than it was prior to divorce. The evidence that this is so is now overwhelming (Maclean 1991). What is their position if they form new partnerships, as many divorced people do? A study in 1979 (Leete and Anthony) showed that 55.5 per cent of the men in the sample and 48 per cent of the women were remarried four-and-a-half years after divorce, and most of them within a year. Leete and Anthony found that the likelihood of remarriage falls with increased age at divorce, especially for women, but the presence of children, at least young children, does not seem to be a deterrent to remarriage. Given that many women do remarry, and many form cohabiting partnerships, it can be assumed that their economic situation improves with the new household but still may fall below the average national family income. Eekelaar and Maclean (1986) found that 15 per cent of remarried parents were continuing to receive welfare payments as their main source of income. Some women are able to resume work, part-time or full-time, in a new partnership where the management of both children and household is shared by two adults, thus raising the standard of living for the entire unit. These women will be able to clear the 'poverty trap' of welfare payments reduced by earnings. Because of the presumption that a man will be supporting the household, a remarried or cohabiting mother will no longer be eligible for income support in any case (and she may not continue to receive the same amount of maintenance for herself from her former husband), but this need not be a concern for her if her partner is in work. Child benefit continues whatever the parents' employment status, but because of the assumption that repartnering means shared income and shared expenses in one household rather than two, the child benefit is reduced for combined families (Family Policy Studies Centre 1991). In spite of such reductions, remarriage, or re-partnering, introduces a positive economic effect as well as a new beginning for the two adults; it does have the potential to reverse some of the economic hardship which follows divorce for women with dependent children. Indeed, the same is true for either parent living alone with children.

Men and divorce

The shock of separation is felt by all members of separating families. The shock waves last longer for couples with children than for childless couples, which is not to say that couples without children part without pain. The loss of a close relationship is a difficult thing to accept, integrate and move on from, but the loss for childless couples need not be repeated over and over, as it is for couples who are parents. Whichever one is the parent no longer living with the children must experience the parting repeatedly and be constantly reminded that ordinary daily life with children has been sacrificed. Whoever wanted the separation, and rarely do both partners want to part, must encounter the aggrieved one every time the children move between them or when they have contact about issues concerning the children. Anger and sadness can last a long time under these circumstances.

In most cases it is the man who no longer lives with his children, while at the same time he has a financial obligation towards them and possibly the mother, whether or not he was the instigator of the separation. He may have to support two households with the same income that previously supported one. He may be homeless for a time. He may have few social supports and struggle with a lack of skills in day-to-day domestic chores. During the separation transition there can be extreme difficulties for men in addition to the financial issues, and in fact, these may loom even larger. Social norms, however, and the sheer need to feed and clothe a family, place a continued expectation that men provide the money, or the major portion of it. Everyone in the family, adults and children, experiences a change downwards in standard of living as a result of divorce, including the man whose income has to spread further than it previously did. But because his income will be likely to rise, providing he has skills and remains employed, his standard of living is likely to recover over time. In any case, the amount of maintenance a man pays to a former wife and their children will be a lower percentage of his income than it is of hers. For most fathers the maintenance paid is 10 per cent or less of their household income, whereas the recipient family would be dependent upon the maintenance for as much as 30 per cent of the total household income (Eekelaar and Maclean 1986). If a man forms a new partnership, his income is stretched again of course, a situation to be discussed later.

Lone fathers are more likely to remain in work than are lone mothers and to have the care of older children rather than infants and toddlers. Their child-care problems are therefore not as difficult to overcome, while at the same time their earning capacity is greater. If their income is low but they are in full-time employment, they will be eligible for family credit (only available to families in which at least one parent is in a full-time job). Four out of ten of all family credit recipients are lone parents and a large proportion of these are lone fathers (Family Policy Studies Centre 1991). Child benefit will be paid regardless of the parent's employment status plus one-parent benefit for the first child in a lone-parent family. But most divorced fathers do not have their children living with them.

In the first stage of separation immediate arrangements have to be made to meet everyone's daily needs. A man might move to his parents' home in the short term, or even stay in the same house and attempt to live a separate life. If he is not employed, both partners are eligible for benefit and both will live at poverty level. If he is employed, he will probably cover some of his wife's expenses even if she receives benefit. If she is earning they will probably try to establish who has been paying for what and discover whether this arrangement can continue. Somehow they manage until the time comes to consult solicitors and set the legal machinery in motion. Part of this will be an assessment by the Child Support Agency when it comes into being in April 1993. Even if never married or divorced, if a lone parent applies for income support, the absent parent will be assessed in terms of ability to cover the costs. When these processes are underway, unresolved issues, lingering grief and anger, will arise as the couple divide material items and have to make decisions, forcing them to confront not only the end of the marriage partnership but also its history and meaning to them. At this time a man may be relieved to have his financial commitment defined, but dismayed to realise that the forces of separation and divorce are almost certain to distance him from his children. He may find ways to have good times with them or he may give up, but when he forms a new partnership himself, a new set of emotional and financial circumstances come into being.

New partnerships

Stepfamily households, when compared to households where one parent is living with dependent children, are better off, but worse off than the average household (Eekelaar and Maclean 1986). The explanation for this does not appear to be simply the strain of paying maintenance to former spouses. When Maclean and Eekelaar explored this question they found that stepfamily households which were below the poverty line were those affected by high rates of unemployment (three times the national rate at the time the study was made), and they also tended to be larger families. Nevertheless, these families had an income which was marginally greater than the lone-parent family which preceded it.

A woman who has been living alone with her children is to some extent rescued from poverty and insecurity when she remarries or forms a cohabiting partnership, and possibly to a great extent. Her life and that of her children enters a new phase as comfort and financial security improve for them, certainly in the short term. Long-term results for security and for children's wellbeing will depend on many factors, but it is highly likely that their immediate living standard will rise. As we understand more about stepfamily development we know that in the first phase all members have a fantasy, different for each of them, but for the adults, at least, related to the fantasy that all marriages begin with: 'They were married and lived happily ever after.' The fantasy for a man who improves the economic standard for a woman and her children is very likely to be something close to that. The children have other fantasies, fears, as opposed to the glowing hopes of the adults, that their parents both may be lost to them – one to the new step-parent and the other to the world outside. And for the woman there may be a price to pay for an improved standard of living. She may have feelings of guilt about the burden she has placed on her new partner. She may feel that she does not have equal rights in decisions about how money is managed, and this following her previous experience as sole manager when she was on her own with the children. And she may feel constrained in dealing with her children, as if they have to be exemplary in their behaviour. This early period will last through many struggles to begin working together as partners and as parent and step-parent.

One young woman tells this story about the beginning of her life as a single parent:

> I went out to cut the grass the first time after he left. As I went round and round I realised that I would always have to do it and I thought about all the other things I would have to do, mending furniture as well as toys and clothes, and all the shopping and

> cooking – just everything. Not to mention the children! I was now the only one to read bedtime stories, take them to school. But you know, I felt happy as well as scared about that. I felt excited at the prospect of making all my own decisions.

Life was a struggle financially for the family: housing was insecure and efforts to generate income herself were met with the well-known difficulties in finding child care – the story of lone-parent families. However, this woman continued to value having her own choices, in so far as the demands of caring for children and the limits of a small income allowed them. When she remarried, her life changed dramatically, becoming financially more secure and, as she put it, 'more interesting'. The first few months were extremely happy in spite of the stresses of early adjustments. As time went on, however, she found herself tense and uncomfortable about her children's normal and natural behaviour and about her own lack of status in the new household. She described this period in these words, 'It was as if we had to be on our best behaviour, to prove that we were worth all the expense and bother.' It took more than a year to begin to talk and be open about the issues, but it was the way the new couple found to work together in making decisions. Clear agreements were made about money and about what to expect from the children. Her knowledge and expertise began to find expression and gradually she began to value her own contribution, which was not equal in financial terms, but was vital to all the family.

Men without children

When a man, himself childless, marries or becomes the permanent partner of a woman with children, the cost of living rises for him. This is the position whether he has previously been married or not, and whether he is paying maintenance to his previous wife or not. The costs associated with his new partner and her children are likely to add to his financial outlay, and although he may move into her home, it is still probable that there is rent or a mortgage to be paid. The financial responsibilities in a family household will be considerable compared with those entailed as a single person. Taking on a family also implies that he is assuming at least some financial responsibility in relation to them, since 60 per cent of men fail to pay child maintenance for their children from a previous marriage or partnership, and among the 40 per cent who do, payment is often sporadic. For stepfathers, helping to support a new family frequently entails a considerable proportion of a man's income being earmarked for household and child-related expenses, or suddenly having to pay unexpected bills. His money is no longer his to spend as he wishes. Where both are earning, many couples do not anticipate an increase in expenses and endeavour to continue their previous financial arrangements, which often results in some degree of financial crisis, producing in turn a crisis in the relationship. To resolve this, recognition with openness in required, and renegotiation of how expenses are to be shared. The example which follows illustrates this.

Daphne met Bill through going to work in his business. At that time both were separated from their previous spouses and they began a relationship which led to marriage after their divorces were finalised. Daphne had two children who lived with them, although they saw their father frequently and he paid their school fees. Daphne's previous husband also had a business, which he sold profitably, and after his remarriage he indulged the children, taking them on expensive holidays and giving them large allowances. He also increased his heavy drinking, becoming an alcoholic, and this eventually resulted in his becoming virtually penniless. This meant that Bill had to shoulder the school fees and the children's maintenance, and he was bitterly resentful, partly because he had not expected to do so when he married Daphne and partly because he felt his stepchildren had never accepted him.

Men with children from a previous marriage

A remarried man who has children from a previous marriage or relationship continues to have a financial responsibility towards his children, if not also towards their mother. While nowadays there is usually an attempt to divide the financial resources equitably at the time of the divorce, this often entails selling the matrimonial home, thus necessitating a move for all the members of the family. However, the divorced and remarried father will, in any case, have a financial obligation to two households. As indicated in Chapter 5 and also in this chapter, many men fail to honour their financial responsibilities towards their first families, but for those who try to do so a considerable financial burden is placed upon them. Until the present time, many women who are divorced, whether remarried or not, are reluctant to pursue their former husbands for failure to pay maintenance because pursuance is expensive, often unproductive and, in any case, the courts are reluctant to imprison those men who default upon their maintenance orders. Although we have described the Child Support regulations which are to be introduced in 1993 and discussed some of the possible difficulties they may hold, it is too early to be precise as to what the effect of the regulations will be upon stepfamilies.

If the partner of the remarried man has an income, both his and hers will be essential in providing for their shared household. If the remarried man is honouring his commitments to his previous spouse and children and the former husband or partner of his present spouse is not, then resentment is inevitable. Most remarried households where both partners have children from previous relationships are under some financial stress, and this makes the decision to have a child of their relationship difficult for them, perhaps even impossible. This, indeed, was the situation for Bill and Daphne.

Bill had two children from his previous marriage, one of them adopted. When the marriage broke up, his former wife returned to her country of origin together with her children. However, when she found it difficult to rebuild her life, the children were placed with his sister, who, with two children of her own, found this a considerable burden. Bill maintained the children and tried to see them as often as he could, becoming increasingly worried about the quality of care and education they were receiving. Eventually, it was agreed that they would return to this country with him, go to boarding school and spend holidays with Daphne and himself. This meant Bill taking sole financial responsibility for his children. Because of these unexpected changes Bill and Daphne put off having children of their own until it was too late. Although Daphne became fond of Bill's children (and they of her), they each resented not being able to have a child of their relationship.

An unexpected pregnancy in a new partnership can throw a carefully planned stepfamily life into some disarray and put considerable stress on the relationship. The example which follows is an illustration of this situation. Derek and Linda had married after Derek's divorce from his first wife and his move to a different part of the country. His two teenage daughters would spend half-term and some of their holidays with him and Linda, with whom they got on well. Derek and Linda both worked and continued to do so after Linda became pregnant and they had a daughter of their own. This pregnancy was planned, but they decided that they would not have any more children. When Linda unexpectedly became pregnant again, they contemplated whether or not she should have an abortion, although neither of them believed such an action to be the right one. Linda found herself particularly distressed: on the one hand, worried about money and, on the other, fearing that she would not be able to manage looking after two small children, having regular visits from her teenage stepdaughters who were in the throes of adolescence and holding down a demanding job. She sought a consultation with one of us (M.R.) and after several sessions, some of which were with both Derek and herself, they decided to continue with the pregnancy.

Both have children from previous relationships

For stepfamilies in which both partners have children from previous marriages or partnerships the financial burden is greatest. In these combination families the new couple will have expenses related not only to their own household but also to those of their own children whether or not they live with the stepfamily all the time. In a typical stepfamily, her children live primarily with her and their stepfather. The children's father may or may not be contributing to their keep, and if he is, this may be inconsistent. The stepfather's own children may be living with their biological mother and may or may not be regular visitors to his new household. Perhaps because of the financial stresses, but perhaps also because such stepfathers not only expect themselves but are expected to contribute to the stepfamily household, they often also take a significant paternal role with their stepchildren. At the same time they may have a diminishing role with their own children and try to resolve this by making the major contribution in their remarried household.

Returning to Bill and Daphne's family shows how this can happen. When Daphne's first husband ceased making contributions for their children, Bill and Daphne tried to meet the additional expense by Daphne resuming her employment part-time so that she could contribute to her children's (by now) higher education costs. Bill maintained their household, to which his stepchildren returned in the vacations, as did his own children in their school holidays. His resentment about the financial burdens often boiled over following lengthy telephone calls to and from his adolescent stepchildren, which, not surprisingly, exacerbated the tension between himself and Daphne. By this time neither of the other biological parents were making any contribution for any of the children. It seems that when the Child Support scheme is implemented things will become even worse for families such as this one, as many will be in a lower-income bracket. If neither maintenance from parents nor family income support is available, which lower-income families would previously been drawing, financial hardship is inevitable. It also remains unclear how this major change in family financial arrangements will influence the attitudes of parents who separate, divorce and form new partnerships.

Traditional gender roles are incompatible with stepfamily life

Parenting in stepfamilies requires a revision of the conventional and traditional roles for both men and women. It is possible that those stepfamilies which survive – and in the United Kingdom half of them do (Haskey 1988), although the statistic is usually stated the other way round – have found many and various ways to be flexible in their family lifestyle. Mothers in stepfamilies who are also stepmothers find ways to balance the needs of their own children with those of stepchildren, who have a mother and do not need and will not accept another. Fathers in stepfamilies do not have to be limited to discipline and control of money.

As well as financial stress in stepfamilies, there are often issues related to where the household income comes from and how it is managed. The traditional role for men in families is that they will both earn the money for the family and control family finances. In stepfamilies some of the money may come from another man, the father who is paying child support for his children living in the stepfamily household. A man whose outlook and expectations are traditional will feel his role as provider is thus undermined. But male parenting in stepfamilies has the potential for much broader scope. Stepfathers have the opportunity to develop relationships with their stepchildren based on something other than money and authority. During a lone-parent household stage, whether full-time or limited to contact times, men find the skills to nurture and listen to children, as do many men in nuclear families now that gender roles are changing generally.

For women who have managed both their own household finances and their children during the lone-parent household stage the expectation that they will fulfil a traditional role in the stepfamily, relinquishing power and responsibility and taking a subordinate position, is frequently simply unacceptable. Nor does such an expectation fit what is required in the stepfamily, where she, if she has children of her own, needs to remain in control of their disciplining and general care. She needs to be able to negotiate with the children's father about their needs, financial and otherwise, and to know how resources are to be allocated. This can be a delicate situation if all the adults take a traditional gender position, as the father paying child support will want to control how the money is used, the mother will feel powerless and the stepfather will feel undermined and probably resentful at what seems an intrusion.

When a woman without children becomes a stepmother and she is earning, some of her income will be used to support the stepfamily household. Her partner's income will, at least partially, be directed towards child support, whether the children live with the stepmother and father or with their mother. Traditional gender roles suggest that the father in this situation will experience a loss of self-respect at having to be at least partially dependent on his new partner (Carter and McGoldrick 1989).

Money as power

The discussion thus far has centred upon the question of the sources of income in stepfamilies and the issue of who controls money. Traditional attitudes can give rise to certain anomalies, and probably conflicts, when one man provides some of the money for the family and another man believes he should control family finance. Traditional beliefs about women and their familial role which hold that they care for the children and free their husband to make the money also hold that women do not manage money. Often the first step a woman makes in pursuit of greater autonomy is to take over some of the management of finance and to have money she alone controls.

Now let us consider these matters in terms of power. It is obvious that to control money is to exercise power; when this is translated into stepfamily matters it is obvious what a minefield it can be. Child-support payment can be used as a means to control contact with children by either the custodial or the non-custodial parent ('residential' or 'non-residential'). A father separated from his children might exercise power by saying that he will make payments when he sees them. Both maintenance and contact may be erratic as he confuses the issues of their need for contact with him and their need to be cared for materially. A mother living with her children might also confuse these issues by withholding contact unless maintenance is paid. Or a father paying maintenance may declare that since he is supporting his children he will see them as and when he wishes. All of these situations are familiar in the course of the work of conciliators, mediators, family therapists and other professional helpers.

Davis and McLeod (1983) found in their study a few non-residential parents who implied that their *inability* to pay maintenance was a source of satisfaction to them. One man said that he would not pay maintenance even if he did get a job; another said, 'I'd be bloody annoyed if I got a job and then had to pay' (p. 219). This is exercising power in a convoluted way, but nevertheless it is an expression of power – 'I would not pay, even if I could!' The desire is to undermine the power and control of the custodial mother, who may have been the partner instigating the separation.

In some instances the effort to control the stepfamily household made by a non-residential parent takes another form. One such father became unreliable in both his child-support payments and in his contact with his children after his ex-wife remarried. When he demanded to see his children at an unplanned time, having failed to keep to arrangements previously made, he asserted that making payments gave him this right. The new stepfather retaliated by saying that henceforth child-support payments would no longer be accepted. He had no legal basis on which to do this, of course; it was an obvious power struggle, the stepfather wanting to reduce the control and influence the other man had over his household, the father wanting to overcome his own feelings of powerlessness by entering into inappropriate battles. Perhaps the end to financial obligation made a great difference to his personal circumstances, but his right to contribute to the support of his children was forfeited. Thus not only money was used in a struggle for power but also the relationship between the father and his children.

Where money disputes develop into unresolved contests, the power of the courts has to be used. In the context of divorce and new partnerships, whether remarriage or cohabitation, the courts have to consider three main factors (amongst others). These are the financial resources and potential for earning that both new partners have, the financial needs and responsibilities which each has or is likely to have and the standard of living which the parties have been used to (papers from the Solicitors' Family Law Association, Education Committee Seminar, 6 October 1989). A new partner may be a liability or a resource financially, but will be viewed by the courts in differing ways in the context of cohabitation or remarriage. It is helpful for us to consider some of the decisions that courts have made.

A significant case on cohabitation was heard in 1988. In it the (former) husband argued to reduce the amount of periodical payments he made because the wife was living with a cohabitee. The court at first hearing decided that the wife would have married her cohabitee except for the loss of the periodical payments which would result and so the original order was varied and the payments were reduced. However, the wife appealed, and the Court of Appeal, while deciding that the wife's needs were reduced as a result of cohabitation, said that it was not for the courts to equate the effect of cohabitation with that of remarriage. While the outcome was the same, the principle applied is different and important and relates to decisions made in other cases which followed. In 1989 a similar case was heard in which nominal periodical payments were ordered to continue and the court's decision included a statement that a court should not pressurise a woman to marry in order to obtain a husband's obligations.

The courts have less difficulty when the disputed payments are capitalised payments and not maintenance. If the husband is sufficiently wealthy to make such a payment and the marriage was a long one to which the wife would have contributed in a supportive way while the assets were built up, she will be granted a capitalised payment, whether or not she is cohabiting or has remarried.

While at present a cohabitee cannot be compelled to disclose her or his means, a spouse can be required to file an affidavit stating all income and assets and all financial responsibilities too, of course. These may include children of a former marriage. The proposals contained in the Child Support Bill are intended to ensure that parents do meet financial responsibilities to children, whether the parents were ever married or not. The position of cohabiting parents surely must change under the regulations of this legislation, and so also will the jurisdiction of the court in child-maintenance decisions. The Child Support Agency, which will be run by the Department of Social Security, will make assessments and orders as to how much maintenance a parent should pay for a child living with a former partner. The court will not make these orders, and appeals will not be allowed except in very limited circumstances (Richard Sax, Solicitors' Family Law Association speaking at the Annual General Meeting of the Stepfamily Association, June 1991).

Under the proposals for the new Child Support Agency, or when money disputes have to be resolved in a court, little privacy is left and perhaps little power to make further decisions. Courts have to try to be fair, but when parties are locked in bitterness, nothing will seem fair to both of them. The future for the separating couple and their children is much more favourable if agreements can be reached with the help of third-party negotiations in the setting of a mediation service or other non-adversarial agents.

Inheritance

In legal terms, where no will has been made, stepchildren have no automatic rights of inheritance because, with the exception of spouses, inheritance goes down the bloodline. However, stepchildren who have not been provided for in a will, but have been dependents of the deceased – usually interpreted as living within her or his household – may be able to make claims under the Inheritance Act (Provision for Family and Dependents) 1975. The legal principle on which decisions are usually based is the 'a child of the family' principle, meaning that in every sense the stepchild was treated as any other child in the family. The maintenance and inheritance position of partners who are not married to one another, their children and stepchildren, is somewhat confused and seems likely to become more so.

What inheritance means to the family, however, is equally important, if not often more so, than the division of money or the allocation of property. The father of one of us (M.R.) left a sum of money to each of his grandchildren, though nothing to his stepgrandchildren. One of them, grown up and living near the old man, had been particularly kind to him towards the end of his life, when he lived in the old people's home where he eventually died. The stepgrandson had regularly visited with his wife and children. In this case it was possible to rectify the situation because a stepuncle, as executor of the will, sought and gained agreement from the other beneficiaries for all the grandchildren, including the stepgrandchildren, to receive the same amount of inheritance.

There may be family heirlooms, such as paintings, jewellery and furniture, whether of significant financial value or not, which have particularly meaningful value to one or other member of the stepfamily. When a member of the extended family dies, executors and other members of the extended family may not be sufficiently sensitive to the meaning attached to such things as books or albums of family photographs, probably of little intrinsic financial value. Some of these objects may be reminders of episodes of family history, such as shared holidays. Gifts given to grandparents by grandchildren or stepgrandchildren may also be reminders to them as adults of happy times in their childhood, or of secrets once shared.

A death in the family often brings increased closeness as grief is shared and acknowledged; it can also be the cause of much bitterness when inherited wealth or keepsakes are not equitably distributed, or if stepchildren are ignored.

Money as a source of conflict

What else has been said, other than that money is a source of conflict? In the context of the stepfamily it is almost surely a source of conflict in the early stages and possibly for many years. This section will review some of the possible reasons and suggest some ways to relieve tensions.

Finances and relationships with children are the two most commonly cited issues that cause tension in stepfamilies. Messinger and Hausen (1976) identified these factors several years ago, and subsequent studies confirm their findings. Difficulties with children are the greatest cause of stress and the factor most commonly leading to divorce in stepfamilies. It seems obvious that the two main stressors, finance and problems with children, are linked in many ways.

A woman whose new husband assumes a financial burden in relation to her and her children feels guilty about it. Both she and her children feel like outsiders, as if their home were not fully their own, and the behaviour of the children becomes difficult when they experience their mother's uncertainty. They do not acknowledge the stepfather or accept discipline from him. The mother becomes the go-between, trying to link her children to her husband, and him to them. He complains of their behaviour to her and she is aware of what is owed to him. No-one in this kind of situation is clear about what is going wrong, except perhaps the stepfather, who may think it is the fault of the children.,

A man may not reveal his entire income in order to avoid paying maintenance. Although he pays child support, he resents money which goes from him to an ex-wife to be hers to control, and most especially if the separation was instigated by her. He is aggrieved. Why should he support her, and why ever should he contribute money to a household in which there is another man (if there is)? His feelings are understandable, but his responsibility to contribute to a home for his children and for their needs exists whatever his feelings. (This is just as true for mothers when they are the non-residential parent.) The children have a right to be cared for through his contribution as well as a right to remain in contact with him. The man or woman who tries to avoid paying maintenance to a former partner is punishing his or her children, although that will not be the intention. These rights and responsibilities are defined and laid out in the Children Act 1989, which was discussed in the previous chapter.

Alternatively, a man who left his family may pay more to his former wife and their children than he is required to pay because of his complex feelings of guilt at having left. This in turn will be resented by his new partner and could lower her standard of living and that of her children or any children they may have together. A man whose income is sufficient to it can literally pay for his feelings of guilt, but that does not end them, and it keeps everyone caught in a guilty atmosphere. Consider, for instance, the family in the following example. A wealthy solicitor leaves his wife and two children of nine and ten. He marries again, a woman who has good income as a doctor, and they eventually have a child of their own. His children go to boarding schools and spend holidays and weekends with their father and stepmother in almost equal proportion to the time they spend in the home they have with their mother. She does not earn and the children are entirely maintained by their father. Money is not short in either household, but how it is managed is never discussed. The stepmother has no voice in the management of her stepchildren, even after many years. The division between the values she wishes to inculcate in her own child and those she sees her stepchildren living by and being encouraged to live by causes serious friction between her and her husband.

In an earlier section of this chapter the significance of gender issues in stepfamilies was discussed and particularly the effect on a step-parent partnership when the couple try to establish traditional male and female roles. A woman who has been self-supporting, in control of her life and decisions, finds herself resenting a position of dependence, and most especially if her views are not respected and listened to. In one stepfamily in which both partners had children from previous marriages, the wife gave up her job and career in order to move with her husband and her children (his spent weekends with them) to a new town, where his career took an upward turn. Because she did not contribute to the family in financial terms she felt she had lost all parity in the marriage and found her life increasingly empty. Her husband assumed a position of authority in relation to her and her children. Hardest of all for her was the fact that she felt criticised as a parent by her husband. Her sense of self-value suffered badly. She sought counselling help for herself and to her surprise the counsellor asked for her partner to attend at least the first session. He did, and several joint sessions followed in which both expressed concerns they had not been able to talk about before, and their ability to negotiate and communicate improved.

Because of the sensitivity of financial issues – whose is it, who controls it, where does it come from? – money often becomes a subject which is not talked about, leading to an increasing spiral of conflict. In our view these issues must be brought into the open and both partners must value all the contributions they make, financial and emotional, and value those in one another. It is difficult to talk about financial matters when a partnership is developing, although that is probably the best time to do it. Some couples who did discuss finance early in their relationship say that their planning discussions did not bear complete relation to the reality as their family developed. But they had established the principle of openness, which helped them to deal with tensions as they arose rather than allowing them to accumulate. When conflicts deepen and communication becomes difficult or impossible, it is time to ask for help from a third person, a counsellor, family therapist, a specialist in family finance or a conciliator/mediator.

Money as an expression of love

After all that has been said about money and conflict it may seem impossible to discuss money in terms of love and affection. The father discussed above whose love for his children became dominated by guilt for having divorced their mother used money to show his children that he loved them as well as a means to assuage his unhappy feelings. Some people who have great difficulty in expressing feelings buy gifts as a way of showing affection. But there is another aspect of the connection between money and love for one's children.

Every parent wants the best they can achieve for their children. Most of us embark on parenthood suffused with ideals. Armed with feelings about mistakes we think our own parents made, about deprivations either material or emotional, we are determined to do better than they did. If a parent grew up in poverty and insecurity the impulse to provide every material advantage to her or his children is very strong. 'I want them to have what I never had' can mean many things, from electric trains to private education, from a room not shared with brothers or sisters to a pet of one's own or, perhaps, enough attention and enough positive confirmation from parents. Being able to give one's children enough, to correct the past through our children, is often frustrated. For example, one man, one of thirteen children himself and among the youngest, says that he remembers little attention from his mother. It consisted almost entirely of her giving directions to the older children about chores which needed to be done. As a father himself, of one child, he is filled with determination to surround his child with loving attention at all times. When his marriage collapsed he suffered extreme grief; he had poured so much of himself into being a good parent that with the loss of family life his purpose in living seemed to be taken away from him. It is possible that since the birth of the child, a time that both partners pinpoint as the beginning of their marriage going wrong, the wife felt diminished in value to him except as a mother. She is looking to a relationship with another man as a way to find confirmation of her own value. The father is desperately afraid of losing the child and feels helpless in being unable to protect her from a disrupted childhood: 'I know what it feels like to be a neglected child. I want better for her.'

Stepfamilies can be good places for children; step-parents can provide needed adult attention and, more than that, they can provide another access to the adult world and an understanding that parents, with their emotional closeness to their children, sometimes have difficulty providing. But the financial reality of most stepfamilies means that giving children a higher material standard will probably be frustrated. Money has to stretch. There is concern in most stepfamilies to be 'fair' to all the children, a difficult principle to carry out in any case, but especially difficult with limited funds. When children live in two households or have grandparents who indulge some of the children and not others (their stepgrandchildren) the amount of control required to 'be fair' is lacking too.

One woman, a stepmother to one stepdaughter and mother to four children from a previous marriage, described her desire to provide for all the children equally. Her first husband had died. As a teacher, she had managed to look after herself and her children and was proud of her success in doing that, but she wanted them to have a better life, one that included a 'father figure' as well as greater material advantages. When she met a man whose wife had died, leaving him with a daughter, it was a time of happiness for them both. The stepdaughter, while living in her father's home, had spent much of her time with both sets of grandparents. Neither she nor her grandparents wanted this to change when the stepmother and her children moved into the father's home. The stepmother, on the other hand, wanted to create one family of five children. She knew she was successful as a mother and the only approach she could see to being a stepmother was to use her tried and tested skills and treat her stepdaughter as one of her own. However, it could not work. The family was two families and there was no way in which all the children could respond to the same set of rules and expectations. Nor could the stepmother control the grandparents. Being 'fair' by setting firm rules and limits for all the children and setting standards for clothing and material possessions was not being fair at another level. The children had different histories and different needs and they had to continue to be met in ways which varied.

As we have seen, the lifestyle for a woman with dependent children changes after a divorce, and almost always in the direction of a poorer standard. A parent wanting to give children a better life than the one the parent had will feel a failure twice over, once by the divorce and again by the lowered standard of living. When a mother with children remarries the family will enjoy a higher standard again. When a man remarries his income has to go further, but in some cases the father's income goes very high while the mother's remains low. When in such circumstances there is a dispute over maintenance payments, which in the past was taken to court, the courts must take decisions based on a first principle in all cases involving children – their best interests. Several cases on record show that the courts try to reduce the amount of very wide disparity between the two households. It is considered not to be in the children's best interests for there to be a gross difference between their parents' households in terms of material advantage. This is a question of fairness to the children, not their mother, but it may seen an unfairness to a second wife to have her income assessed and considered by the court as a resource in varying a maintenance order. But in a case where, for example, the father's income was thirty times greater than his former wife's, and his second wife had an income of her own which was more than double the income of the former wife, the court held that it was 'not desirable for the children that their parents should have totally different standards of living' and ordered an increase in the amount of maintenance payment (SFLA document).

Money as an expression of rights and responsibilities

One aspect of parental responsibility is that of continuing to make financial contributions for the care of children after divorce. There are, as already discussed, many different levels of provision, and what is contributed can have different meaning for all members of the stepfamily household, as well as for the parent making the contribution and her or his new partner. At the basic level money may be provided for food, clothing and 'a roof over their heads', while at another a parent may provide school fees, extracurricular activities and holidays. These are some of the ways in which parental responsibilities can be met through payments. Where the parents cannot come to an agreement about periodical payments for children, the courts can make orders for their financial provision. These may be made against either or both parents of the child (or children) who is deemed to be a 'child of the family'. In the past either parent has been liable to be ordered to make payments, and this has been restated under the Children Act 1989 and reinforced by the Child Support Act 1991 (discussed in Chapter 5).

In the past parents have often been resentful about payments because these are frequently understood to convey rights regarding the children. Sometimes it has been assumed that making financial payments guarantees unrestricted contact with the child, or even control over the way money is spent. Under the Children Act 1989, which makes the welfare of the child the highest priority, together with the new principle of shared parental responsibility, the child is not the possession of the parents. Rather, it is to the child that rights belong. However, the new financial responsibilities under the Child Support Act could be seen as giving a non-residential parent more power again in the control of money and how it is used. Will these principles change attitudes in society? And will they affect the attitudes of parents in some anger and distress as a result of the failure of their marriage?

Summary

Money always has implications for stepfamilies at various levels and not only because finances after divorce and remarriage or repartnering are often constrained. In an attempt to assuage guilt after divorce, parents often buy children presents; a step-parent too can use gifts to attempt to buy a place in the children's affections and a role in their lives. There are diverse meanings attached to the payment or non-payment of money, or of money or valuables which are given or withheld, which may be perceived by members of an extended family as symbols of love, power, disqualification, guilt or anger. Meanings, and the strength of emotional reaction, will vary from family to family, but money representing love or power or both is very common.

This chapter has attempted to cover the following issues:

- Following divorce or separation, women with dependent children have a lower standard of living. When women form new partnerships the situation may be relieved with improved housing and greater financial security. While a woman is thus 'rescued' from poverty, she may have guilt feelings about the burden on a new partner.
- Men, following separation (and divorce) do not usually experience the same reduced standard of living as a woman since they are more likely to remain in employment and men's wages are higher than women's.
- For a man without children of his own to support, taking on stepchildren means his costs rise but his income may not. In any case, it is no longer his to spend entirely as he wishes.
- A man who does have children from a previous partnership has a financial obligation to two households. If his new partner has an income it will be essential in providing for their shared household. This may make the decision to have a child in the new partnership very difficult or even impossible.
- If both partners in a stepfamily have children from previous partnerships their financial burden is greatest and most complex.
- Traditional roles for both men and women do not fit the facts of stepfamily life. Money and where it comes from and how it is managed is one of those facts.
- Money can become a means of wielding power between separated couples who have not resolved, or begun to resolve, their anger and bitterness about the ending of their relationship.
- Inheritance in stepfamilies, especially those which form when

stepchildren are adults, is a significant issue. Wills can serve to include or exclude stepchildren from equal membership in a family.

- Money is a powerful source of conflict and because of the sensitivity of financial issues, it often becomes a subject which is not talked about, leading to an increasing spiral of conflict.
- Paradoxically, money can be an expression of love. Such expression can be frustrated in stepfamily life, where money is often short and not always under the control of the two adults.
- Money is an expression of rights and responsibilities. Children have the right to be financially supported and cared for by their parents and to remain in contact with both parents following parental separation. Money often becomes a battleground rather than an expression of parental responsibilities toward their children.

Helpers are directed to the above summary, but the authors wish to make it clear that this chapter on financial issues should not be used as a definitive guide for helping separating couples to know what their financial settlement, or their welfare rights, should be. Expert advisors are needed for what are suggested possibilities here. Rather, it is hoped that this chapter can assist individuals, couples and those who try to advise them to understand the complex meanings of financial questions.

CHAPTER SEVEN

Exes and extras

This chapter will explore the characteristic complexities of family structure and relationships in stepfamilies. The stereotypical form of family – the simple, small structure of mother, father and their children – is the one presented as the 'normal' family through social institutions and the media, advertising, plays, films and literature. It may be the ideal but it is not numerically the most common. If households, rather than biological relationship, were to be the starting point for describing and counting families, we would find that other family forms, and that includes the stepfamily, together number a greater proportion of the total number of households than the two-parent nuclear family does. However, the definition of 'family' has evolved over several centuries, as Chapter 1 shows, to its most narrow meaning of two parents and their children. In this 'normal' family, the parents of the parents live elsewhere, perhaps at some distance, as do other members of the families of each – their brothers and sisters, aunts, uncles and cousins. In the dominant culture in the Anglo-European world, therefore, 'family' conjures up a picture of a fairly small number of people living in a household on their own, with relations living in other small households; and, of course, many millions of people do live in this way. The ideal for families goes further still however, and much further than the reality most people experience.

The 'ideal' family is made up of a happily married couple, married in their early twenties 'for life'. He is older than she, and better educated and a little taller. They share the burdens of household and parental responsibilities in a quite particular way, along the lines of traditional expectations for men and women in families, described in Chapter 1 as 'segregated conjugal roles'. The husband/father earns the money and controls it; the wife/mother takes care of the home and the children and does not work outside the home or concern herself with decisions relating to much else. She is the emotional centre of the family, always available, with responsibility for everyone else's emotional and psychological wellbeing. The man is involved in the outside world as provider, protector and decision maker. The wife and children are his dependants. Now, the fact is that not many families fit this ideal. In 1981 the Study Commission on the Family reported that only about 15 per cent of households would even begin to correspond to such a picture, and that figure appears to be getting smaller. The 1988 General Household Survey found a mere 8 per cent were composed of a married couple and their dependent children in which the man was the breadwinner and the woman was solely a homemaker caring for their children (Office of Population Censuses and Surveys 1990a). Most women work outside the home and many households are made up of adults without dependent children, of homosexual as well as heterosexual couples, or one adult with children, or two adults with children part of the time, or a group who live as a family but are not biologically related, and so on. The definition of 'family' is far more complex than the one which is held as the norm; indeed, it may even be impossible to establish a single definition which would encompass the many forms of family life which exist, even in a single culture. When multi-cultural factors are taken into account, a single definition is even more difficult to contemplate. What is obvious is that it must be a very wide one.

In this chapter the position is taken that the idealised family is in many respects a myth; at the very least it is an oversimplified and inaccurate picture which ignores the complexities of actual family life, including stepfamily life. This cultural ideal not only ignores diversity, it leads to presuppositions that only those families which structurally correspond to it – that is, the two-parent family and their biological children – can function well for their members, particularly the children. Suppose, however, that 'complex' does not equal 'bad' or 'pathological' or 'dysfunctional'? The proposition here is that what is important is not the shape a family has but how the sense of belonging and connection works for its members. A single definition of 'family' may be difficult or impossible to establish, but it is not contentious to state that families provide identity for their members by means of the intimacy created in the group. Families are about belonging and mutual attachment, and about creating a context in which a child or adult can be accepted and encouraged as an individual.

In some families the pressure to belong, to conform to all the requirements of membership and loyalty, is at the price of individuality. In this kind of family, being different – for example, having more or less ambition than parents envisaged or siblings attain – is not easily tolerated. There may be high levels of tension and conflict in such a family when one or more members departs from familiar patterns and values. In other families the sense of being cared for and nurtured in a special group of intimates – the family – is weak and the individual's identity may suffer in other ways. When a person does not feel valued by her or his family that person's self-confidence will be low. The balance between emotional closeness and distance is hard to find and maintain for any family. Too much closeness can be stultifying and suffocating; too much distance can be lonely, leaving the individual without sufficient emotional and psychological supports. Getting the balance between belonging to the family and being a separate individual is particularly difficult in a stepfamily because the stepfamily begins at some point when its members have already reached various stages of individual development and it will contain family cycles from the previous families which may not match well. There are special issues along the way towards integration which make it difficult to achieve. One of these is the risk that a stepfamily will have too much distance in its manner of relating. A girl of sixteen, when asked what she would most like to change in her stepfamily, said, 'I wish we could be together more, and talk more without being self-conscious. We are so far apart.'

In spite of the many hurdles which must be overcome, it is possible for a stepfamily to become a reliable unit which fulfils the needs individuals have in terms of group identity and security of affection, as well as individual development. Before examining stepfamily complexity in more detail, there is another belief about family life which has an impact upon stepfamily integration which needs to be considered.

The extended family ideal

If the notion of 'family' is examined further, it can be seen that the extended family network of grandparents, aunts, uncles and cousins is also idealised. It is frequently lamented as something lost, something which used to exist in times past when relations lived together in multiple households or in close proximity, forming a network which gave its members identity in a clan, provided practical help in times of sickness or misfortune of other kinds, and shared and celebrated the joys of life. The ideal represents a yearning for a safe, secure affectionate family group and a belief in some golden age when families did not 'break down'. To what extent did this ideal ever exist, and where? If it has changed, what is the pattern of change? Is it really lost?

Most individuals, if not all, understand themselves in the context of a web of family relationships inherited by either birth or adoption. Each of us carries our family around inside ourselves, even if we live many miles away from other members. In that sense, the extended family always exists as a frame of reference, even if only in memory, and whether or not the memories are happy. Usually, however, when the extended family is lamented, what is being referred to is a close-knit interdependent group, living together or very close by one another, and what is believed is that this was, until the fairly recent past, a universal experience. There is little evidence to support this belief. The simple family form of parents and children, or parent substitutes, has been the predominant one in most of Europe and certainly in England, as far as living arrangements are concerned, for as long as records permitting study of family households have existed (Laslett 1977). If anything, as records show, households became more complex, rather than less, from the sixteenth century to the beginning of the twentieth, due to the presence of servants in households rather than to an extended family group living together. This factor has been discussed in Chapter 1. Until industrialisation radically changed patterns of employment most family groups, it can be argued, may have lived near to one another in the same or neighbouring communities as a minority do now. Following industrialisation, however, the search for employment and the demands of employers meant that younger families moved away from parents, establishing themselves in other communities, perhaps at a great distance, and this process continues to the present time. In modern western society whole families seldom migrate when one member goes elsewhere because of a job. There are exceptions, an example of which would be Asian families who may migrate together and follow when one or more members acquires employment.

In the past when emigration occurred from Britain to North America it was often in family groups, some of whom continued across the country together, ultimately settling in the same area, with relatives helping one another with house building, harvesting, births, deaths and so on. However, each household consisted of a simple family of parents and children and in most instances, the period of time when families remained living in close proximity was usually not more than a generation or two. One of us (D.S.) had the experience as a child of growing up in a community in the midwestern United States which consisted almost entirely of families related to one another by birth or marriage. There now remains barely one member of the family which once dominated it.

The belief that the past was a time when extended families, large groups of related people, lived together appears not to be supported for the western world, although it is very likely that related people living in proximity was once more common than in current western post-industrial society. The myth based upon this unsupported belief is that extended families were always comforting and supportive and that the stress and alienation of modern life was unknown. But whether or not members of extended families are in frequent contact, or in contact at all, there is meaning attached to all such connections and relationships by every person. One only has to see the efforts made to trace lost members or information about ancestors to recognise the need to answer 'To whom do I belong?' and 'Who belongs to me?'

That 'belonging' is not exclusively a biological connection is supported by many people who were adopted as babies or children and some who grew up in a foster family, and also by those who have step-parents. In a stepfamily the children have a primary loyalty to their mother and father, the grandparents and other relations from each, and a secondary loyalty, in time, to their step-parents. If the various sets of grandparents and stepgrandparents accept the stepfamily the sense of belonging to a wide network of people, some connected by a biological link and some connected by links of affection only, will develop. We hear little about such stepfamilies since more attention – in the media and in the literature pertaining to research and clinical studies of families – is paid to problems in stepfamilies in which no sense of belonging ever developed. There are sources of information – such as biographies, oral histories and some research studies – which show that family ties and identity in stepfamilies can and do exist (Burchardt 1989; Smith 1990). Researchers have found that children in stepfamilies have distinct perceptions of family strength in their stepfamily structure; these researchers warn teachers, therapists, social workers and others against making assumptions that children in such families have no family pride (Knaub and Hanna 1984).

Research into stepfamilies is often discouraging, however, and must be evaluated by a comparison of studies. At the time of writing, a study using information from the National Child Development Study (NCDS; based on 17,000 children born in Britain in one week in 1958) is receiving wide attention. The Family Policy Studies Centre found that those children who became part of a stepfamily by the age of sixteen (they reached that age in 1974) showed certain features when compared with those who had continued to grow up with both their parents, or with a lone mother. Children in stepfamilies tended to leave home earlier, that is before the age of eighteen, because of conflict at home; girls were at twice the risk of having a baby while still a teenager and four times more likely to marry before the age of twenty; both boys and girls were twice as likely to leave school early (Kiernan 1992). The differences remained after consideration of the effects of social-class expectations for marriage or education. It seems to be a picture of escape from unhappy family situations. But before stepfamilies are burdened with yet more of a scapegoat role for the negative effects of divorce and repartnering on children another study must be mentioned. This also is a longitudinal study and compares children in the United States and Great Britain whose parents have divorced. This study indicates that negative effects (in terms of learning difficulties and behavioural problems) can be discerned long before the parents actually separate (*ibid.*). At a seminar at the University of Cambridge in June 1991 at which both writers were present, there was a report on what is now a significant body of research showing that the effects of parental divorce upon children must be considered in both immediate and long-term time periods. This seminar also emphasised that changes in children's behaviour are apparent long before the divorce itself occurs. It appears that unresolved and continuous conflict between parents, and between parents, step-parents and stepchildren, is at the root of the long-term disadvantage children suffer. What is needed is more understanding of how to help couples and families cope with conflict and how to make help both available and respectful.

In 1983 a small study of adolescent children in stepfamilies was published (Lutz 1983) which found that the greatest degree of stress experienced by these children was in hearing one of their parents criticised by their other parent and a step-parent. In this group at least, the family structure itself was not a source of significant stress, nor was explaining their stepfamily to the outside world, nor having membership in two households (those of their two parents), all factors often assumed to cause high levels of stress for children and adolescents. What this study indicates is the significance of the loyalty issues; children remain loyal to both their parents and this loyalty must be respected by parents and step-parents alike. In a conversation with one of us (D.S.) a young man, now in his thirties, was reflecting on his experience of growing up in a stepfamily from the age of seven and had this to say:

> A fear I always had was that my father would have another family and forget all about me. But the hardest thing was when my mother and stepfather ran him down. It confused me and made me feel miserable and lonely, especially because I really came to love my stepfather. Even now I find it hard to forgive him and my mother for – well not protecting me from the problems they had with my father. I sometimes felt I was responsible for those problems.

Stepfamilies past and present

There was a time when the existence of stepfamilies was due almost entirely to the death of one parent. The stepfamily could assume the appearance of an 'ordinary' two-parent family plus children. Because most households did not include the grandparent generation, the extra grandparents in a stepfamily could be, if desired, discounted much of the time. Or perhaps the complexity, however unacceptable, was taken for granted when the stepfamily could approximate the approved family form. Now that divorce has replaced death as the reason most marriages end, a more complex and awkwardly shaped stepfamily has emerged, one which is difficult to disguise or manage in day-to-day life. The post-divorce stepfamily has former partners, the 'exes', who cannot be left in the past if there are children from those previous relationships. If both partners in a stepfamily have children, there will be two living former spouses each holding powerful emotional connections and parental responsibilities for some, but not all, of the children. There may be several sets of grandparents and stepgrandparents. The difficulty of managing the complexities and the desire to 'disappear' into society leads some stepfamilies to sever relations with former spouses and their families, with the result that children lose contact with one living parent and also, of course, grandparents. On the other side, the challenge of keeping contact is great for the non-residential parent, and that parent often gives up. Estimates are that as many as half of the children whose parents separate lose contact with one parent within two or three years (Law Commission 1986).

Children do not lose parents now in late-twentieth-century life in greater numbers than they did in the past, when parents often died. We do not have a problem which is greater than at any previous period, for it seems that children are less likely, not more, to lose natural parents through divorce (Laslett 1977). Obviously, when parents go on living, even though they are divorced, children need not lose them at all. What changes is the amount of time spent with each parent. The ways in which contact and time are organised are crucial to the child's quality of life, but the total loss which death signifies is not part of the adjustment the child must make.

Even with the divorce statistic of one divorce for every three marriages, two in three marriages surviving may be a higher rate of survival than is represented by the death rate in the past. If two marriages in three do last throughout the lifetime of at least one of the partners, we need not condemn ourselves so very harshly, especially when we consider that in the nineteenth century the average length of a marriage was about twelve years. Therefore, in earlier times, when couples promised one another to remain faithful 'until death us do part' it was against the threat of death, not the threat of having to live together for four, five or six decades! The cultural significance of the stepfamily we are learning about now is that individuals locked in an unsatisfactory and unfulfilling marriage are not willing to spend a long lifetime in it. We demand unrealistic satisfactions from marital relationships, there is no doubt, but we also demand to be released from miserable and clearly unsuccessful ones.

Women are not destitute without a husband, as they often used to be when widowed, although they are likely to be poorer after divorce. This and other financial issues were explored in the previous chapter; for the purposes of this discussion it can be stated that with the exception of mothers with small children, women are now more able to support themselves or supplement a low income than in the past. Men as a lone parent with children are not as rare a phenomenon as was once the case, and single parents, mothers or fathers, might have a steady lover who does not live in the home full-time. Both men and women may make a choice to remain single, preferring life as an autonomous adult. And many men and women, having experienced an unsatisfactory marriage, try again, forming a stepfamily through either living with a new partner or remarrying. The meaning of marriage has changed from an arrangement based on economic exchange or property accumulation and the procreation of children, to one based on satisfactions within a close, interdependent union which includes sexual satisfaction but may not include having children. That many couples appear to achieve it is perhaps the statistic to astound us, not the divorce rate.

Yet the suffering that divorce entails and the effects on both adults and children must not be minimised. The fact that society allows divorce does not mean it approves of it. There is enormous social approval attached to marriage – or long marriage – while only tolerance is attached to ending one. Thus for adults divorce means failure to achieve one of society's most cherished ideals as well as the ending of a relationship which must at one time have provided a degree of satisfaction. For the parents of the couple and other family members divorce also signals a failure and loss, and for the couple's children, divorce is almost impossible to conceptualise. As described in earlier chapters, there will be confusion and sorrow for a time, and the sorrow may recur over many years. Children usually feel that they caused the separation and divorce through their own bad behaviour. While they are not conventional in their thinking and do not hold society's ideal and condemnations, they want both their parents together. One little girl of eight who had both a father and stepmother and mother and stepfather, and had grown fond of both her step-parents, said that she wished for two large houses next to one another so that her mother and father could be in one house and her step-parents in the other.

The helplessness and dependence of childhood means that the fear of being abandoned is the greatest fear children have (Visher and Visher 1979), and when parents separate children do feel abandoned. If parents can explain what is happening in the child's own language and, if possible, demonstrate that neither parent is disappearing, children appear to recover from the effects of divorce (Walczak and Burns 1984). Many years later, when they are adults themselves, they may have understanding and acceptance rather than bitterness, but while they are growing up, most children will long for their parents to be together. That is not to imply that parents should stay together no matter what the cost to them as individuals, but that the importance to children of both a mother and father does not end when a marriage ends.

In the following example one child became the focus of conflict between divorced parents and as a result lost contact with one parent. In a family of two sons the parents were both closely involved with the children but the marriage became untenable and the parents separated. One son had already left home and the other was just entering adolescence. He remained with the mother and the father set up a new home nearby; for a time both children were in close contact with both parents. The acrimony increased between the parents, however, as they tried to settle property issues and negotiate when decisions had to be made, particularly regarding their younger son. It became more and more difficult for the boys to move back and forth between the two homes until finally, when the father's new partner joined him in his home, the younger son refused to visit. His mother was criticised in his father's home, even denounced, as he saw it, while in the mother's home, the criticism took the form of silence with regard to the father. Verbal battles between the younger boy and his stepmother had become frequent; his school work and school attendance deteriorated. The stepmother no doubt felt she was helping to deal with a difficult child, but her actions made the boy feel further alienated from his father. A complete break resulted and for a time the two boys were locked in battle also, as the older boy aligned himself with the adults in criticising the younger one. In this situation the younger boy was bereft of the father who had been very involved in his life when he was little and also of his brother. In time the two boys became cautiously reconciled. The estrangement continued between the father and son, however, which the boy mourns, while at the same time trying to remain loyal to both parents. No solution appears available apart from accepting the loss.

When stepfamilies follow the death of a parent there will be loyalty issues for the children just as there are in the example above, when divorce disrupts the parenting relationship. Stepfamilies which result from death are not easier to integrate, merely more able to appear to conform to the model of family life which is socially acceptable. A stepmother appealed for help from the telephone counselling service managed by the National Stepfamily Association. Her family is a stepfamily which followed the death of both former partners – we might refer to this as the 'traditional' stepfamily and it seemed to be the answer to the dreams of both adults. It was not for the children, however, and relationships became very tense. The public image of a 'normal family' belied the private reality of resentments, anger and blame. The family accepted a referral to a family therapist and began a process of coming to terms with the opposing feelings of different members, allowing them to be expressed, but requiring standards of behaviour necessary for the group to stay together. What might have happened to this family in the past? Support from other family members, or from the clergy, might have been utilised, and helpfully so, but it is reasonable to suppose that the unique stepfamily issues would not have been explored. Now the rise in the numbers of stepfamilies following divorce is forcing us to examine the complexity of stepfamily life in a more open way. With parents and former partners still living, the roles of all the adults become harder to define and to name. Do children have two 'mothers', two 'fathers', and numerous grandparents? How do adults in a new relationship withstand the contact with former partners? What if this is not possible? Some relationships are destructive and contact perpetuates the risks for everyone. There are emotional hurdles to overcome that few of us are prepared for when we marry the first time; a second marriage might be described as an emotional minefield. Indeed, the divorce rate for second marriages is slightly higher than for first ones. And yet about half of all remarried families do appear to survive. Many stepfamilies are created by cohabiting couples, about whom statistical information is difficult to acquire. They are not ignored in this book, however, as the issues for them in creating a satisfactory family life for themselves and their children are the same.

The family seen through a diagram

There are many ways to tell the story of a family, and one of those is a family tree, a diagram showing the development, chronology, off-shoots and links members of a family have with one another and with members of other families. Using such a diagram to describe a stepfamily immediately shows the complexity of relationships, but by making a visible representation of the complexity, it becomes comprehensible. A family tree, referred to as a genogram in family-therapy literature (for example Carter and McGoldrick 1980), shows three generations or more, revealing patterns of marriage and remarriage and generational links over time.

A child of seven whose parents had divorced and formed new partnerships said of her stepfather, 'He is nothing to me. My mummy is my mummy and my daddy is my daddy. A stepmother is someone who is not your mummy, a nothing.' She was sad and confused. With an adult (D.S) she was helped to draw a family tree. Starting with herself, she added next her sister, a half-sibling. She then put her mother on the diagram, the parent she and her sister have in common. Her father was next, then her sister's father (her stepfather) and stepbrother. As the lines of relationship and connection were added, and grandparents and stepgrandparents, aunts and uncles appeared, she became more confident and delighted with the discovery that other members of her family network lived or had grown up with a parent and step-parent. It was *her* family, and it was *normal*. She wanted to add some important friends and a child minder to her picture, then labelled the page in red with her name and her sister's, followed by an exclamation mark.

A simple description follows of the construction of family trees and the symbols used. Squares represent males and circles represent females. The simplest possible figure would be a two-generational one of two parents and their children and would have this appearance:

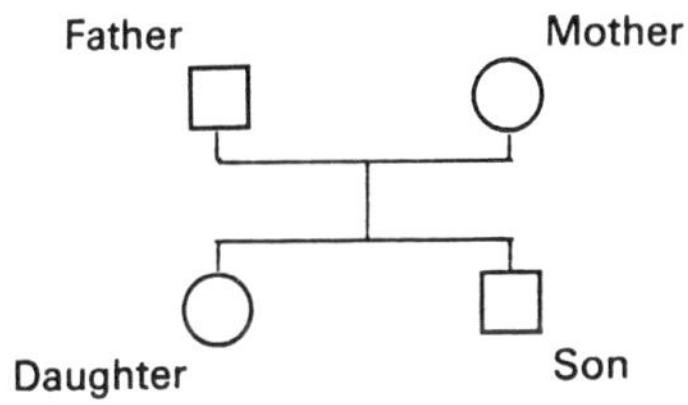

If the third generation is added, the network of grandparents and the sisters and brothers of the parents becomes visible (see Figure 7.1). If a member of the family has died, a cross in the circle or square indicates that, and if the brothers and sisters of the parents in the nuclear family have married and had children, the family tree grows to include them (see Figure 7.2). In Figure

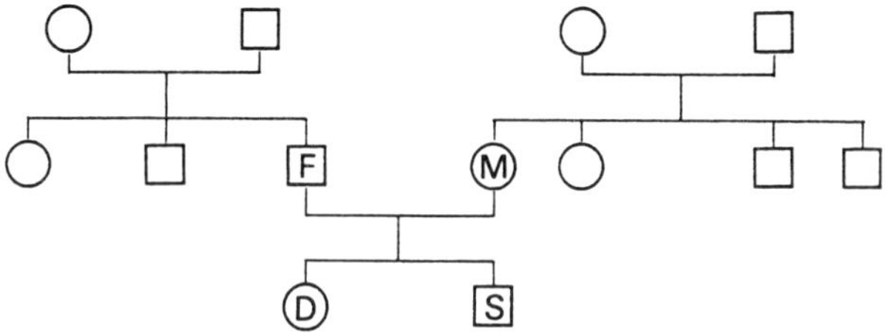

Figure 7.1

7.2 the family tree shows that the mother's mother has died and that her sister is married with two sons, one brother is unmarried and the other brother is married with no children. On the father's side, both parents are living, his brother is married with three children and his sister has one child.

In this family the number of children is small and there is only one death and no divorces in the three generations displayed. It is a fictitious family; almost any family will contain more complexity than this. Imagine the couple separated and divorced – shown by a double diagonal line on the family tree – and they each form a new partnership. One of them becomes a step-parent. The tree now looks like Figure 7.3. The son and daughter in the first diagram now have a larger and more complex family, with a stepmother and through her, a step-brother and stepsister. They also have a stepfather, with whom

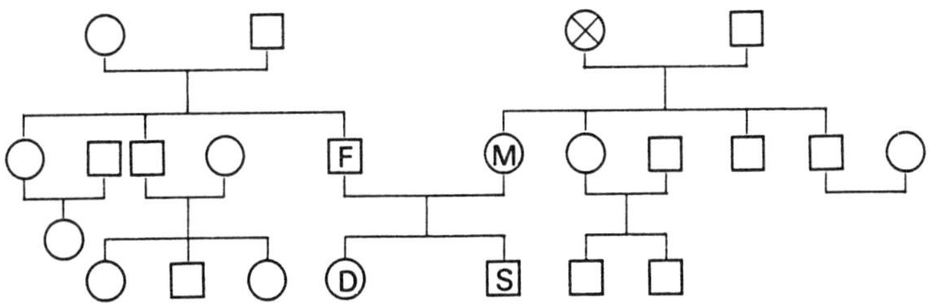

Figure 7.2

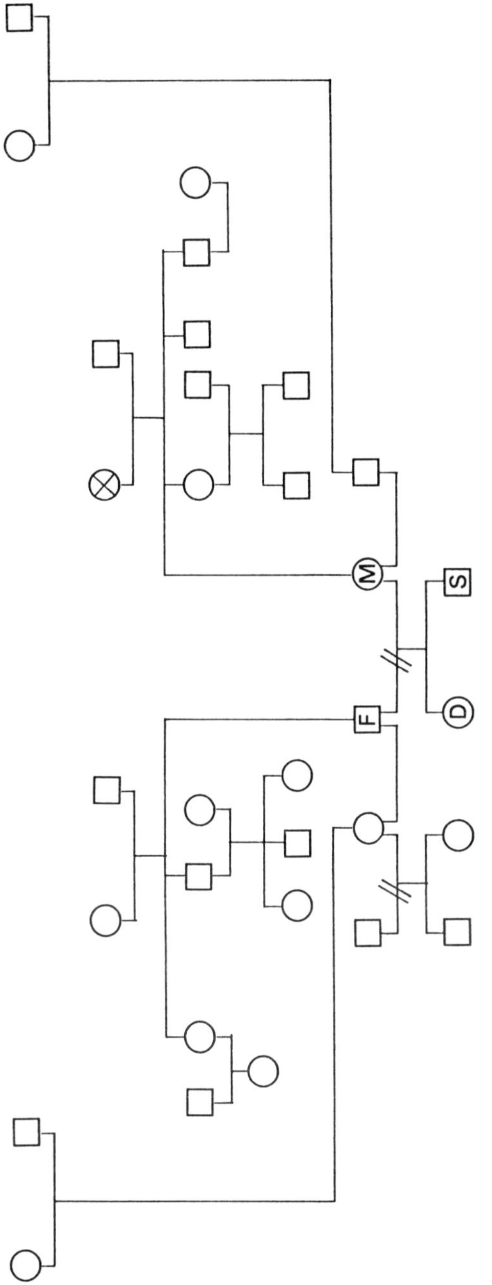

Figure 7.3

they probably live. In addition to their grandmother and grandfather on their father's side and grandfather on their mother's side, they now have two sets of stepgrandparents. As the family tree shows, their stepfather has not been married before. His parents are grandparents, that is, stepgrandparents, for the first time. The other members of the family are adding the steprelationships to their pre-existing links.

The family tree in Figure 7.4 shows an actual family, and displays four generations. The mother, father and child in the centre of the tree have separated and the two parents have each formed new partnerships. The mother has another child and acquired a stepchild in her new family. Both parents have grandparents still living as well as parents, and the mother also has a stepfather. Reading the family tree from the bottom, we can see that there are three children in the youngest generation, none of whom has the same two parents. In their parents' generation, the father of the child in the centre has parents who were each in previous partnerships and he therefore has three half-brothers, sharing a mother with two of them and a father with the other. One of his parents was divorced and the other widowed before forming the partnership which produced him. This is not a complete version of the family network, since not all the parents and grandparents are shown. They may all be in contact with the children from time to time in a stepfamily network, as they are in this family. The significance of all the links is not biological, but what is contributed in terms of care, affection, knowledge and enrichment to each individual.

A pictorial family tree is commonly used to trace ancestry and to show genealogy, noting births, marriages and deaths, with dates of all these events. When stepfamilies are described on paper, the significance of relationships other than biological ones becomes obvious. Drawing a family tree can be a positive experience for members of stepfamilies and one which families can do for themselves. It helps to describe and acknowledge important people who do not have a conventional position. Putting on paper what is ill-defined gives it a meaning and normality. It emphasises what is shared and valued, the commonality of interests and concern, while at the same time it recognises those variations in relationship and loyalty which are characteristic features of stepfamilies.

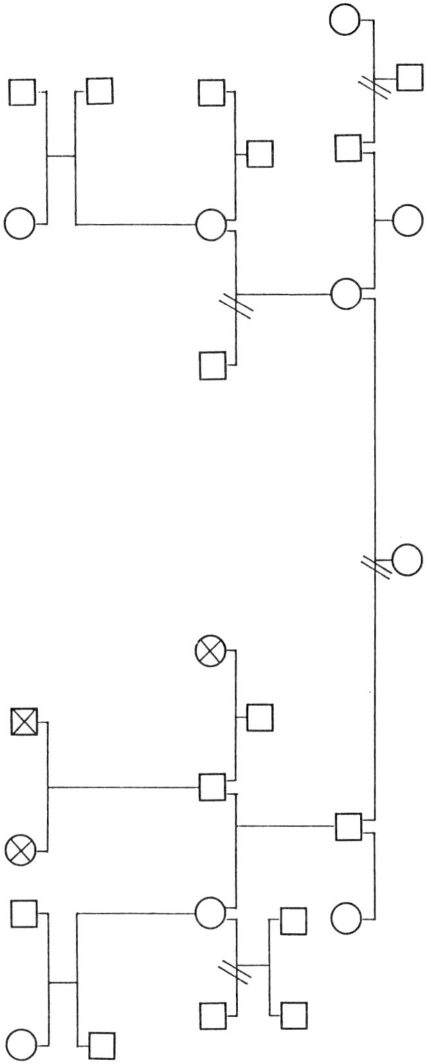

Figure 7.4

Stepfamilies from the inside

The emphasis in this chapter thus far has been on the way stepfamilies appear from the outside – upon society's expectations and views of them and how these views may be at best erroneous and at worst negative and even denigrating. It would be sentimental and naive, as well as useless, to suggest that if only society's attitudes would change, the life inside a stepfamily would go smoothly with no trouble integrating children, parents, step-parents, grandparents and stepgrandparents. After all, there is enormous social approval for marriage in general, and no end of difficulty for many couples in making it work for them. If attitudes changed suddenly so that no stigma attached to stepfamilies, formally married or living together, there would still be many dilemmas facing adults and children in forging the bonds which create family identity. Adding caring adults to the lives of children is surely positive for them: the problem is how will they be added, and how will the many players on the sometimes crowded stage of stepfamily life determine how that life will continue?

There is the matter of duplicate roles – or rather, two players and one role. If a child has both a father and a stepfather, does the child have two 'daddies'? What does it mean if a stepchild refers to both a stepfather and a father as 'dad'? Obviously, a person has only one biological parent of each sex – one mother and one father. Unless the child is very young when a step-parent enters the scene, the child will be quite clear about who is mother and father, and who a stepmother or stepfather. Even when the birth parent, or parent *from* birth (a parent who adopted a child soon after its birth), is distant emotionally or geographically or both, that person's identity will be understood by the child. One young woman said of her stepmother, 'She has been more of a mother to me than my own mother.' The mother is not forgotten, although she is distant and a less nurturing person for the young woman than her stepmother is, and there is no confusion between the two figures. Another young woman who has had a stepfather since she was a small child uses the name 'dad' for both her father and stepfather. She says, 'The world expects people to live with their Mum and

Dad' and so she does not explain that she lives with a stepdad except to close friends. 'But I know which is which when I say "Dad".' This girl is trying hard to protect and please everyone, and the strain is great. The difficulty is that the pain and loss from the ending of her parents' marriage has never been sufficiently resolved; she sees her mother's sadness and it seems to her that the stepfamily is a guilty secret.

Step-parents can become deeply important, can even become under some circumstances the 'psychological parent', that is, the parent figure with whom a child or adult identifies, turns to for comfort or nurturance, and who is more 'alive' and emotionally available than a birth parent. When a step-parent becomes a psychological parent it means that the child has mourned the loss of a parent who either has died or become very distant (Draughon 1975; Visher and Visher 1979) and the step-parent has become a reliable replacement. For most step-parents becoming, or attempting to become, a replacement for the birth parent of the same sex is inappropriate because there is a parent already 'psychologically alive' for the child. However, a step-parent role can be fulfilled in many ways and need not be limited to parent–child expectations, although, of course, it is always an adult–child relationship (until the child is an adult also) with the responsibilities towards children any adult has.

Adults, wanting to forget the past and progress quickly towards family identity in a stepfamily, commonly and mistakenly assume a child will forget a separated parent, and they thus expect 'instant love' and attachment (Visher and Visher 1979; Crosbie-Burnett 1989). Adults, trying to start afresh in family life, will encourage loyalty to a person who, in the child's eyes, is a stranger. 'This is your new daddy' does not fool a child, but can frighten and confuse. A conflict of loyalties almost certainly will be established and anger may go on for years. One woman, now in her forties, describes with great feeling such an introduction which took place many years ago. Parents may divorce one another, but they cannot divorce a child; parents may die, but their memory lives within their children until or unless grieving is completed and the loss accepted. It is not only a desire to shed an unhappy past that makes adults want children to accept a step-parent as a parent's replacement; they do not know what else to do. Our socially prescribed pattern of family life says

'You live with your Mum and Dad.' We are presented with one model for family life; there seems no alternative but to try to fit a stepfamily into it.

Fathers and stepfathers

The traditional role for fathers in the ideologically 'normal' family is rather limited and ill-defined when it comes to what fathers actually *do* with their children. Fathers are expected to provide authority and finance for the family. His job, traditionally, is to earn and control money, enforce standards of behaviour, and his concerns are mainly in the world outside the family. Beyond this his role in the family is vague. Although many men now choose to have a more active part in child care and many women earn part of the family finances, the prevailing norm remains unchanged. Therefore, when a man becomes a stepfather, what that means to him and to his partner and how he is to relate to his stepchildren will probably be determined by the same norms as apply to fathers. The limitations of these will actually hamper integration in the stepfamily; neither money nor discipline is under his control. If a stepfather tries to become a disciplinarian too soon the children will resist and their behaviour will worsen instead of improve. When stepchildren are at mid adolescence when the stepfamily forms, it may never be appropriate for a stepfather to have a disciplining role. It is not uncommon, however, for mother and stepfather to expect that he will 'get the kids in line'. One stepfather said he felt he 'became an ogre the minute I walked through the door'.

When children are very young, a stepfather has more opportunity to build a friendly relationship which will include setting limits on the child's behaviour, providing he becomes active and involved in family life. Stepfathers may leave the care of children to the mother, and this may be what she expects, but then if the couple decide to have a child of their own, the stepfather/father may find he wants to do more and be more involved with his child. That he has a different relationship with his child than with a stepchild is natural but may cause distress to him, his partner and to the stepchild. He cannot change his deep feelings but he can give all the children attention and time. A counsellor who is sensitive to stepfamily issues or a group of step-parents and parents meeting to talk over their concerns might be helpful in accepting differing attitudes and tolerance towards children.

Becoming a stepfather is a challenge which gives a man the possibility of thinking about the role of a father and of men in families generally and of being innovative in working out his own ways of doing it. Many enter the stepfamily with high ideals and others with perhaps few plans to be much involved with stepchildren, some even with initial indifference, but most find daily life with children a messy, demanding and noisy buisiness. Whatever expectations a man previously held about their role will probably have to be re-evaluated. In the first place, the children's mother has a powerful tie to the children, one which is older and stronger than the one she has with the stepfather. He is a new member of the cast and often feels like a bit player. If he is harsh with the children the mother may try to protect them from his harshness. The children will be resistent to the stepfather's efforts to control them. If the children are in contact with their father they may compare the stepfather to him, but with time the stepfather can gain the trust of the children, especially if he brings contentment to their mother. In some instances the stepfather may be an antidote to an abusing father or to a cold and indifferent one, but even in these cases the stepfather does not replace the father outright.

For both stepfathers and stepmothers, the ages of the children when the stepfamily forms determines much of the way the step-parent enters and functions within the family. In their Sheffield study Burgoyne and Clark (1984) found that even in recently formed stepfamilies, if the children were young, the parent and step-parent tended to talk more confidently and unselfconsciously about their family life than those with older children: 'Neither step-parents nor their stepchildren were as likely to question the legitimacy of their parental authority and they also had fewer and less persistent anxieties about the long-term effects of their divorce and remarriage on their children' (p. 152). When the children are older than five or six and have known their own father, the stepfather will have to *create* an appropriate place for himself in the lives of his stepchildren, that is, a place which works for them and for him, while respecting the place their father already has. A stepfather to children who have not known a father has a challenge too, in being an outsider to the close life the mother and her child or children have had together. Many issues of day-to-day life are affected – how much intimacy is possible, how much touching, who comes into the bathroom when it is already occupied, whose food preferences and table manners prevail – as well as decisions about such issues as schools and educational performance and who 'lays down the law' when needed.

In the family whose story follows, the man is a stepfather to his partner's son by her first marriage, and together they have a daughter. At the time of writing they had been together for fifteen years; their stepfamily status is not a predominant issue for them any longer, although at times the past intrudes and troubles one or more of them.

Harry and Anna were both previously married and Harry was a stepfather in his first marriage also. He has occasional contact with the young woman who was a small child when he was married to her mother. Harry had grown up without knowing his father and is conscious of having no model to draw upon; he is determined to provide for his daughter and stepson (from his second marriage) what had been missing in his own childhood. No-one has training for the job of parent; the learning for this essential task takes place in the family in which one grows up. From his family Harry brought to his role as father and stepfather a desire to give wholeheartedly and to be an active father but no model of fatherhood. He also brought a dread of arguments and conflict. Conflicts were not resolved in his family – his father had left and his mother avoided any confrontation. He has difficulty being a disciplinarian with either his daughter or stepson, largely leaving that job to their mother.

Anna married her first husband when she was a student, and married out of loneliness rather than confidence in herself and her partner. In the marriage she felt imprisoned, dominated and controlled. As she matured, the constrictions became intolerable and she left, taking the couple's baby son. Her childhood experience contributed both to the pattern of her marriage and its character as well as to her decision to end it. Anna had observed her parent's marriage, her mother's lack of freedom to express herself or develop her own activities and her father's need to control every facet of her life and of Anna's. When she became an adolescent Anna discovered she could have some power and control of her own by not eating. Anna brings to parenting a lack of confidence in her own value. She has a fear of 'spoiling' her children by making all their decisions for them – as her father had done – but at the same time she has a desire to cater to their every demand. She understands that Harry's feelings for his daughter are not as intense as those for his stepson and does not blame him, but at the same time, she feels she needs to compensate for this and becomes overwhelmed by the task she has set herself. Anna appreciates Harry's efforts to be a good father and stepfather and his support in the early years of their marriage, when there were tense meetings with her former husband; Harry and Anna have worked hard to avoid criticising him in the child's hearing and have given support to the continuing relationship between the two. Harry's loss of his own father makes him want to protect his stepson's right to know his father.

It has been many years since Anna left her first husband and established a relationship with Harry; the contacts with her first husband are no longer very tense or dreaded. Harry has based a relationship with his stepson upon shared activities and concerned attention. He is the boy's 'social' parent (Burgoyne and Clark 1984), distinct from his biological or psychological parent. Harry adores his daughter, while his feelings for his stepson are milder, which at times causes him to feel uneasy, although he knows he brings important adult care and enrichment. While Anna accepts the difference in his feelings for the two children, at times she has blamed herself for having removed from her son's life the opportunity to grow up with his own father. These self-doubts arise out of love for her son but she knows her first marriage was untenable. When she accuses herself of a selfish act in extricating herself from it, she remembers that in her heart of hearts she believes her mother should have left her father in order to live a happier and more fulfilling life.

The feelings of doubt, confusion and regret plus the evasion of disagreements led Harry and Anna to seek therapy. They have since found ways to negotiate differences of opinion and feelings and to accept and value their particular family and their individual histories. The family now has a history of its own, with relationships which are nurturing and reliable. The concerns Harry and Anna now have are those of most families with adolescent children. The stepfamily is no longer the ready explanation for every worry and problem. At times, Anna feels she and her son are an economic burden for Harry, but she realises when she has these thoughts that what she is actually striving for is a more equal partnership and more independence and control for herself. The issue is not the stepfamily, but one of sharing economic responsibilities and gaining the consequent self-respect.

Control, independence, self value, all contribute to a sense of having power, as opposed to being dependent and therefore powerless. In stepfather families, does having power – that is, power to make decisions about money, or children, to make demands, including those for sexual contact – function in a different way from that between biological parents? Theoretical explanations for power relations in couples emphasise comparative resources between the two, cultural norms for men and women in couples, the development of commitment over time and available alternatives (Crosbie-Burnett and Giles-Sims 1991). Using this theoretical framework to examine power sharing in eighty-seven stepfather families with at least one resident adolescent stepchild yielded some interesting results, perhaps not conclusive because of small numbers, but certainly intriguing. The couples in the study were found to have an egalitarian style for making decisions and this is consistent with other studies of remarried couples: that is, the remarried couples reported their second marriages to be more egalitarian than their first. A major basis for greater power – certainly, for women – was satisfaction with the increased responsibility and independence they experienced during the single-parent phase. For both men and women the alternative to being in the stepfamily is a return to being single, either with or without children. To the extent that this is an attractive and viable alternative, dependence upon the new couple and family life is less and power thereby is increased. In other words, 'I can live without you, I can live on my own' enhances self-esteem, which in turn enhances a couple's relationship. The major difference in power relations in stepfather families, however, was found to be in the domain of parenting, where the wife was dominant. Some stepfathers, wishing to replicate cultural norms for men in families, attempted to gain power in the household by excluding financial support from a non-residential biological father (see Chapter 6, p. 143) or by insisting on adopting a stepchild. Wishing to adopt a stepchild is not by any means always a move to be more powerful, but it was one aspect these researchers found in the families they studied. A mother's or a biological father's resistence to adoption or to refusing child maintenance might be an attempt to keep the stepfather from gaining power in the family. But a woman who had found her independence satisfying and wanted a balanced relationship in a new partnership might resist the pressure to minimise her power for those reasons.

Mothers and stepmothers

Cultural expectations for mothers are explicit. When women become stepmothers they draw upon a set of ideals that are pervasive and universally familiar. Whether or not they have ever been a mother and whatever experience they bring from childhood, women have knowledge of what is expected of them as a mother, and that is full commitment and responsibility for the physical and emotional care of their children. They know that mothers are expected to ensure a happy childhood and are held accountable for the adults their children become. The day-to-day care of babies and young children is a mother's job, even if some fathers choose to take part in it. Later, when the children are older, overseeing educational performance is primarily theirs also. Schools are organised on the basis that mothers are available at all times and it is they who most often meet with teachers when there is concern about a child. There is much joy in the performance of these tasks, but also much hard work and worry. 'Why didn't someone tell me about this constant state of anxiety?', asked a woman in her thirties, a mother for the first time, who was trying to continue her career in journalism with the help of a child-minder. She thought she had made every preparation for coping efficiently with a child. She was not prepared for the feelings which accompany having total responsibility for another human being, nor for the fact that her partner was not feeling the same way.

Mothers are revered and motherhood idealised. The expectations and responsibilities attached to the ideal are probably impossible for any woman to meet, and when these are transferred to stepmothers, whose very name 'stepmother' carries a burden of denigration, the situation *is* impossible.

Typically, stepmothers expect themselves, and are expected by their partners and others, to fulfil the role of a mother, including having the same feelings of selfless love and devotion which all mothers are supposed to have. Unloving mothers are monsters, an unthinkable travesty of the ideal for women, and when a stepmother finds that her feelings for a stepchild include resentment and even dislike, she feels monstrous. Warned that she should not expect to love her stepchildren quickly or in the same way as she does her own, a stepmother can be relieved of some of the guilt and self-denigration many women in this position experience. One stepmother, already an experienced mother with two children, was grateful for the advice given her by a wise friend not to expect to feel the same strong devotion for her husband's children. This saved her from having unrealistic beliefs about her task, but she was surprised all the same at the extent of care she was expected to provide and did assume. Their father had been a capable single parent but handed over parenting responsibilities upon remarriage. The stepmother had imagined they would be a 'team' of parents, continuing to manage their respective children. Instead, she found all the decisions involved with children's activities became hers, and it seemed to her that she had no choice, no basis for negotiation about what was expected of her, because to do so would have been to be the wicked, rejecting stepmother.

In another stepfamily, the stepmother looks back upon the beliefs she once held about what she would be able to provide for her four stepchildren with some amazement. She had lived for many years with her daughter when she married a man, also a lone parent, and together they had three adolescents and a child of nine to integrate into one household. The stepmother had high ideals about creating 'one big happy family' under her management of it all, as well as her ability to feel affectionate towards the children. There were many rows and disagreements over daily issues and underlying ones as well, some of which included contact with the other parents. Very soon two of the children decided to live with their mother, and the stepmother's own child also moved out to live independently. The stepmother's dream and her self-esteem were in tatters; she and her partner have had to review their expectations about their joint life and the kind of parenting all the children need at their various stages of development.

As with stepfathers, stepmothers with young stepchildren usually find their task less complex, at least in terms of what to do with the children. Young children have specific needs for care and attention which can be met directly; their resistance to new people in their lives can be more readily overcome than with older children and adolescents. Unlike stepfathers, however, the stepmother will be at the centre of child care with considerable obligations thrust upon her. Here, as an example, is Mary's story.

Mary had three children, and was living on her own with them, working full-time and managing on a small income, when she met a man with two small children, one just older than her youngest and one a toddler. They lived with their mother. Mary and Tom decided to live together and on occasion all five children were with them. Mary enjoyed these times and actually delighted in the chaos and noise of five children under eleven, but then it quite suddenly became a permanent situation when Tom's first wife died in an accident. With no time to prepare for the changes in the household or the responsibility of two shocked and bereaved children, Mary and Tom made all the practical arrangements. Mary was staggered to find herself a permanent stepmother with overwhelming demands to meet emotionally and practically, and these included Tom's shock and the children's grieving grandparents. The mother's parents resented and disapproved of Mary, which she had to bear while caring for the children day by day. They varied in their needs according to their ages, the younger one accepting Mary more readily as she comforted and cared for him, but the older child was withdrawn and remote. She needed very sensitive attention, and Mary's own children had also to be helped to come to terms with the sudden change and the demands made on their mother's time and attention. The two extra playmates had become permanent intruders. Mary began to resent the demands and the fact that she was never alone with her own children. She had lost an intimacy with them which she sorely missed. Mary has never tried to eradicate the memory of her stepchildren's mother; on the contrary, she has encouraged the children to have pictures of her about and to talk about her openly. Nevertheless, Mary has resented being compared to her by the older child especially.

After a long period of adjustment the family began to knit. Tom became more involved once his initial shock and grief had passed and he and Mary began to work more closely together. They had a child of their own, a conscious decision to link their two families. This brought about another period of adjustment for each member. Five of the children have now progressed through adolescence and all six have a close identity and loyalty with one another.

Mary's family is a complex stepfamily, the 'combination' type (Robinson 1980) in which both partners have children from a previous relationship and there is a child from the new relationship. They combine death and divorce as the reasons for the existence of the stepfamily. The parent figures include a mother to four and stepmother to two, a father to three and stepfather to three, a non-resident father and a mother who has died. There are also the grandparents and other family members: the two sets of grandparents Mary's stepchildren have, and those of her own children, making a total of four which the children share in varying combinations. Some of the grandparents show a preference for the children they are biologically related to, others try to be even-handed with gifts and visits.

Grandparents and stepgrandparents

In many respects this is a very challenging and confusing role in the stepfamily constellation. Being a grandparent, so the conventional belief goes, is the twilight of parenting, the restful time, when the heavy work of bringing up children is finished and the pleasures of grandchildren can be enjoyed. It is not so simple, which is not to say that grandchildren are not enjoyable. Grandparents are included or excluded from the lives of their grandchildren on the basis of decisions the children's parents may make; like step-parents they have few rights entailed in their role. (The Children Act 1989 does provide the right to grandparents to apply for residence or contact orders; see Chapter 5.) On the other hand, when circumstances dictate, they may find themselves totally responsible for grandchildren if, for example, parents die or for some reason are unable to care for their children. During the process of parents' separation and divorce, grandparents are often crucially important in providing continuity for the children and a safe and reliable refuge from overwhelming changes. Again, when a stepfamily forms, grandparents frequently mean safety and continuity for children.

Grandparents may not always be a benign influence. They may intrude or criticise in destructive ways and behave towards their adult children as if they were still children. They may disapprove of the choice of partner their child makes and carry that disapproval in to the next stage, when the young couple become parents. In many families, however, there is a kind of partnership between the generations which is 'good enough' in terms of mutual respect and advantageous support.

Becoming stepgrandparents usually means loss and sadness for this generation also, especially if the precipitating reason was the death of a beloved child or a bitter divorce between a child and a partner. Older people have years of life experience, but that may not prepare them for the role of stepgrandparent. For some older people, the biological link is all-important; they can see no need to have a relationship with children they are not related to. For others, the absence of expectations means they do nothing, or too much. In one stepfamily of five children, one set of grandparents is critical and unsupportive of the stepfamily and wants contact only with the children to whom they are related. Another set wants to do all the right things and is scrupulous about gifts of equal value to all five children and has all the children for staying visits. A third set sees only their own grandchildren when they visit their non-residential parent. The fourth set has no contact at all with any of the children. As it happens, some of the children in the family have two sets of grandparents whom they do not have to share with their stepbrother and sister. The others have one set, the ones trying hard not to discriminate, who are shared. After a few months, the decision was reached that those children needed visits with their loving grandparents just for themselves sometimes.

Children and stepchildren

Children do not have obligations while they are of dependent age in the sense that adults have towards children. There are no role obligations for children, but as they grow out of infancy there are expectations placed upon them, that they will conform to standards of behaviour set for them at home and at school. In the context of the family such expectations include attitudes towards parental authority and loyalty towards other family members. Becoming a stepchild means that another set of expectations suddenly comes into play. Between the family of origin and the stepfamily is the period of transition known as the 'single-parent' or 'lone-parent' family. Each of those transitions would have brought new requirements that the child had to learn and to which she or he had to conform.

Living with a single adult who has the entire responsibility for the household, a child often has an important status, sharing tasks in ways which are more than good training, but actually necessary to the running of the household. In one of the stepfamilies mentioned earlier in this chapter, the father lived for a period of three years with his four children, during which time they cooked meals and helped with washing and other tasks on a rota basis. When their father married again, their idealistic stepmother wanted to rescue them from this toil and took over the kitchen as well as, from their point of view, their father. The children resented the loss of status and felt banished. On the other side, the stepmother and her daughter were closely interdependent, had been a household of two, and they both felt intimidated by the large family group. In addition, the daughter felt she had lost her mother. All the parent–child relationships in this stepfamily have had to go through a period of turbulence in order to be re-established on a new basis.

One parent and a child usually develop an emotional closeness which is different from that which preceded it in the two-parent household. This can be positive and develop nurturing abilities in both boys and girls. Overdependence of an adult upon a child is, of course, inappropriate and harmful, the most extreme example of which is a sexual relationship, which is not a common feature in single-parent families. The change from one parent to one parent and a step-parent introduces another set of expectations for the child – to accept the new adult, perhaps to accept discipline from her or him, even to love the person, to share the parent with the new adult and not object, to accept reduced status in the family, possibly to share with stepbrothers and sisters, to keep destructive feelings under control, especially resentments about the displacement of the other absent parent. These and other issues relating to transitions and integrations in the stepfamily will be discussed again in the next chapter. Here, the emphasis is on the complexity of expectations placed upon each member of a stepfamily, including the children, and that this complexity is a characteristic feature of every stepfamily, not an indication of failure.

Summary

In stepfamilies there are more than enough players for the various roles and there are confusing expectations with few guidelines. Stepfamilies cannot fit the traditional ideal for families with father at the 'head', mother caring for everyone's emotional needs and two pairs of grandparents who keep a respectful but loving distance. There may be several sets of grandparents with interest in some but not all of the children. Individual stepfamilies have found their own unique ways of dealing with the complexities. Stepmothers and stepfathers can find ways of caring for children without competing with the child's birth mother or father.

There are parent figures outside the stepfamily household, of tremendous importance to one or more of the children, who may intrude upon the life of the new stepfamily. Ex-partners are not ex-parents, however. Even without frequent or continuous contact with one parent, a child will continue to want reassurance of both parents' affection and concern. When that is not possible or forthcoming, the child will need help in coming to terms with the loss.

CHAPTER EIGHT

A family by stages: transitions and transformation

Earlier in this book, in Chapter 2, there is a description of the stages which are typical of stepfamilies as they progress from being a collection of new and unfamiliar strangers to being a dependable group of intimates. Chapter 2 also provides examples of families at the various stages, some of whom are obviously grappling with issues which cause tension and conflict in stepfamilies. It is obvious from these and other case examples throughout this book that while many stepfamilies reach a point of integration, few, if any, progress smoothly, some fail and give up and some appear to remain fixed at a certain stage, experiencing the same difficulties over and over again. Being 'stuck' might be the situation for years, until children grow up and live independently, parents and stepparents become less sensitive and anxious about family relationships or some other change brings about an easing of the problems. Perhaps some problems are never fully resolved, but instead become familiar over the years, recognisable as a part of personal and family history. This would apply, of course, to all families, not only stepfamilies. There are not many individuals who look back on childhood with unmixed feelings; warm memories are almost always mixed with sad or angry ones. Bringing up children is the hardest thing most people do, and no-one can promise to create a perfect environment for a child. There is too much uncertainty in the world, with risks of economic decline and other stresses from outside the family, as well as those from inside – death or ill health in a child or parent, for example, or the ending of the parents' relationship.

Since stepfamilies all have their inception in the death or failure of a relationship – Chapter 3 discusses issues of loss fully – the picture of a stepfamily can look unrelievedly sad. Some sad feelings may remain too, becoming part of the mixed feelings the past usually evokes. But there is in stepfamily life an optimism also, one which must have its roots largely in the power of affection between two adults. 'The triumph of hope over experience', as Dr Johnson cynically described the re-marriage of an acquaintance, may also be stated as the eternal strength of belief in love and new beginnings. Most stepfamilies set out in this spirit, at least the two adults do, and if the stepfamily is to survive, their relationship must carry the burden of helping the children, previous partners and extended families to share their optimism through the bewildering and threatening changes which follow.

New rules

All families have rules about how to behave, about what is and is not acceptable. Rules for behaviour are unique to each family, creating traditions and norms that members of a given family recognise as belonging to them and identifying the family to which they belong. In one family everyone is expected to be present for meals and sit down together, and in another meals are informal. In one family the rules may be many and specific, and in another they may be vague, and thus it is possible to say that families have different styles in their ways of operating, their codes of behaviour. In addition, there are two kinds of rules: those which govern everyday behaviour and are expressed in verbal instructions and other overt ways: and those which are not usually overtly expressed but which are nevertheless understood, although not necessarily at a conscious level, by all the members of a given family. The second kind of rules, unspoken ones, pertain to such things as who in the family speaks first and longest, which issues can be talked about and which will cause tension if raised or who has greatest authority and power. More than anything else, the unspoken rules are the ones which control intimacy and conflict in a family and how these and all emotions may be expressed. Some families seem to shout and argue all the time while in others voices are never raised. The rule governing the first might be something like, 'The way to be listened to in our family is to make the most noise', while for the second family it might be, 'We cannot allow any unpleasantness.' In some families touching is rare while in others it is an everyday experience to hug and caress all around the family. Spoken rules tend to apply primarily to children, an example of which is 'Eat your vegetables first, then you can have pudding' although those relating to money and how it is spent will exist between adults.

Both kinds of rules, the spoken and unspoken, are necessary and important in providing predictability and connection as well as controls, organisation and identity in a family. Rules of each kind change in time as members grow older and have different requirements, and it can be seen that if rules do not change, relationships within a family cannot develop well. But a family will tend to retain a style of relating and even hand it along from generation to generation. For example, in a family where it is acceptable to argue openly about differences of opinion but not to express anger with one another over personal irritations, the rule will be reflected in gatherings or households where several generations are present. One might observe the family arguing about politics while grandfather fails to pass the potatoes and no-one can ask him to do so for fear of offending him.

Unless a rule is consciously changed – or challenged – it will, as stated above, characterise several generations. A couple in the first stages of their relationship bring together two sets of family rules of both kinds, and therefore part of their adjustment to one another involves becoming aware of differences in codes of behaviour and gradually creating their own, either replicating the familiar ones from their families of origin, or creating an alternative family style, using some but not all of the rules with which each grew up. Often the first serious conflicts between a new couple arise over what seem to be petty issues, something like how and when the washing up is to be done. 'In our family', says one, 'we clean up after ourselves; we don't leave it for someone else.' The other hears a statement which not only criticises her or his behaviour, but seems to condemn an entire clan while excluding membership in another! With time, reasonable flexibility and not too much defensiveness, the couple compromise, and a new rule exists which may not only govern how they share the labour in their household, but how they can ask one another for help.

Family rules are the result of deeply shared experience in everyday domestic activity. When a stepfamily forms there is usually a clash of rules, a sudden demand for change rather than a gradual adjustment. There is an impact of different and unknown rules coming together suddenly, with no habits of sharing everyday routines, but with deeply held and probably conflicting expectations of 'how things ought to be'. An improvement in stepfamily tensions often comes about when these rules change, not merely as a result of everyone getting older as in a non-stepfamily, but because there is an awareness of a need and a willingness to make a change. Stepfamily life requires an openness and flexibility about all the little matters often thought too unimportant to discuss as well as the big issues that hurt and perplex and are too difficult to discuss. Papernow (1984) found that of the stepfamilies she studied in her work on the stepfamily cycle of development, those which progressed at the fastest pace and continued to progress without either becoming 'stuck' or extruding a member in order to resolve a problem, were those with the greatest amount of openness in expressing and dealing with issues as they arose.

If both partners in a stepfamily have children, sometimes referred to as the 'combination stepfamily' (Robinson 1980), there will be many pre-existing rules about children's behaviour and how discipline should be exercised. There will also be rules about intimacy and its expression which may be contradictory. Suddenly, no-one knows what to expect in everyday situations. One stepmother, for example, described how she had felt unable to deal with an apparently simple problem when her young stepson came for weekend visits. She did not allow her children to bring toys to the table during meals; her partner had no such rule and so his son brought a game, book, small car or whatever to the table as he usually did at home. The stepmother's children glowered as their mother remained silent at this infraction of her rule. The father remained unaware of the cause of the tension until the stepmother finally spoke up. When she did, it was accepted and the air cleared. What had become unbearable was the tension and silence which had developed at meal times, not the different rule in itself.

The above example is one of a simple rule of the spoken type, and although it was resolved without difficulty, it had given rise to some distress. When the clash is one of rules in the second category, the unspoken kind, the difficulty is much harder to discover and resolve, especially if the contrast of rules is around the very issue of expression. In one stepfamily, one parent and her children had a fairly noisy, chaotic but affectionate way of relating. When the children were upset or fractious they were liable to cry loudly or otherwise make a lot of noise, demanding and receiving a great deal of attention from the mother. The other parent also had children who visited regularly but lived with their mother. These children were much quieter, more restrained and controlled, with physical contact at a minimum. The two adults were critical of one another as parents and of one another's children. They had no method, no basis or rule for how to express this criticism and negotiate differences. The father/stepfather became tense and disapproving but could not say what he found difficult to live with. The mother/stepmother expressed her disapproval in derogatory terms of what seemed to her the 'uptight' behaviour of her partner's children. The differences in their personalities was one of the things which attracted them to one another – she loved his quiet organisation and he loved her spontaneous warmth. Translated to the children of each, the differences became irritations. Finding ways to enjoy the other's children, to express interest and allow affection a chance to grow, only followed long sessions talking about what each expected from children and considered 'normal' in this case, with the help of a therapist.

It is not only in 'combination' stepfamilies that a clash of rules occurs. Either partner, whether a parent or not, may be critical of the other concerning ways of managing the children, money, the house, free time, other family members, former partners and so on, but especially the children. There is no more severe critic of parenting than one who has never been a parent; we are all so deeply influenced by the experience of childhood that we want to correct the mistakes we perceive our parents to have made. Becoming a parent, experiencing the combination of love and responsibility that parenthood entails, usually modifies the severe judgements we make. Many step-parents admit that in the early stages of life in a stepfamily they expected too much of the children or felt their partner could do a better job of bringing them up. The inexperienced parent brings rules from her or his own parents and family, and very likely some unrealistic ideals, and tries to impose them on children who already have a few years of another set of rules and expectations. The children's mother or father is torn between protecting the children from the step-parent's critical and maybe harsh approach and wanting to maintain the new relationship. If the stepfamily couple have a child of their own, a new situation may arise in which there seems to be one set of rules for the older children and another for the new child. This kind of divisiveness can be very destructive for the development of the older children and for the partnership. In most stepfamilies there is an awareness of the risk of this situation, or its existence, and efforts are made to correct it. Where it exists without awareness there will be anger and resentment and probably ongoing conflict between a step-parent and stepchildren.

With an effort at being open and direct about 'the way things are' members of a family can begin to have a new and different experience of one another even after many years. For example, a couple who married and separated when both were in their early twenties sought counselling eighteen years after their divorce. Their separation had been abrupt and painful and had occurred at the time of the birth of their second child. The first child was barely two. The woman, Elaine, married again and had another child a few years later. He, Phil, also married again and had another family. Over the years Phil's contact with the children of his first marriage was spasmodic and almost always accompanied by acrimonious exchanges between Phil and Elaine. Arrangements were often cancelled at the last moment. The financial support Phil was obliged to provide was sometimes withdrawn by him because he felt it was the only power he had in the situation. From his perspective, Elaine undermined him as the children's father, actively discouraging their contacts with him; from hers, Elaine felt that each contact with Phil disturbed the children and made them unhappy. She was not aware that her own distress and unhappiness at the contact times were conveyed to the children so deeply that it seemed like theirs, and not hers. To the credit of both, a complete 'cut-off' never occurred.

Several things happened to bring about the determination in both Phil and Elaine to change the pattern of their relationship. One was the passage of time, certainly, because as the children grew into young adulthood and began to make their own decisions, some of the buried issues were exposed to questioning. But in addition, both Phil and Elaine had experiences which caused each of them, quite independently, to seek to understand problems that arose for them in work and relationships. Elaine's bitter anger and sadness about the ending of her first marriage had become an intolerable burden for her. She wanted to feel free of it, and significantly, her daughter said very clearly at a first meeting with a family therapist (D.S.) that she wanted her mother to stop being sad. She was moving into adult life; not only did she want to have an easier relationship with her father, she also wanted to feel less responsible for her mother. The other child, a boy, much to Phil's distress, had taken his stepfather's name, because, the boy said, 'It is Mum's name.' The issue of the name the boy used was poignant for Phil. He felt annihilated and rejected, as might be expected, but in his particular case, painful questions were aroused about a name and the identity it symbolises since he had been adopted as an infant and until well into his adult life did not know the names of his birth parents.

The rules, the controls over how each person was able to behave with the others, needed to change in the family. Without a change like this there is a kind of paralysis of emotional and psychological growth; painful feelings continue, with results which are damaging. Phil and Elaine's children, one or both of them, now old enough to control contacts with their father themselves, might have become permanently estranged from him, or alternatively, might have taken his position and condemned their mother for the years of stress associated with Phil. The rule which seemed to say 'The past must never be forgotten *or* forgiven' needed to become something like this: 'The past can be questioned; what was good can be talked about and what was bad need no longer be an influence.' Phil and his second wife and Elaine and her husband agreed to work together and met in order to begin making easier links. It was difficult and tense, but the meeting itself signalled a difference; the rules were changing.

Patterns of change

In a family, whether a stepfamily, single-adult family, part-time stepfamily, three-generations in one home or any other form of family living, the members relate to one another in transactional patterns, controlled by family rules, which are repeated over and over (Minuchin 1974). These are sequences of behaviour so familiar that it seems there is no alternative, no other way to behave, even if awareness of them exists. It is these repeated ways of relating and behaving which determine the way a family responds to the demands of its own inevitable development, adapting and transforming itself at every stage. Each new stage of development is marked by changes in individuals and the family as a whole, as described in Chapter 2 of this book. Each new stage is a transitional crisis. Most people know, without studying human growth and development, that a family is transformed by events and time: that which happens to individuals in a family happens to the family also. When a child is born, two people become parents and have an entirely new dimension added to their relationship, a new identity in the world – as mother or father – and a new set of tasks to perform; their parents become grandparents and so on.

The most profound adaptations families have to make are those which involve adding members, or losing them. The birth of a child may or may not be planned or welcomed, but will usually be celebrated eventually; the certainty is that each person's place is altered by the addition of a new member. The death of a family member, whether a child or an elderly grandparent, diminishes the entire group, requiring adjustments from every member. Each person in the family will have had a unique relationship with the one who died and will respond according to what the loss means, but the entire family changes, structurally and transactionally. Whatever role the lost person performed will be taken on by others. For example, in one family the lost person was the one who always remembered everyone else's birthdays and anniversaries. Cards and greetings always arrived on time and links throughout the extended family system were maintained over wide geographical distances, links which this one member seemed to symbolise.

When she died her daughter discovered her mother's address book and greetings continued to arrive. But in addition, other members of the family also began to communicate directly with one another, each one, as it were, acting upon the memory of what the loved person had meant to the entire family. When the person had a less positive role in a family the response may be to create a silence about her or him, or a secret grows up around the dead person. Although the secret may be known by only one member, all relationships throughout the family are affected.

Obviously, as the family as a whole adapts and is transformed, each individual is developing and adapting too. Many different transitional requirements are being made simultaneously. A family may be at the stage of the first child starting to go to school when a grandparent dies. Or a young adult is leaving home at the same time as another child in the family is entering adolescence, or when a parent retires. The family as a whole adapts to these many changes in its 'parts'. Referring to these periods of alteration as crises may seem to be an overstatement, but they are crises in the sense that it is a time of confusion, when the old ways no longer fit new requirements, while the new ways have yet to be developed (Hoffman, personal communication). The transition is a turning point, a crucial period of increased vulnerability; relationships may collapse if adjustments are not made, but they are also times of heightened potential (Erikson 1968). Unused potential is tapped and new competences discovered.

Some transitions in family development are predictable and some are not; some are accompanied by a gradual transformation and evolution and others by a plunge into the unknown. Those which come as a shock produce great stress, a sudden change in structure requiring immediate adaptation, such as an accident resulting in the death of a member of the family. Sudden redundancy, rapidly progressing serious illness, a handicapped child, a frail elderly relative coming to live in the household are all examples of common human experiences which cause shock waves in a family system. The transition required by separation and divorce is similar in its impact. The transition is like a dislocation in family structure, and forming a stepfamily is a further transition. If divorce and remarriage (and the same is true for cohabiting couples) follow quickly, the rapid changes in structure and relationships constitute a double transition (Robinson 1991). Burgoyne and Clark (1984) found in their study of stepfamilies in Sheffield that a rapid move from one partnership to another puts extra stress on the new stepfamily. Confusion, distress, anger and sadness about the end of the old and beginning of the new is at a maximum level.

A time of natural, or predictable, change often triggers another change. Awareness of long-standing issues or old ways of relating that no longer apply might be produced by some event or ritual. A wedding is a ritual which signals to the world – and especially to the families involved – that two people have formed an alliance of intimacy. 'Coming of age' rituals signal to the entire family that one of its members is no longer a child; new expectations and responsibilities flow from marking the fact and it is then no longer appropriate to direct and control the young person in ways which are appropriate for children. The ritual is a kind of punctuation in the life history of both family and individual. Of course, it does not always produce the implied changes in behaviour, but it does create a context for change. In the family already described in which change was sought eighteen years after a divorce, it was the 'coming of age' party of one of the children which set in motion a new 'transactional pattern'. The parent and step-parent of the young person invited the other parent and step-parent and all the combined children to the party. For the first time they were all in the same room, celebrating the life of a person who was dear and important to them all. Never before had all these people been together. The new partners, and later on the younger children, had been shielded from the tensions which had always surrounded previous meetings, the purpose of which had been to collect or return the shared children. The birthday party was not a relaxed day, nor could it be, with no previous experience except antagonistic exchanges and no practice whatsoever. Something new and different was created, however, which has grown.

The determination to act on a perceived stressful situation is an important stage of development in a stepfamily. It follows the earlier stages of new beginnings, assimilation and awareness (see Chapter 2 for a description of all the stages). At the first stage the family is new and unfamiliar and everyone has a fantasy about how it will or should be – the adults with hopes and beliefs that all will be well, and children with dark fears and sometimes hopes that somehow they can get the new stranger to go away so that their two parents will re-unite. The second stage – assimilation – is when the step-parent feels like an outsider to the unit of their partner with the partner's children, but is trying to develop a relationship with stepchildren, and probably being rebuffed. The third – awareness – is the period marked by distinct feelings that something is wrong and needs to be changed. There is often at this stage an awareness that the stepfamily has not been accepted as a legitimate group, by the children or by their other, non-custodial parent, or by the extended family, or all of these. Authority over the children, decisions about them, financial matters, relations with ex-partners, all may be going badly, with no clear approach to finding solutions. The dreams and fantasies that the stepfamily would solve all problems, that affection would develop quickly between the children and a step-parent, that the new couple could sweep away all resistence to their union, give way to the reality of an uncomfortable acceptance that all is not well. Restructuring the stepfamily, getting mobilised to make a change, airing the difficulties, is the next stage.

In almost every case the transitions from one stage to the next will not be successful if attempted too quickly, and they cannot be skipped over. Unfortunately, a timetable for these stages is impossible to give except as a suggestion. What can be said with certainty is that stepfamilies cannot develop affection, loyalty, traditions – their own rules of operation – instantly, which is what adults who create them wish to happen. It will probably take two or three years to reach the restructuring stage. The relationships are too new and tenuous to be challenged in the early stages (think, for example, of the step-parent who immediately attempts to discipline the children; when the lines of authority become clearer, when bonds begin to strengthen, when the presence of the step-parent is taken for granted, discipline has a chance of success). It is often the step-parent who is the first to press for a change of some kind. The telephone counselling service operated by the Stepfamily Association reports that most of the calls come from step-parents, and most of these are women, who, whether they are also mothers or not, call about difficulties they are experiencing with stepchildren. They long for a change but do not know what it should be. Dreams of bringing together two families to create 'one big happy family' have faded; often they express a feeling of being unsupported by a partner whom they do not want to challenge because that might cause strain in the new relationship. Time and the changes it brings in each individual's development will eventually encourage moves towards greater sharing or increased tolerance of the stepfamily reality.

When some other transition occurs or is impending, a signal is usually made, and if the time is right, action can follow and the stepfamily can move on in its development. For example, adults (mostly women) in stepfamilies asking for advice often mention that a baby has been born recently to someone in the family, not necessarily to the stepfamily couple. In one case the birth of a baby to the previous partner brought to light the resentment a stepmother felt for her own childlessness. She had made a choice to have no children but became distressed about it when it appeared to be a decision she could not reverse. Her income was needed to supplement money going to the children of her partner's previous marriage. She felt she was not valued for what she provided either by her partner or his children. She wondered if having a baby would make her more important in everyone's eyes, a 'real mother', but the financial constraints were great. In fact, she enjoyed her work and the status that went with it. It was at home she felt of little significance. She began to realise that the change she really wanted was to have more understanding from her partner and asked him to join with her in meeting with a marital counsellor, to which he agreed with some persuasion.

In another case, a mother asked for help with her distress over the difference in her partner's treatment of their shared child and the child of her previous marriage. She wanted him to feel the same towards both children. Although he was kind to his stepchild, he was far more attentive and joyful with the child of the new partnership. He held her often and played with her, while he rarely cuddled his stepchild. When the mother could accept that it was natural for his feelings to be less intense for his stepchild and finally talked with him in a way that did not accuse or blame him about her own concerns he became more relaxed with both children. An aspect of the situation which had not occurred to the mother was articulated by him also, and that was that he had been jealous of the affection between her and her child, had felt excluded by it and he had also been envious of the bond between his stepchild and her own father. When his baby was born he felt that finally he had a child of his own. His possessiveness abated as the two shared and admitted their concerns and then both he and the mother began to take pleasure in the relationship between the two children.

And in yet another, a woman, Ruth, asked for help in making the decision to have a child. She and her husband, Nick, both had children from previous marriages. Her children lived with them; his came for weekends and long periods during holiday times. Ruth was somewhat disgusted by Nick's behaviour with his own children, which she found overindulgent and sentimental. In her view, he set no limits for his own children and far too many for hers. They argued constantly about this and other matters, frequently focusing on Nick's guilt for having left his first wife for Ruth. Nick did not deny this, but took it for granted that both he and Ruth were in the wrong for succumbing to their attraction to one another and would therefore have to make sacrifices to those he saw as 'victims' – his first wife and his children. Ruth believed that Nick was perpetuating his guilt needlessly, and in fact it had been several years since he and Ruth had married. They were 'stuck' at a stage of awareness of difficulties in their stepfamily, unable to agree upon ways to make changes. During their married life Nick's financial support of his first wife had never been settled; he sometimes made extra payments without consulting Ruth or even telling her. Although their relationship was stormy, and in spite of the fact that Ruth felt she came after his first wife and his children in Nick's affections, she wanted a child. The value she placed upon marriage was in adding children to it. At another level she hoped having a child of their own would resolve the conflicts between her and Nick, giving her and her child equal status with his previous wife and their children. She became pregnant without having Nick's agreement and he was angry at being, in his opinion, manipulated. Ruth's opinion was different, of course. In her view, Nick enjoyed their sexual relationship without taking any responsibility for contraception. Therefore, she believed she had a right to choose pregnancy. Tragically, the pregnancy ended in miscarriage. Ruth was distraught and accused Nick of being relieved. Their marriage continued for another year before they separated.

Ruth and Nick never progressed beyond the earliest stages of stepfamily development. They began, as all stepfamily couples do, with the fantasy stage, both believing that all problems would be overcome by the power of their feelings for one another. They wanted their children to form 'one big happy family'; they wanted to love the other's children and be loved by them in return. When these fantasies gave way to reality Nick Ruth continued to be shocked by the difference between it and their dreams, and the fact that the previous bonds between parent and children, on the part of each of them, were more powerful and more intimate than their love affair. Neither ever came to feel the other was a partner in parenting. Ruth described herself as a 'single parent' although married. The fantasy of sharing life's burdens and joys was rudely shattered by the mutual exclusion of what was of deep importance to each of them. Although each was aware of something being wrong and both wanted to improve their relationship, neither could make a change. They remained like people who want to mount a moving carousel but cannot find a safe way to do it.

Unable to find a solution to their problems, Ruth and Nick ended their marriage, but in other families the reaction to what seems to be intractable tensions is to extrude a child. In others it may be to eliminate all contact with an ex-partner. If the first stage of stepfamily development is a fantasy one – 'Everything will be all right now and we can live happily ever after' – the next ones might be described as lingering fantasy, or 'If only', stages. 'If only we did not have to cope with her ex-husband' (or someone else); 'If only my partner would understand how I feel about . . .' and so on. At these stages someone, usually the step-parent, is aware that the hope of making one 'ordinary' family is foundering. The parts seem not to fit together. A long period of feeling dissatisfied, that something is wrong, may follow, until some action is taken. In the example which follows, the stepfamily stayed together for many years before strong links of attachment were established between all members.

This stepfamily was formed after the death of one parent and the divorce of another. The four children involved lived in one household, but some had weekends and holidays with their non-custodial father while the others obviously did not. Fortunately for the couple, Jane and Paul, one set of grandparents/stepgrandparents, lived nearby and had the children to stay so that the couple had time alone occasionally. Nevertheless, there were difficulties. Which parent was to correct which child, for example? Which set of table manners was to dominate? If one child refused food cooked by a step-parent, who was to insist that everyone had the same menu? Children in stepfamilies often refuse food or complain about it. It seems to be a way to express loyalty to an absent parent. In this family, the dead parent, a mother, was seldom spoken about. Sad feelings about her would arise at meal times when some favourite dishes never appeared. In the early stages the parent and step-parent were unaware of such issues. They were intensely involved with one another and believed they could overcome the children's resistance quickly, while the children were hoping the stepfamily might vanish and things return to a previous state – that father and mother might re-unite, that the dead mother might magically re-appear.

There was a good deal of intrusive contact from the father of two of the children; he would telephone frequently, cancel visits at the last minute, fail to appear for visits or demand visits when the stepfamily had planned an activity. At such times the divisions in the stepfamily were painfully apparent. Jane and Paul sometimes criticised her children's father within the hearing of the children. The different levels of closeness and intimacy between the parts of the family were highlighted by other things as well, such as when a child was ill and needed extra attention. The child would call for the parent and reject the attentions of the step-parent. Or at moments of triumph and happy anticipation a child would not seek out the step-parent to tell, but the parent the child had shared such moments with before. As time wore on, Jane and Paul became confused and angry with one another's children and critical of the other as a parent. When the children quarrelled they blamed one another, and privately worried that the family would fail.

Feelings of failure in Jane led her to seek therapy. It is, as has been shown, often the mother/stepmother who asks for help from outside because it is the woman whose role it is in the family to ensure everyone's happiness. It is so frequently the woman who, in her role as stepmother, becomes depressed and goes to see a doctor or counsellor that two mental-health workers have found a label for this depressive syndrome: the 'Cinderella's Stepmother Syndrome' (Morrison and Thompson-Guppy 1985). This is not to suggest that a woman who becomes a stepmother is a depressive personality, but that many woman, perhaps most, who become stepmothers experience depression because what they expect of themselves and what is expected of them, is simply impossible. Jane wanted her stepchildren to accept her 'mothering' them just as her own children did. Paul expected Jane to take the place of 'mother' in the house for all the children equally. It was fortunate that Jane found a therapist with some knowledge of stepfamilies who did not reinforce the traditional 'mother role'; instead, Jane realised she was not the only parent with responsibility for nurturing the children. Jane and Paul began to understand what was happening and then to work together. It became accepted and natural that their respective children would seek their parent and not their step-parent at times, and that the same principle also applied to questions of discipline. When a quick matter of correction could be dealt with either of them handled it, but when a child needed strictness and punishment, each parent dealt it out to her or his own, but according to some agreed-upon rules.

The therapist was important in helping Jane and Paul move from one stage to the next. They had been struggling with the problems of amalgamating two families, two sets of spoken and unspoken rules, many already established patterns of behaviour, and they were at risk of becoming bogged down at a stage of being aware that changes were needed but not knowing what to do about it. They were silently struggling – except when a row broke out – and not empathising with one another. To empathise with another person is to know in one's own feelings what that person is experiencing: this is different from sympathising, when one knows another is suffering and one is sorry, but does not have the same feelings. Jane and Paul discovered they had the same sense of failure at times. This enabled them to consult rather than blame, to complain but not hopelessly. Rather, complaints became the preamble to looking for ideas, new methods and for understanding. All was not smooth at this stage, the 'action' stage. Possibilities were created, but not final answers, and there was a long period of turbulence.

For Jane, Paul and their children, the long haul through the middle stages of stepfamily life – creating stronger new alliances while preserving important old ones, finding solutions to the daily issues, respecting the past which was not shared by all, making the family a place where the demands and disappointments of the world outside can be shared – required many years. For a long time the children distinguished between parent and step-parent markedly. The warmth and ease of each parent with her or his own children did not extend to their stepchildren. One child, Simon, was particularly tense with his stepmother. It is often puzzling as to why one particular child appears to withhold membership in the stepfamily, to remain outside, silent or angry when others participate in family routines. Such a child may be the one with most vivid memories of an absent or lost parent, as was the case with Simon. An unspoken but deeply felt rule may have come into existence that this parent cannot be talked about freely. The child (of whatever age), in order to maintain loyalty to the absent parent but live in the stepfamily must then exercise a self-control which inhibits spontaneous expression. The result will be an angry child, and this seemed to be the case in Jane and Paul's stepfamily. Their relationship was strong and thus they could withstand an onslaught of what seemed like hostility from one child. The solution they found was simply to wait until time took its course and Simon left home.

Stepfamilies often ask for help with one child whose behaviour is difficult and different, as one or both of the parents see it, from that of the other children. The 'difficult' child often bears a physical resemblance to a former partner, the child's non-custodial parent, or has characteristics and traits similar to that person. If there are continuing and unresolved conflicts with the former partner, the child then is burdened with reminding both parent and step-parent of this difficult problem. The child can be used as a scapegoat, carrying the blame for something which s/he has no responsibility. Another possibility is that one member of the new couple objects to traits and behaviours in the other but never expresses this. The same traits in a stepchild may seem intolerable, however, resulting again in scapegoating of the child. Couples in stepfamilies tend towards ignoring their personal differences because they have so much to adjust to at once. A child can become the target for adults' unexpressed annoyance and frustration. Another factor which appears to contribute to one particular child's difficulties is the age and stage the child had reached at the time of the parents' separation. In the early sections of Chapter 2 is a description of individual development, from which it can be seen that parental separation will have a differing impact at the various stages. For example, a child who is old enough to understand a verbal explanation of what is happening to the family, and we know that children need and benefit from this kind of information, will react differently from a very young child who needs the consistent presence of parent figures in order to feel secure. Words are not as reassuring to a child of one, two or three as the physical nearness of the parent. Whatever the contributing factors, when one child presents particular problems to the parent and step-parent, the solution may seem to be for the child to leave the home or, if non-resident, not to visit often. If the child is an adolescent it seems a logical answer.

Burgoyne and Clark (1984) found in their Sheffield study a group of stepfamilies in which the children were adolescent when the family formed. A feature of this group was that the parent/step-parent couple were looking forward to the children leaving home. These families were experiencing difficulties characteristic of the early stages of stepfamilies, with the additional pressures of children at adolescence. Theirs was the 'double transition' (Robinson 1991) mentioned earlier, a juxtaposition of changes. A feature of adolescent turmoil is the challenge to parental control and authority. If a stepfamily forms at this stage of children's development the parental system is not well enough defined to withstand the inevitable pressures. The challenge from adolescents may seem like a threat to the new couple, and especially the step-parent. The adolescents themselves were not included in the Sheffield research. They may have wanted to leave home too, as adolescents frequently do, imagining that restrictions upon their activities would not exist once they got away from parental controls. In a stepfamily, however, adolescents may leave home before they are prepared through education and maturation to live independently, or they may leave too finally. One reason for this is suggested by the group of families Burgoyne and Clark found – older parents with older children – but there may be other factors not yet clarified by research studies. Because adolescence is a testing time for all parents, the strain on relations between step-parents and an adolescent stepchild is especially great; the bond is weaker before the stress begins. Persistent conflict appears to drive the adolescent out, which can be detrimental to her or his life chances if education is curtailed or there is an escape into early marriage or pregnancy. The National Child Development Study research makes this very suggestion (Kiernan 1992) with respect to the stepchildren in their sample; that is, the researchers found a tendency for stepchildren to make such transitions as leaving home, leaving school, forming a partnership, having a baby earlier than their counterparts in lone-parent families or traditional two-parent ones. It is not the stepfamily *per se* which should be seen as causal, and indeed the cause is not clear. What seems to be the cause is a pattern of conflict within the family (Kiernan, personal communication).

In Jane and Paul's case, although they had been a stepfamily for several years when the eldest child, Simon, became adolescent, Simon, as has already been described, seemed to remain resistant to the family identity and they looked forward to his departure. He had the added disadvantage of being the first to test the ability of the parental couple to cope with adolescence and it was a difficult time for them all. Jane and Paul were relieved when he left to go to college, but the 'leaving' was too final, too marked with unresolved anger. There continues to be tension around the relationship between him and both parents. In spite of this, there is also affection and concern. The children developed strong links over the years which have survived into adult life; there is a loyalty and friendship between them which makes their steprelationship irrelevant.

Moving on

What might a stepfamily be like that has progressed through to being integrated as a unit of intimates, identified with one another in the special way we call 'family'? Jane and Paul have a long history together, as do their combined children. They have many shared memories now, outnumbering those they do not share. In the early years it was the other way round. The stepfamily identity is no longer significant but the identity with one another *is* significant and provides security. What once was threatening and unknown is now deeply familiar and accepted.

This stage, called 'resolution' in Papernow's (1984) scheme, is not free of problems – life never is – but problems related to the stepfamily itself are rarely experienced. Membership in the family is secure and is sanctioned by every other member. Mistakes made in the beginning, when the family was forming, may cause reverberations at times, but the resolution stage is marked by acceptance – of both strengths and weaknesses. This implies that no-one has become a permanent outsider. Certain events, however, may be a painful reminder of stepfamily status and temporarily throw one or more members back into memories of the stages when fearful doubts about being an undisputed part of the family existed. These events, for example weddings and other ceremonies, highlight the fact that stepfamilies as a family form are not sanctioned outside the family, by society in general. For example, a woman whose stepdaughter married in a very traditional style found that she was excluded from the seating arrangments for family members and from photographs of the family group. Although she and her stepdaughter had been part of the same family and household for several years and had developed a reasonable and affectionate relationship, there was no acknowledgement and no evidence that the stepmother existed in any of the wedding protocol. Conventional wedding etiquette does not provide guidance as to where to place step-parents. As other aspects of modern stepfamily life, it is the families themselves who create new traditions.

Here is another example which demonstrates the way people adapt old traditional ways to fit new realities. A traditional church wedding was planned by a couple in which the groom had both a stepmother and stepfather. His father and mother had divorced, married again and had children in their second marriages. Wedding dress was formal, the bride entered on the arm of her father behind the maid of honour, the bridegroom and best man awaited her in front of the alter. What was different was that the tradition of seating the families of the bride and groom had been expanded to include the step-parents. The 'new' couples sat together, with their respective children, and all of the parents and step-parents signed the register.

As we know, many stepfamilies are formed by couples who do not marry, but live together, sharing home, income and children. Such a stepfamily progresses through the same phases of development, of course, as does a married couple. In one instance it was not a social ritual which had an impact upon the family after many years, but the birth of their own child. Mary and Don met after Don had been divorced. He had two daughters and was determined to maintain contact with them, to 'keep faith' with his children, in spite of the anger and bitterness which prevailed between him and their mother. When the children's mother learned of Don's attachment to Mary, she confronted Mary in a fury, blaming Mary for the ending of her marriage. It was not possible; Don and Mary had not been acquainted at the time, but anger and pain rarely need logic to find an object. When Don and Mary decided to live together the anger shown by the children's mother, Lora, did not decrease for a long time. At first Lora refused to allow the children to visit Don if Mary was present. Overnight stays were therefore not possible; Mary either did not accompany Don when he had the children for a day or she agreed to make other plans for herself. As Don and Mary became closer and more involved in sharing one another's lives, it became not only difficult and artificial and a source of great resentment to Mary that she was 'got out of the way', but a deception in which the children were involved. Don and Mary asked Lora to meet with them and discuss the situation. They met, all three in a tense and nervous state. The result was that the children began to have more meaningful visits with their father and contacts with Mary when they visited him. They also began to have longer times in Don and Mary's home, spending weekends and parts of holiday periods. It was the beginning of stepfamily life for Don and

Mary and Don's children, albeit as a part-time stepfamily, and it was not easy. Of course, Don and Mary thought they had cleared the way for themselves but they yet had to go through the fantasy stage as all stepfamilies must.

When Mary found that she was still excluded, now not physically but by Don's attentions to his children when they were present, she was astonished. To add to this, the children carried with them into their visits Lora's hostility towards Mary. They were loyal to their mother; they knew it was hard for her to accept Mary. By resisting Mary's friendly overtures, by ignoring and shunning her, they could avoid being angry at their father for having Mary in his life. Things went on in this way until Mary confronted Don about ignoring her when the children came to visit. She described her feelings about the children's behaviour towards her. In response, Don tried to tell Mary that he needed her to love the part of him that was a parent, to support him in his role as father. They worked out a kind of bargain that eventually had enough success to comfort them both. They began to make decisions together about the children and their activities. Don began to take more care of the children in terms of feeding and washing, rather than leave those tasks, usually a mother's, to Mary. He also assumed responsibility for correcting the children if they needed it, particularly when they were rude to Mary.

Slowly a warmer and more relaxed relationship developed between Mary and Don's daughters. They began to share activities without Don once in a while. Mary found that as the girls grew older she could help Don understand their femininity, the developing woman in each of them, not only with such obvious matters as menstruation but with what it is like to be a girl, and she began to feel she had a kind of pact with Lora to do the best she could for Lora's daughters. As the stepfamily made this progress towards integration, Mary's wish to have a child of her own grew, and thus another difficult phase occurred as Don and Mary coped with different needs and wishes. Don felt no desire to have more children. He finally accepted Mary's right and his own wish to spend his life with her and they had a child.

During Mary's pregnancy there was a resurgence of the girls' resentment of Mary, perhaps a renewal of their conflict of loyalty. Lora had not married again or formed a long-term relationship. It was a help to the girls when she explained that she felt happy about her life as it was, but they, especially the younger of the two, continued to treat Mary with the old coldness. It is probable that they feared her claim upon Don would now be greater than their own. As for Mary, she also experienced a resurgence of the old resentments. She wanted to have Don to herself while she was pregnant. In a sense, she and the girls were a threat to one another during this time. After the child was born all these fears and resentments seemed to fall away. The family moved into a new stage of development and a new connection as they shared the new member. The structure of the family changed and each individual member acquired a new dimension to her or his self-concept. Lora, the outsider in this new phase, was for a time unhappy again. The loss of her marriage to Don and her grief about that was aroused, but temporarily. She had gained in self-esteem in the intervening time by pursuing a career and had achieved a satisfying sense of independence and self-sufficiency.

Births, by their very nature, alter and unbalance family structure and therefore can cause a reaction in a stepfamily. After the stage of resolution has been reached, however, it is not likely that this would jeopardise the family or cause long-lasting disturbance. There may be a period of sadness or of jealousy at the attention a new baby requires. Once the relationships have become reliable and a source of intimacy, the new child reinforces the connections. At earlier stages of development a baby in a stepfamily unit can be more stressful, as has been described in previous sections of this chapter.

Perhaps the most likely event to destabilise a stepfamily at later stages, however, is a will left by a parent or grandparent which excludes non-biologically related family members. Chapter 6 includes a section on the importance of wills and the impact of inheritance in stepfamilies. Advice is seldom offered to grandparents who are also stepgrandparents and probably seldom considered. Suddenly stepgrandchildren, perhaps loved and accepted by the grandparents in life, can seem like outsiders again when their stepbrothers and -sisters, or half-brothers and -sisters, are remembered in a will but they are not.

Because events and rituals linked to family life are often a destabilising factor in stepfamilies at a later stage in their life cycle, it is appropriate to conclude this chapter with a brief discussion of the significance of rituals in general. However much individual variation there is in the habit of ritual, or differences in religious and cultural practice, there is deep awareness of the importance of rituals in the organisation of human life. The family is the context in which the process of cultural transmission of rituals begins.

Family rituals serve to create and maintain social structures for individuals, families and communities (Roberts 1988). They can help to manage contradictions, simultaneously celebrating opposing meanings – for instance, at weddings when at one and the same time a child is being 'lost' and a new family member is being 'gained'. Rituals also serve to provide containment and support for the expression of strong emotions, the foremost example of which is mourning. At funerals the prescribed ways of behaving and special verbal expressions are shared by the bereaved and those who mourn with them, within limits which are circumscribed by time and place. People weep and hold one another, acknowledging sorrow in a place where such expression is sanctioned and understood by everyone present. Besides helping to resolve contradictions, face strong emotions and bring people together to do these things, rituals can also support the transition from one stage of development to another – from one state of being to the next.

Rituals which mark growth have three symbolic stages: first, the separation stage in which an individual is separated from her or his own group; second, a liminal, or threshold, stage, in which the person is often isolated, being neither one thing nor the other; and third, a re-integration stage, when the individual returns to day-to-day life, but with a new status (*ibid*). Many cultures have rituals which mark the transition from childhood to adulthood in which young people are segregated from their families, considered neither child nor adult, then during the threshold stage are taught by adults how to try out the new roles of adulthood. New learning is passed on to them in this phase of initiation, and from this they return to everyday living with a new identity, that is, new privileges and new responsibilities. Often the return to the community is marked by a new name or clothing and with a celebration. In traditional western marriage ceremonies the separation, isolation and coming together with a new couple identity are expressed through the convention of the couple not seeing one another before the wedding ceremony; the clothing worn by the bride, who is 'given away'; the signing of the register and procession led by the newly married couple; and the final celebration and cutting of the cake to symbolise the sharing of their new life together.

When thus described, such rituals may seem odd, even slightly ridiculous, and yet they mark and manage situations in which powerful emotions can be safely expressed. There are as yet no generally recognised rituals for divorce, other than the legal pronouncement of the decree absolute. In the United States some couples do send cards to family and friends announcing their divorce. For couples who never married, there is no public acknowledgement of their private arrangement at all when they separate, unless they invent their own. Their separation has, of course, no legal status unless the two owned property together and seek legal advice to settle the division of their assets. Increasingly, remarriages are recognised through some kind of ceremonial, such as the service of blessing, in which the couple's children by previous relationships may take part. It is at least possible for stepfamilies to design their own family rituals which recognise the transition to their new status, as one couple did, for example, by writing to members of both their families and to close friends, enclosing photographs of themselves and both sets of children. They designed the service of blessing together with the minister of their church and acknowledged the past in statements which each made. Perhaps ceremonies such as this, in a secular context as well as a religious one, will be the rituals of the future, encompassing such themes as membership, healing, identity, the expression or negotiation of beliefs and celebration (Imber Black 1988).

Rituals, then, help to manage change. Transitional passages are critical, demanding adaptations which are often unknown in advance and must be discovered through experience. The transitions from nuclear family to separated parents to stepfamily – and, for the children, possibly two stepfamilies – are complex and painful. What is more, they often come one on top of the other and coincide with other life changes. Change, or transition, is difficult – a leap in the dark. Perhaps rituals are a metaphorical way of holding hands while taking the leap. But if change always involves struggle and a degree of loss, it also involves growth – a 'leaving behind', but a 'becoming something new' as well. If both are valued and appreciated, change can be in part a welcome challenge. As a child in a stepfamily once said, 'Change is always happening, but it isn't always bad.'

Summary

This chapter has described the concept of family rules, both expressed and implied, which control behaviour in important areas of daily life such as expressions of intimacy and authority. Stepfamilies bring varying sets of rules together which are already functioning for one parent and her or his children, but which are new and unfamiliar to the step-parent. If both parents have children there are increased complexities in bringing two different methods of operation together.

Stepfamilies progress through transitions as all families do, adapting relationships to the demands of growth and change. However, transitions in stepfamilies are often characterised by more than one set of changes at a time as the stepfamily's inception may coincide with significant individual developmental transitions. When stepfamilies try to integrate quickly and expect relationships to develop instantly in an effort to manage change, resentments in children and others increase. All families adapt as time and growth occurs, but stepfamilies have particular needs for understanding both from inside and from the wider social context in their transitional progress.

Examples have been given of families at various stages of stepfamily development, some of whom progressed to a stage which satisfied members' needs for intimacy and belonging, and others which remained fixed at earlier stages, where connections between step-parents and stepchildren were conflictual or where the two adults did not share parenting responsibilities.

Finally, this chapter described the meaning that rituals can have in family life and how some of these are not applicable to stepfamilies. Stepfamilies, therefore, often create their own ways of marking events in the passage of life.

CHAPTER NINE

Stepfamilies – the family of the future? Possibilities and guidelines

The 'breakdown of the family' is an emotive phrase. It strikes fear into the hearts of everyone who believes that a plurality of family forms means that society has become disorganised and disintegrated. Some religious thinkers, legal and social planners, many politicians and theorists of many persuasions are worried that the rise in numbers of divorced couples and stepfamilies means a falling moral standard. 'Family breakdown' can refer to a single family, or to an entire generation of families, but it frightens most of us at some level, because we all know the profound importance of the earliest relationships in life. The phrase also evokes a common and cherished belief that at some time in the past families were more enduring than they seem now to be, that there was once a 'golden age' of family life where warmth and security existed and could always be relied upon (Skolnick 1991). There never was such a golden age, although it can be argued that periods of rapid change or times of war are more traumatic for families than others and influence how they must live and function. A long view of human history shows 'the family' adapting to cultural changes, political and socio-economic forces and varying ideals – religious, philosophical and psychological – and surviving as the basic social institution. It changes, but also remains the same. The phrase 'breakdown of the family' means 'breakdown of the family as we know it', for it refers to changes of the norms at a given period which pertain to the family, and not the demise of this most fundamental social unit

Stepfamilies are currently at the frontier of changing attitudes about the meaning of 'family'. Changes in the law relating to marriage and family are a result, in part, of social pressure, that is, of pressure from families themselves; and in part, they result from an effort to control and organise a population, pressure from outside the family. Divorce law was altered to make divorce more accessible because society demanded it. Laws relating to the way property is managed were changed in the nineteenth century, heralding the end of marriage as a means to accrue wealth, or, for poorer people, a way to survive economically. Expectations of the marital relationship have become centred on personal fulfilment, and because death no longer releases so many people from unsatisfactory marriages as was the case in the past, a tolerance of divorce exists – something which has to be sanctioned, if uneasily. The acceptance of divorce has made it impossible to ignore the existence of stepfamilies, the families which follow. Although they are labelled and stigmatised as the result of failure, little by little their successes are being acknowledged and their particular stresses understood. Long-held and cherished concepts of 'normality' or 'ordinary' as applied to families are challenged by the increasing knowledge about stepfamily life as well as by awareness of their numbers. Families which form after the divorce of one or both partners have many complicated issues to deal with, particularly in the early stages, and some founder, but many survive and stabilise, fulfilling the needs their members have for intimacy and nurturance.

The fact that many couples end their stepfamilies is the result not only of the difficulties of merging two families with all the complex issues of parenting and wider family relationships, or that they are compared to an idealised picture of a 'normal' family; but there are also the factors which contribute to the ending of first marriages. Much is demanded of marriage – for companionship, sexual satisfaction, financial security, support in personal development, stimulating company and the sharing of child-rearing. When any area is proving unsatisfactory, all others are affected. Stepfamilies represent the quest for success in this most complex of human endeavours – creating the right partnership. Some individuals are not able to sustain relationships for many reasons and go from one to another, and without doubt this is damaging to them, to their partners and to any children who may be involved. Some people choose autonomy and satisfy needs for closeness and intimacy through work or relationships which allow scope for independence. The meaning of marriage and domestic partnerships changes, laws and social conventions alter, but the need adults have for stable life in a couple relationship continues.

It is highly likely that people will continue to marry and divorce and marry again in spite of social disapproval and social stigma. As was pointed out elsewhere in this book the numbers of families which correspond to the conventional ideal for a 'normal' family – husband as breadwinner, wife as homemaker and their children – are few, only about 8 per cent at any one time (OPCS 1990a), so the ideal certainly does not represent a numerical majority. But what values are represented by it? The existence of the many families which do not conform, and the focus here is on stepfamilies, gives us the opportunity to think about what is desired and required of family life whatever the shape and form it has. In fact, stepfamilies *force* us to 'ask awkward questions about our conceptions of the "normal" family' (Burgoyne 1987: 3), and we then discover some interesting gaps in sociological knowledge.

Research into stepfamilies demonstrates the amount of assumption and lack of knowledge about families in general and how they function *from the inside*. Jacqueline Burgoyne and David Clark (1984), in their Sheffield study of stepfamilies, found they were learning from the families themselves what the images of 'normality' were that the stepfamilies were trying to achieve. It was a bewildering and complex array of standards in child care and development, marital relationship, extended family ties, legal and economic knowledge, and some were dealing with such difficulties as violence and child abuse. Burgoyne and Clark found that research into the ways any family copes with all these aspects was hardly available and rarely integrated (Burgoyne 1987). Since stepfamilies draw upon the cultural model of a two-parent family and most want to provide the best family environment they can for their children, the natural direction is towards trying to reduce contact with the 'extra' parents. Many stepfamilies have found this is impossible for various reasons and have had to forge ways and means of incorporating levels of relationship, of creating flexible boundaries so that children can move between parents and sets of parents. There is no model for this kind of family functioning, no cultural standard or value which says it is good, yet stepfamilies do it and many do it well. Research such as Burgoyne and Clark's is beginning to catch up with *how* they do it. (And see Pasley and Ihinger-Tallman 1987 for a collection of research papers on stepfamilies and step-parenting.)

There is a need to understand more about how families, and especially stepfamilies, create emotional security and sustain it over time. As more is understood about stepfamilies, there is increasing appreciation of the wisdom contained by those which survive. Burgoyne (1987) provides several reasons to be grateful to them, which we list and expand in the following paragraphs.

- Stepfamilies remind us that there is more to ending a marriage than a legal procedure. In this book we have attempted to explore the transitions involved, social, psychological and emotional and economic. At a personal and familial level, it is possible that in a sense a marriage never totally ends. Living intimately together, even unhappily, becomes part of each person's deepest self and part of the histories of the families involved. Surviving stepfamilies demonstrate that the past, with all its successes and failures, can be 'lived with' and become a dynamic part of the present, but does not have to dominate it.
- Stepfamilies expose social and cultural myths about families and parenting. One of those is that being a parent is natural and easy. People who find parenting a hard, demanding task usually feel they are failures at a job they should know by instinct how to manage. In fact, it is probably true to say that all parents feel at some time or other that they have failed. This is especially acute for women, for whom motherhood is expected to be a natural and total vocation. Talking about and asking for help with parenting is something many people find hard to do. Burgoyne and Clark found that the parent and step-parent couples they met did talk about their children because they had to. They also shared the tasks of child care more than is usual in nuclear families. Having to cope with many difficult daily issues for which there is no acceptable model, no formula and no experience to draw upon means that the parent and step-parent couples must find their own, and learn as they live through the various stages.

- Surviving stepfamilies provide a challenge to the expectation that the marital or couple relationship should provide for the entire range of emotional, physical and psychological satisfactions for the partners, and that the same two people should be able to provide for all the care of their children.
- The step-parent role has an inherent capacity to contain both closeness and distance from child-rearing; this can be a benefit to children's individual growth and provide an additional adult model for them.
- There is an interpersonal respect in stepfamilies which allows for closeness with other parent figures and other family connections while maintaining reliable links to the parent/ step-parent couple (Carter and McGoldrick 1989).
- What is personal satisfaction from each and every member's perspective? This is a complicated question which stepfamilies force us to talk about. What do adults and children, women and men, want and gain from the intimacy involved in living together? Families provide a home, food and shelter, but also other needs, more difficult to define, are met within the family context. Most people, and especially children, need predictability and safe limits. Children need discipline within a context of connection and concern. People of all ages need emotional and psychological acceptance and affection. At its inception, stepfamily life cannot satisfy these needs and wants, but in time it is possible. What is important and significant is not the shape of a parcel, but what is inside. What is significant to individuals, families and society is the way the private and intimate life of the family – stepfamily and every other form – manages growth, closeness, distance, role expectations, social stigma and the many other pressures from a changing and often threatening world.

The organisation for stepfamilies, the National Stepfamily Association, finds through its telephone counselling service and the letters which arrive in numbers every week, that many step-parents, both men and women, want help to understand their confusing role, and there is much concern expressed by these step-parents about their stepchildren. It is a fact that the majority of callers and correspondents are women who often say that getting a partner to discuss parenting issues is difficult; men tend to turn the job of caring for the children over to a woman. With an effort and determination to open the subject, and frequently with support from a helpful outsider, a positive change almost always follows. What is becoming clear through the work of the Association and research, is that those stepfamilies which progress to a stage where the stepfamily identity is accepted and relationships valued and secure are those in which communication about children and parenting was thought about and approached openly.

One of the most astonishing achievements of surviving stepfamilies is in meeting the challenge of providing a positive but realistic picture of the non-residential parent. It is possible that one aspect of the step-parent role which is most positive and not sufficiently exploited is, as listed above, the capacity to have a warm relationship with a child but a greater distance from child-rearing than a birth parent, making it possible to perceive a child's needs with a wide perspective. It is this greater objectivity which helps many step-parents to support and maintain a stepchild's relationship with a non-residential parent.

As stepfamilies forge alternative and more varied parental roles, the limitations of the traditional ones became obvious and constraining. It seems sad that men are presented with a cultural model which is limited to authority and money. Emotion in men is often ignored and discouraged in male socialisation. Obviously, men love their children and can be nurturing parents. And mothers can do specific and special things with children as well as nurture them. When a child has a mother to do the physical and emotional nurturing, a stepmother is freed to focus on skills and activities which can be shared with a stepchild without competing with or supplanting the mother, or assuming responsibility for the child (Smith 1990). The basic parental responsibilities belong to the two parents who gave the child birth. Even when one of them is not fulfilling her or his responsibilities a step-parent need not, and probably should not under most circumstances, assume the burden. A step-parent's relationship to a stepchild needs to be worked out over time and according to the particular family situation, and not to the traditional patterns for mothers and fathers.

A summary and case studies

We have tried to explore some of the mythology which has developed in relation to stepfamilies over the ages. In the first chapter we have shown that there have always been stepfamilies created through death followed by remarriage, while the numbers of stepfamilies following divorce and remarriage have been relatively few until this century. Now, newly formed and forming stepfamilies have a major task in overcoming the folkloric and deeply entrenched prejudices against them as well as the fantasies and fears which are commonly held by children. In the second chapter we explored the losses which are the starting point for all stepfamilies.

Whether the loss is the result of a death or a divorce it must be faced and mourned at individual, couple and family levels. It takes time to come to terms with grief, the length depending on a particular situation but also on the amount of anger the loss has invoked. Because stepfamilies are usually quite complex, it also takes time for appropriate attachments to grow and develop, and, initially at least, these are vulnerable and need supporting. Most stepfamilies, by definition, are part of a network of households which are more or less linked, and the boundaries between them often become contentious, particularly in the early stages. These boundaries need both to become more permeable than those of a nuclear family and to be respected so that each household is able to maintain sufficient privacy for themselves (Visher and Visher 1988). There are many different kinds of stepfamilies: some stepfather households, some stepmother, some both, the 'binuclear' (Ahrons and Rodgers 1987) family with children of both partners, and when children are born to these families, they become the 'his, hers, and ours' stepfamily. Not all stepfamily households are full-time. While this arrangement appears to allow a new couple opportunities to pursue their individual lives, they are by no means free of tensions, tensions which inevitably increase when children visit.

Stepfamilies need time to create their own identity through family rituals and explicit and implicit rules. Providing these are respected by both of their parents, children can manage living in two households where rules are different; this has a potential benefit because children thus have more choice in developing their own values as they mature. Family rituals, which are occasions for reinforcing family solidarity – for example, through the exchange of gifts as symbols of love, as celebratory or healing occasions – can prove awkward and even painful for stepfamilies unless attempts are made by the family network to redefine ritual events in order to include them. While we live in a society where there are expectations and guidelines for nuclear families embedded in the culture (whether individual families conform to them or not) and often demonstrated by family rituals, stepfamilies must find their own, and often at times of great vulnerability for them. Family life-cycle rituals, such as Barmitzvah, and family celebrations and holidays, such as birthdays, Christmas and Thanksgiving, are times when conflict in family loyalties can be most evident, as are the demonstrations as to who is 'in' or 'out' of the family network.

Weddings often provide a grave challenge to the stepfamily network. Grief or anger which has lain dormant and unresolved can be expressed by the way seating or receptions are arranged, or by the same token, can demonstrate that all members of the family have a place and are accepted. One of us (M.R.) attended the wedding of a bride whose father had been married four times and her mother three; she is the child of the second marriage for each of them. The bridegroom had also previously been married, but with no children. At the wedding were both parents and some step-parents, plus a number of step- and half-siblings. Everyone seemed genuinely to care for the bride and to have surmounted the original traumas sufficiently to attend and take part in the festivities with amity.

Money can mean power and love as well as provision of the necessities of life. It is a complex and 'loaded' issue in stepfamilies and few are able to live at the level of the original nuclear family although they will probably have a higher standard of living than a single woman living with children did prior to the stepfamily. There may be differences of income between stepfamily households which will mean that stepchildren are materially disadvantaged, while their stepbrothers or -sisters have more. Nevertheless, stepchildren who are treated equitably alongside those children who reside with their parent, if they have their turn to special treatment at times, can manage to cope with the inevitable differences relating to money and gifts.

In many respects, stepfamilies are leading the way in redefining gender roles in families because the traditional role expectations for men and women are not workable in the stepfamily context. The male breadwinner and female homemaker household is less and less common in the general population in any case, but in stepfamily households a woman may have managed finance herself either as a single person or as head of a single-parent household. She may not wish to relinquish this aspect of personal control. A man may have cared for his children either full- or part-time and wish to continue his important role with them and not hand it over to his new partner, who is after all, a stranger to the children in the early stages.

Some stepfamilies, particularly those where the children are young at the time they are formed, seem to be able to integrate sufficiently well after a relatively short period (Burgoyne and Clark 1984), while others never seem to do so, and still others remain at a fixed developmental stage for several years without appearing to be able to overcome conflicts and move on (Papernow 1984). It often seems to promote bonding in a stepfamily, after an initial period of upheaval, if the parent and step-parent have a child of their own. There are stepfamilies, apparently functioning well, where some of the older children are rarely seen or mentioned and through this cut-off can hardly be considered part of the family (Visher and Visher 1988); and yet the parent, step-parent and the younger children have a satisfactory family unit. Others, by using one child as a scapegoat or by making one child into a surrogate additional parent can more or less manage the demands of family life. Jealousy, divided loyalties and guilt are perhaps the cause of most emotional difficulties in stepfamilies, and yet these are also common in nuclear families and, if recognised, allowances made and mutual support given, these powerful emotions can be contained.

A remarried couple with four children, two of his and two of hers, who had married following her divorce and the death of his wife, invested a great deal in creating a good enough family for their children. Neither of them had had a happy childhood themselves and they were determined that this should not happen to their children. They were on the whole very successful, but around the time that the children began to prepare to leave home, the parents became aware that they had never given sufficient time and attention to their own marriage. Each of them was professionally successful, but neither felt that the other gave them what they needed of affection and companionship. They had a number of years marital therapy, eventually coming to one of us (M.R.) for help in parting. It seemed most unclear whether they actually did want finally to separate. In a way, they had attempted to manage this by the husband, Paul, getting a job which, through promotion, necessitated him living away from home during the week. This left the wife, Marjorie, at home with his children (hers having left home by this time). But by now Paul and Marjorie were quarrelling constantly, each bitterly hurt by what they felt was the other's lack of care for them, and even when one made an overture to the other it was either rebuffed or diminished by reminders of bad times in the past. The therapist pointed out that they had several options available to them: they could use his move to decide to separate and make plans to visit lawyers with a view to starting legal proceedings; they could continue to have expectations of one another which neither could fulfil (nor had fulfilled), and these were likely to be even more unrealistic because of the time they would now be apart; they could by agreement use the separation to make plans jointly (something they had never really been able to do) as to how they use the weekends more profitably for them as a couple as well as for the children; or they could spend the rest of their lives continuing in the way they were presently behaving. She asked them to share with the other how each felt about these options, and when they began to criticise and undermine one another in their usual manner, the therapist asked their permission to interrupt to stop them.

Having obtained their agreement, she helped them to listen to each other's tentative attempts to explore the implications of each of the choices. Eventually, they decided upon a structured separation which they began to explore and to make rules as to how to manage. They agreed to spend most weekends together, but that if either wanted to be alone, this would be timetabled in advance with the other. On Paul's arrival home on a Friday evening, they would have a meal together and plan the week-end. Neither would bring work home, and Paul would have time with his children on his own. They would have Sunday lunch as a family, and so on. This was all written down, but they were surprised at the therapist's suggestion that they made up a catch phrase to use should either of them break this agreement. This became 'I am going on strike' which helped them to manage their conflict without destructive argument and to find ways to discuss what had happened.

Just under half of remarriages end in divorce, and there is no way to discover how many informal marriages also end in further separation. Half-empty is also half-full, and we are learning about the stepfamilies which survive. There are many reasons for stepfamilies to break down, but such an additional upheaval can lead to increased trauma for the children and another heavy burden of failure for their parents and step-parents. Too often, because of the lack of norms and guidelines for stepfamilies, the agencies to which they turn for help fail to understand their complexity and the extra burdens they must carry, and make assessments which are based on the model for nuclear families instead of recognising that stepfamilies are different. Yet some families seem to be able to surmount all these complex difficulties, given time.

The Green family

Nan and Mark had each been previously married, and each had two children from that marriage. They decided not to marry formally and had been together for nearly seven years when they asked for help. They were experienced parents with an adolescent daughter, a son on the verge of adolescence and two little girls of nine. The distribution of the children between them was the key to the difficulties they were experiencing after seven years. Nan had two daughters, the adolescent girl, Trish, and a nine-year-old, Lily. Mark's children, who had lived with him following the separation from their mother, were the boy of eleven, Tom, and Sarah, aged nine. Having two children of the same or nearly the same age is not unusual in stepfamilies, but it can bring special complications, which it did for the Green family. In every stepfamily to which both partners bring children, the birth order of the children is disturbed by the two families joining together. In this one, Trish remained eldest, but Tom became the 'second child', although the first born in his family with his mother and father. The two little girls became a special and exclusive unit, almost akin to twins, developing an attachment to one another which was extraordinarily close. Having been only two when the families came together, they barely remembered a time when the other was not present. But in fact they were not always together, because each set of children regularly had contact with their other parent, Trish and Lily visiting their father once a week and some part of every school holiday; Tom and Sarah spending every weekend and school holidays with their mother and her new partner. In their mother's household, Tom and Sarah had a stepfather and a sister of six and brother of two. Tom was the eldest again there, and of four children, while Sarah had been displaced twice by her mother having two more children. Trish and Lily had a slightly less complicated situation to which to belong. Their father had a new partner who was not always present, since her work meant she had to be elsewhere, and they did not have children. Trish and Lily thus often had their father to themselves, while Tom and Sarah always had to share both their parents with step-parents and other children.

Nan and Mark came to a meeting with one of us (D.S.) feeling defeated. Both were sad and expressed the fear that separation was not far off. Nan had expected to be able to manage four children with no difficulty and was shocked and depressed to find that she had come to resent Sarah's presence. Earlier in the family's history it had been Tom who presented a hostile reaction to her and the stepfamily, but she had been able to overcome his resistance. He now 'fitted in', but for about three years it had been Sarah who was 'different' and the 'outsider' to all family plans, from mealtimes to special activities. She would refuse to talk to Nan or participate willingly with anyone but Lily.

As the story unfolded, the therapist learned that Nan was estranged from her family of mother, brother and sister, and that her father had died when she was quite young. Her source of closeness and intimacy was her children and Mark. Mark was grieving over his father, who had died within the last year. He appeared to be grieving also over some loss of closeness with his children. When he had lived with them as a single father he was, as he put it, able to 'mother', but he and Nan had evolved a style of family life which allowed him little scope for 'mothering', that is, for being in direct care of the children. Nan and Mark demonstrated considerable warmth towards one another and sensitivity towards one another's children. Nan's statement that she could no longer live with her feelings towards Sarah brought terrible sadness to Mark, but not condemnation of Nan.

The therapist gently began to challenge Nan and Mark's belief that separation was the only change they could make and to explore their feelings of being distanced from their own children by the desire to create 'one family'. Nan felt Sarah was between her and her child, Lily. She was perceptive about Sarah's need for Lily and about Sarah's loss of her mother's daily presence at an early age. She felt that what Sarah needed from her was the one thing she could not give her – a close relationship with a mother, and at the same time, Sarah's presence seemed to prevent her from providing the same thing to her own child. It is possible that Nan did not sufficiently value Mark's contribution because she had not experienced an affectionate father herself. It is also possible that Nan believed, as most women are taught, that only women can nurture children. Therefore she took over the 'mothering' from Mark, and he had allowed this to happen, wanting to provide a 'normal' family for the children. Both Nan and Mark needed time with their own children. They needed also to allow the other to take major responsibility for each one's children. So, for example, in the week following the first meeting, when a communication with Tom and Sarah's mother was needed, Nan turned it over to Mark, a change in the usual pattern. Nan was, in the words of one stepmother, 'trying to be everybody's everything', and she blamed herself for what she believed was her failure. Mark and Nan were able to help one another with the children, thus acting together as parents in their stepfamily; the change they made was in feeling they had to do and be the same with each child.

Although we hope this may by now be apparent, it seems important at this stage to state our belief that counselling or therapy, whether with individuals, couples or families, is intended to give the clients an opportunity to reflect on their situation within a relationship which is both supportive and trustworthy. As family therapists who work with stepfamilies, we regard the work we do as having an educational aspect and so we may give explanations and make suggestions, although the responsibility for change rests with the clients and them alone. It is only in situations where the worker has some statutory responsibility for child protection (for instance, most social workers in social-services departments) that an assessment of the quality of stepfamily functioning is necessary. Nevertheless, stepfamilies, particularly at the early stages of their development, often lack the supportive assistance which can help them with the difficult choices which individual members have to take, and also to make the important decisions which are the building blocks for their future. Such a couple were David and Sally, who asked for help because their own relationship was in difficulties.

David and Sally

It was David who telephoned a therapist (M.R.) and said he had separated from his wife, that there were difficulties over his daughters and this had led to problems in his relationship with his new partner. He was offered an appointment for himself and his partner, Sally, but the therapist wondered whether he had not resolved whether his marriage was over. He thought the marriage was finished, but he wanted to improve the relationship with Sally, and a long appointment was arranged.

David was a good-looking man in his early forties, a successful manager, who married Sarah when both were young. They had two daughters, Carol and Gail, aged thirteen and nine. The marriage began to deteriorate after Carol's birth. David was ambitious and became deeply involved in his work, while Sarah devoted herself to the baby. Neither of them was very good at talking about feelings, and David, like many men, still finds this difficult. Until the time of contact with the therapist he had not thought feelings were important and had left emotional concerns to Sarah. He had an affair with a colleague which he dismissed as unimportant, but Sarah discovered it and was very hurt. Gail was born as a result of an attempted reconciliation, but they continued to be dissatisfied with their relationship, although both were devoted to their daughters. After another affair, David met Sally and despite all the difficulties they were having, he knew he wanted to make his life with her.

Sally, a woman in her mid thirties, seemed withdrawn while David was talking, and was only responsive when he turned to her for help when he was finding it difficult to describe his feelings. However, when telling her own story and particularly when discussing their relationship, she began to relax, and it was possible to see what a vital and attractive young woman she was. She had also been married, but without children, about which she was glad, because her former husband had been verbally and sometimes physically aggressive. She had been through a difficult and painful divorce which had left her with few financial resources. As a result of the failure of her marriage she had discovered that she was not as confident and sure of herself as she had been, and this had led her to therapy, where she felt she was gaining insights about herself and life in general.

David and Sally's relationship had begun as an affair lasting two years during David's marriage. They had been living together for about seven months. Leaving Sarah and the children had been a very difficult decision for David and one which made Sarah angry and bitter. They had been to a mediation service, where they were helped to reach an agreement for David to see the children about twice a week. It had also been agreed between David and Sarah that the girls should not meet Sally until they became used to their father not living with them, but recently the children had been visiting Sally and David's home. Sally criticised their behaviour. David, after several visits, accepted that they were rude towards Sally, but did not know what to do about it. The children speak little to Sally, complain about her cooking, tease the dogs (beloved to Sally) and demand all David's attention. David knew that he tried to make up to the girls for leaving them and indulged them as a result, but his guilt was very powerful. When the therapist commented that perhaps for the first time in his life David was beginning to attend to his emotions and was finding this difficult, his eyes filled with tears. Sally was trying to help him, but her criticism of his children made him resentful and angry and caused rows, at times in front of the children. Sally was upset because she did not know how to build a relationship with David's daughters or give him her own understanding of what was happening to him. Visits from the children were causing dread in both of them.

The therapist suggested that David might find it helpful to see a therapist on his own, just as Sally was doing. He was reluctant, but agreed. The therapist then, after asking if they wanted to hear what she thought about their situation, talked about the difficulties in becoming a stepfamily and the time needed to sort things out. She thought they were rushing too fast, and pointed out that for the children the separation was quite recent, that while David was certain about the ending of his marriage, for the children and Sarah the change was confusing and painful; all were at different points in facing the losses involved. David did not know how to help the girls, and the therapist encouraged him to talk to them in a way they could understand about separation and divorce and reassure them that it was not their fault. She said it was a good idea for David to spend time alone with his daughters, but that it was also important for him to help them to build a relationship with Sally and to set some limits on their behaviour. Children often behave younger than their age when distressed and she helped both David and Sally to understand this, and she then commented sympathetically to Sally about the difficulty all stepmothers face in finding a role for themselves – she was not alone in her predicament. Both began to relax and Sally became less defensive. The therapist stressed throughout the interview the importance of the relationship between David and Sally, and at its end, David agreed warmly to the idea of a therapist for himself.

The educative approach in one session helped this couple to realise that in their new stepfamily each of them needed to confront the issues and work out some of the choices they would have to make. David had not really begun to understand his own grief for the loss of his day-to-day relationship with his daughters; Sally, never having been a parent, was finding it difficult to understand two distressed little girls and easily felt left out and jealous of David's affection for them. She also did not know how to fulfil a stepmother's role, and David's expectations that she should be a 'mother' to them as Sarah was did not help. With a new set of ideas to draw upon, they could begin making changes.

Guidelines for stepfamilies and those who work with stepfamilies

Adults in stepfamilies need to remember that they need time to become familiar to the children and to expect to grow slowly. They often need encouragement to give themselves time together without children always being present. They need to accept the past, to respect one another's history and learn about loyalty to previous attachments. They need to allow the children to be loyal to and love both their parents. This means that the step-parent may be rejected at times. This is difficult to bear, and to enable a step-parent to do so requires support from partners. Both require helpers from outside the family who have knowledge and understanding of the impact of unrealistic expectations and also loyalty issues upon the development of satisfactory stepfamily life.

Step-parents often need encouragement to find the role which is best suited to the stepfamily of which they are a part. This will be related to the age and stage of development of the children and whether or not they have an active parent outside the stepfamily household with whom the step-parent must not compete. Step-parents can bring a greater objectivity to the parenting process because they are at times able to view the behaviour of both parents and children in a more neutral manner and may be aware of aspects of which the parents are not. Step-parents can befriend children rather than 'parent' them, and as such can be used as a sounding board for subjects which are emotionally sensitive for parents and children, particularly in adolescence. Often a step-parent has never seen their positive potentials until someone outside the family points them out.

Bibliography

Adcock, M. (1992) 'Public law and the stepfamily', in B. Dimmock (ed.), *A Step in Both Directions?* London: National Stepfamily Association.

Adcock, M., R. White, and A. Hollows (eds) (1991) *Significant Harm.* Croydon: Significant Publications.

Ahrons, C. (1980) 'Redefining the divorced family: a conceptual framework for post divorce family reorganisation'. New York: *Social Work* **23**, pp.437–41.

Ahrons, C. and R. Rodgers (1987) *Divorced Families: Meeting the challenge of divorce and remarriage.* New York: W.W. Norton.

Anderson, H. and H. Goolishian (1988) 'Human systems as linguistic systems: some preliminary and evolving ideas about the implications for clinical theory'. New York: *Family Process* **27**, pp. 371–93.

Anderson, J. and G. White (1986) 'An empirical investigation of interaction and relationship patterns in functional and dysfunctional nuclear families and stepfamilies'. New York: *Family Process* **25**, pp. 407–22.

Bateson, G. (1979) *Mind and Nature: A necessary unity.* New York: E.P. Dutton.

Bentovim, A. (1991) 'Significant harm in context', in M. Adcock, R. White and A. Hollows (eds), *Significant Harm.* Croydon: Significant Publications.

Berger, B. and P. Berger (1953) *The War over the Family.* Harmondsworth: Penguin.

Bird, R. (1991) 'The Child Support Act 1991 – an outline'. *Family Law* **21**, November, pp. 478–90.

Bohannan, P. (1971) *Divorce and after: An analysis of the emotional and social problems of divorce.* New York: Doubleday and Anchor.

Bohannan, P. and R. Erikson (1978) 'Stepping in', *Psychology Today*, New York, January.

Bott, E. (1968) *Family and Social Network* (2nd edn). London: Tavistock.

Bowlby, J. (1979) *The Making and Breaking of Affectional Bonds.* London: Tavistock.

Bowlby, J. (1980) *Loss: Sadness and Depression*. Vol.III of *Attachment and Loss*. London: International Psychoanalytic Library, Hogarth and the Institute of Psychoanalysis.
Bowlby, J. (1988) *A Secure Base*. London: Routledge.
Bradshaw, J., and Millar, J. (1991) *Lone Parent Families in the UK*. London: Department of Social Security Research. HMSO.
Burchardt, N. (1989) 'Structure and relations in stepfamilies in early twentieth century Britain'. *Continuity and Change* **4**(2), pp. 293–322.
Burgoyne, J. (1987) 'Stepfamilies and contemporary family values', *Concern* **61** (winter 1986–7), pp. 3–4.
Burgoyne, J. (1991) 'Afterward: does the ring make any difference? Couples and the private face of a public relationship in postwar Britain', in D. Clark (ed.), *Marriage, Domestic Life and Social Change: Writings for Jacqueline Burgoyne*. London: Routledge.
Burgoyne, J. and D. Clark (1984) *Making-a-Go-of-It: A study of stepfamilies in Sheffield*. London: Routledge and Kegan Paul.
Carter, E. and M. McGoldrick (eds) (1980) *The Family Life Cycle: A framework for family therapy*. New York: Gardner Press.
Carter, E. and M. McGoldrick (eds) (1989) *The Changing Family Life Cycle: A framework for family therapy* (2nd edn). Boston, Mass.: Allyn and Bacon.
Central Statistical Office (1989) *Social Trends*. London: HMSO.
Children Act 1975. London: HMSO.
Children Act 1989. London: HMSO.
Children Come First, Vol. 1 1990. London: HMSO.
Chodorow, N. (1978) *The Reproduction of Mothering*. Berkeley: University of California Press.
Clark, D. and D. Haldane (1990) *Wedlocked?* Cambridge: Polity Press.
Clulow, C. and J. Mattinson (1989) *Marriage Inside Out*. Harmondsworth: Penguin.
Coleman, M. and L. Ganong (1987) 'The cultural stereotyping of stepfamilies', in K. Pasley and Ihinger-Tallman (eds) *Remarriage and Stepparenting*. New York: Guilford.
Craig, W.J. (1943) *The Oxford Shakespeare*. Oxford: Oxford University Press.
Cretney, S. (1990) 'Money and divorce – a quarterly retrospect: needs and principles', *Family Law* **20**, March, pp. 89–102.
Crosbie-Burnett, M. (1989) 'Application of family stress theory to remarriage: a model for assessing and helping stepfamilies', *Family Relations* **38**, pp. 323–31.
Crosbie-Burnett, M. and J. Giles-Sims (1991) 'Marital power in stepfather families: a test of normative resource theory', *Journal of Family Psychology* **4**(4), pp. 484–96.

Davis, G. and A. McLeod (1983) 'Divorce: who supports the family?', *Family Law* **13**, pp. 217–24.

Department of Health Adoption Discussion Papers: *No. 1* (September 1990) *The Nature and Effect of Adoption; No. 2* (September 1990) *Agreement and Freeing; No. 3* (November 1991) *The Adoption Process; No. 4* (in press) *Intercountry Adoption*. London: HMSO.

Dimmock, B. (1992) 'Integrity at risk: research, stepfamilies and the media', *Newsletter of the National Stepfamily Association* **28**.

Divorce Law Reform Act (1969). London: HMSO.

Draughon, M. (1975) 'Stepmother's model of identification in relation to mourning in the child', *Psychological Reports* **36**, pp. 183–9.

Edwards, S., C. Gould and A. Halpern (1990) 'The continuing saga of maintaining the family after divorce', *Family Law* **20**, January, pp. 31–5.

Eekelaar, J. (1991) 'Child support – an evaluation; *Family Law* **21**, December, pp. 511–17.

Eekelaar, J. and M. Maclean (1986) *Maintenance and Divorce*. Oxford: Clarendon Press.

Eekelaar, J. and R. Dingwall (1990) *Reform of Child Care Law: A practical guide to the Children Act 1989*. Bristol: Jordan.

Emery, R.E. (1988) *Marriage, Divorce and Children's Adjustment*. Newbury Park: Sage.

Erikson, E. (1950) *Childhood and Society*. New York: W.W. Norton.

Fisher, T. (1990) *Conciliation within the UK: Policy and practice*. Bristol: National Family Conciliation Council with Family Law.

Fisher, T. (1992) 'Stepfamilies: the role of mediation in the light of the Children Act 1989 and divorce law reform proposals', in B. Dimmock (ed.) *A Step in Both Directions?* London: National Stepfamily Association.

Ganong, L. and M. Coleman (1987) 'Effects of parental remarriage on children: an updated comparison of theories, methods and empirical research', in Pasley, K. and M. Ihinger-Tallman (eds) *Remarriage and Step-parenting: Current research and theory*. New York: Guilford.

Grice, A. (1992) 'Absent fathers face a £400m demand', *Sunday Times*, 18 October 1992.

Haskey, J. (1988) 'Trends in marriage and divorce, and cohort analysis of the proportion of the marriages ending in divorce', *Population Trends* **58**. London: HMSO.

Humphries, S., J. Mack and R. Perks (1988) *A Century of Childhood* (A Channel 4 Book). London: Sidgwick and Jackson.

Ihinger-Tallman, M. and K. Pasley (1987) *Remarriage*. Beverley Hills and London: Sage.

Imber Black, E. (1988) 'Ritual themes in families and family therapy', in E. Imber Black, J. Roberts and R. Whiting (eds) *Rituals in Families and Family Therapy*. New York: W.W. Norton.

Jackson, E., M. Mclean, and R. Dingwall (1990) *The Resolution of Financial Disputes on Divorce: A cross national review of current models of policy and practice*. Oxford: Centre for Sociolegal Studies.

Jackson, S. (1950) *The Lottery, or the Adventures of James Harris*. London: Gollancz.

Jacques, E. (1965) 'Death and the mid life crisis', *International Journal of Psychoanalysis* **14**, October, pp. 502–74.

James, A. (1991) 'Continuity, change and contradiction', in B. Dimmock (ed.) *A Step in Both Directions?* London: National Stepfamily Association.

Keller, E. (1985) *Reflections on Gender and Science*. New Haven, Conn.: Yale University Press.

Kiernan, K. (1992) 'The impact of family disruption in childhood on transitions made in young adult life', *Population Studies* **46**, pp. 213–34.

Kiernan, K. and M. Wicks (1990) *Family Change and Future Policy*. London: Family Policy Studies Centre with the Joseph Rowntree Trust.

Klein, J. (1956) *The Study of Groups*. London: Routledge and Kegan Paul.

Knaub, P. and S. Hanna (1984) 'Children of remarriage: perceptions of family strengths', *Journal of Divorce* **7**(4), pp. 73–90.

Kohlberg, L. (1976) 'Moral stages and moralization: the cognitive–development approach', in T. Lickona (ed.) *Moral Development and Behaviour Theory, Research and Social Issues*. New York: Rinehart and Winston.

Krauss, R. (1960) *Open House for Butterflies*. London: Harper.

Kubler Ross, E. (1970) *On Death and Dying*. London: Tavistock.

Laslett, P. (1977) *Family Life and Illicit Love in Earlier Generations*. Cambridge: Cambridge University Press.

Law Commission (1966) *The Field of Choice*. London: HMSO.

Law Commission (1986) *150,000 Children Divorced a Year: Who cares?* London: HMSO.

Law Commission (1990) *Family Law: The ground for divorce*. London: HMSO.

Leach, E. (1983) 'Are there alternatives to the family?', in A. White-Franklin (ed.) *Family Matters: Perspectives on the family and social policy*. Oxford: Pergamon.

Leete, R. and S. Antony (1979) 'Divorce and remarriage: a record linkage study', *Population Trends* **16**. London: HMSO.

Lund, M. (1984) 'Research on divorce and children', *Family Law* **14**, February, pp. 198–201.

Lutz, P. (1983) 'The step-family: an adolescent perspective', *Family Relations* **32**(3), pp. 367–75.

McGoldrick, M. (1989) 'Women through the family life cycle', in M. McGoldrick, C. Anderson and F. Walsh (eds) *Women in Families: A Framework for family therapy*. New York: Norton.

Maclean, M. (1991) *Surviving Divorce: Women's resources after separation* (Women in Society Series). Basingstoke: Macmillan.

Mansfield, P. and J. Collard (1988) *The Beginning of the Rest of Your Life*. Basingstoke: Macmillan.

Masson, J. (1991) 'Stepping into the nineties: implications of the Children Act 1989 for stepfamilies', in B. Dimmock (ed.) *A Step in Both Directions?* London: National Stepfamily Association.

Messinger, L. and J.C. Hausen (1976) *Therapy with Remarried Families*. Rockville, Md: Aspen Publications.

Mills, D. (1984) 'A model for stepfamily development', *Family Relations* **33**(3) pp. 365–76.

Minuchin, S. (1974) *Families and Family Therapy*. London: Tavistock.

Morrison, K. and A. Thompson-Guppy (1985) 'Cinderella's stepmother syndrome', *Canadian Journal of Psychiatry* **30**, pp. 355–63.

Murray Parkes, C. (1986) *Bereavement: Studies of grief in adult life* (2nd edn). Harmondsworth: Pelican.

Murray Parkes, C. and R. Weiss (1983) *Recovery from Bereavement*. New York: Basic Books.

New Encyclopedia Britannica, The (1989), vols 10 and 11. 15th edn. Chicago: Encyclopedia Britannica.

OPCS (Office of Population Censuses and Surveys) (1990a) Calculation from the *General Household Survey Report 1988*. London: HMSO.

OPCS (1990b) *Population Trends* **61**. London: HMSO.

Papernow, P. (1984) 'The stepfamily cycle: an experiential model of stepfamily development', *Family Relations* **33**(3), pp. 355–64.

Parker, S. (1991) *Informal Marriage, Cohabitation and the Law, 1750–1989*. Basingstoke: Macmillan.

Parkinson, Lisa (1990) 'Mediation matters', *Family Law* **20**, December 20, pp. 477–9.

Pasley, K. and M. Ihinger-Tallman (1987) *Remarriage and Stepparenting: Current theory and research*. New York: Guilford Press.

Phillips, R. (1991) *Untying the Knot: A short history of divorce*. Cambridge: Cambridge University Press.

Poster, M. (1978) *Critical Theory of the Family*. New York: Seabury Press.

Priest, J. (1990) *Families outside Marriage*. Bristol: Jordan.
Putting Asunder: A divorce law for contemporary society (1966). London: SPCK.
Rimmer, L. (1981) *Families in Focus*. Occasional Paper No. 6, Study Commission on the Family. London: Family Policy Studies Centre.
Roberts, J. (1988) 'Definition, function, and typology of rituals', in Imber Black, E., J. Roberts and R. Whiting (eds) *Rituals in Families and Family Therapy*. New York: W.W. Norton.
Robinson, M. (1980) 'Stepfamilies; a reconstituted family system', *Journal of Family Therapy* **2**(1), pp. 45–69.
Robinson, M. (1991) *Family Transformation Through Divorce and Remarriage: A systemic approach*. London: Routledge.
Robinson, M. (1993) 'A family systems approach to mediation during divorce', in A. Treacher and J. Carpenter (eds) *Using Family Therapy* (2nd edn). Oxford: Blackwell.
Roll, J. (1991) *What is a Family? Benefit models and social realities*. Occasional Paper 13. London: Family Policy Studies Centre.
Sheinberg, M. and P. Penn (1991) 'Gender dilemmas, gender questions and the gender mantra', *Journal of Marital and Family Therapy* **17**(1), pp. 33–44.
Shorter, E. (1975) *The Making of the Modern Family*. London: Collins.
Skolnick, A. (1991) *Embattled Paradise: The American family in an age of uncertainty*. New York: Basic Books.
Skynner, R. (1976) *One Flesh: Separate persons*. London: Constable.
Skynner, R. and J. Cleese (1983) *Families and how to Survive Them*. London: Methuen.
Smith, D. (1990) *Stepmothering*. Hemel Hempstead: Harvester Wheatsheaf.
Social Trends, No. 19. London: HMSO.
Solicitors' Family Law Association (1989) *Stepfamilies: The impact of the new partner on the family*. SFLA Seminar Papers, October 1989. London: SFLA.
Solomon, M. (1988) *Narcissism and Intimacy: Love and marriage in an age of confusion*. New York: W.W. Norton.
Staves, S. (1990) *Married Women's Separate Property in England 1660–1833*. Cambridge, Mass.: Cambridge University Press.
Stern, D. (1985) *The Interpersonal World of the Infant: A view from psychoanalysis and developmental psychology*. New York: Basic Books.
Stone, L. (1990) *The Road to Divorce: England 1520–1987*. Oxford: Oxford University Press.
Terkelson, K. (1980) 'Towards a theory of the family life cycle', in E. Carter and M. McGoldrick (eds) *The Family Life Cycle: A framework for family therapy*. New York: Gardner Press.

Thompson, P. (1975) *The Edwardians*. London: Routledge and Kegan Paul.

Thompson, S. (1946) *The Folktale*. New York: Dryden Press.

Vaughan, D. (1987) *Uncoupling: How relationships come apart*. London: Methuen.

Visher, J. (1984) 'Seven myths about stepfamilies', *Medical Aspects of Human Sexuality* **18**(1), pp. 52–80.

Visher, E. and J. Visher (1988) *Old Loyalties, New Ties: Therapeutic strategies with stepfamilies*. New York: Brunner Mazel.

Visher, E. and J. Visher (1979) *Stepfamilies: A guide to working with stepparents and stepchildren*. New York: Brunner Mazel.

Walczak, Y. and S. Burns (1984) *Divorce: The child's point of view*. London: Harper & Row.

Wallerstein, J. and J. Kelly (1980) *Surviving the breakup: How children and parents cope with divorce*. New York: Basic Books.

Walters, M., B. Carter, P. Papp and O. Silverstein (1988) *Gender Patterns in Family Relationships*. New York: Guilford Press.

Whisman, M. and N. Jacobson (1990) 'Power, marital satisfaction and response to marital therapy', *Journal of Family Psychology* **4**(2), pp. 202–12.

White, R., P. Carr and N. Lowe (1989) *A Guide to the Children Act 1989*. London: Butterworth.

Whiteside, M. (1988) 'Creation of family identity through ritual performance in early remarriage', in E. Imber Black, J. Roberts and R. Whiting (eds) *Rituals in Families and Family Therapy*. New York: W.W. Norton.

Index